The Scramble for Africa

Third Edition

M.E. Chamberlain

Routledge
Taylor & Francis Group

LONDON AND NEW YORK

First published in Great Britain by Longman Group 1974
Second edition published 1999 by Addison Wesley Longman
Third edition published 2010 by Pearson Education Limited

Published 2013 by Routledge
2 Park Square, Milton Park, Abingdon, Oxon OX14 4RN
711 Third Avenue, New York, NY, 10017, USA

Routledge is an imprint of the Taylor & Francis Group, an informa business

British Library Cataloguing in Publication Data
A catalogue record for this book is available from the British Library

Library of Congress Cataloging in Publication Data
Chamberlain, Muriel Evelyn.
  The scramble for Africa / M.E. Chamberlain. – 3rd ed.
    p. cm.
  Includes bibliographical references and index.
  ISBN 978-1-4082-2014-6 (pbk.)
  1. Africa–Colonization. 2. Africa–History–1884-1918. 3. Europe–Colonies–Africa.
  I. Title.
  DT29.C45 2010
   960'.23–dc22

                                        2009048609

ISBN 13: 978-1-4082-2014-6 (pbk)

Set in 10/13.5pt Berkeley Book by 35

Introduction to the Series

History is narrative constructed by historians from traces left by the past. Historical enquiry is often driven by contemporary issues and, in consequence, historical narratives are constantly reconsidered, reconstructed and reshaped. The fact that different historians have different perspectives on issues means that there is also often controversy and no universally agreed version of past events. *Seminar Studies in History* was designed to bridge the gap between current research and debate, and the broad, popular general surveys that often date rapidly.

The volumes in the series are written by historians who are not only familiar with the latest research and current debates concerning their topic, but who have themselves contributed to our understanding of the subject. The books are intended to provide the reader with a clear introduction to a major topic in history. They provide both a narrative of events and a critical analysis of contemporary interpretations. They include the kinds of tools generally omitted from specialist monographs: a chronology of events, a glossary of terms and brief biographies of 'who's who'. They also include bibliographical essays in order to guide students to the literature on various aspects of the subject. Students and teachers alike will find that the selection of documents will stimulate discussion and offer insight into the raw materials used by historians in their attempt to understand the past.

Clive Emsley and Gordon Martel
Series Editors

Contents

PART FOUR   DOCUMENTS   97

Acknowledgements

I should like to acknowledge my debt to Dr A.F. Madden of Nuffield College, Oxford, who first aroused my interest in Commonwealth Studies, and Professor G. Shepperson, formerly of Edinburgh University, who kept a friendly eye on the development of Commonwealth and African courses in Swansea.

The first edition of this book would probably not have been published without the encouragement of Alun Davies, Professor of Modern History, and the practical help of Mrs P.M. Thomas and Mrs Kathleen Rees, History Department secretaries and Mrs Glenys Bridges, the cartographer in the Geography Department in the then University of Wales, Swansea (now Swansea University).

For later editions I should like to thank Mrs Jane Buse, a History Department secretary, and Professor David Eastwood, my successor as Head of Department, for their continued support.

Publisher's acknowledgements

We are grateful to the following for permission to reproduce copyright material:

Plate 1 courtesy of Wikipedia/GNU Free Documentation license; Plate 2 courtesy of Corbis/Paul Almasy; Plates 3, 5 and 10 courtesy of the Mary Evans Picture Library; Plates 4 and 12 courtesy of Getty Images/Hulton Archive; Plate 6 courtesy of The Bridgeman Art Library/Bibliothèque des Arts Décoratifs, Paris, France; Plate 7 courtesy of the Royal Commonwealth Society/L Firolli; Plate 8 courtesy of The Bridgeman Art Library/Private Collection; Plate 9 courtesy of E M Clements; Plate 11 courtesy of Topfoto/Topham Picturepoint; Plate 13 courtesy of Topfoto/The Granger Collection; Plate 14 courtesy of The Bridgeman Art Library/Musée de l'Armée, Paris, France/Giraudon; Plate 15 courtesy of the National Portrait Gallery; Plate 16 courtesy of The Bridgeman Art Library/Royal Geographical Society, London, UK; Plate 17 courtesy of The Bridgeman Art Library/National Army Museum, London; Plate 18 courtesy of The Bridgeman Art Library/Leeds Museums and Galleries (City Art Gallery), UK.

Document 27 from R.E. Robinson and J. Gallagher (1962) 'The partition of Africa' in F.H. Hinsley (ed.) *The New Cambridge Modern History*, Vol. XI, Material Progress and World-Wide Problems, 1870–98, Cambridge University Press, pp. 593–4, 639.

In some instances we have been unable to trace owners of copyright material, and would appreciate any information that would enable us to do so.

Chronology

Events of significance for whole African continent

1869   Opening of the Suez Canal revolutionised geo-political picture. Quickest route to India and the East was now by way of the Mediterranean and the Red Sea. But some British military authorities still considered the Cape route safer

1870–1   Franco-Prussian war. United Germany emerged as arguably the strongest Power in Europe and some in France looked to an overseas empire to restore French prestige; others saw it as a dangerous distraction

1873   Financial crisis led to Great Depression which lasted for nearly thirty years and led some to think that the solution to Europe's problems lay overseas

1878   (June–July) Congress of Berlin. Great Powers met to avert danger of war from flare up in the Eastern Question. A number of private deals were struck, notably the Cyprus Convention, by which Britain withdrew her objections to France taking control of Tunisia in exchange for France acquiescing in Britain leasing the island of Cyprus from the Sultan of Turkey

1884–5   (November 1884 to February 1885) Berlin West Africa Conference drew up the ground rules for the European acquisition of territory in Africa. Although technically only applying to the coasts of West Africa, the provisions of the Berlin Act (February 1885), such as 'effective occupation', were applied to the whole continent

1904   (April) Anglo-French *Entente*, in reality a series of colonial bargains, in particular relating to Egypt and Morocco

Egypt and Sudan

1875   (November) British government acquired the Khedive of Egypt's shares in the Suez Canal Company. This gave them a strong, but not a majority, holding

1878   *Caisse de la Dette Publique* set up to safeguard interests of those who had lent money to Egyptian government. System known as Dual Control established with an Englishman and a Frenchman supervising the Egyptian revenue and expenditure

1879   (February) Egyptian army mutinied

(June) Sultan deposed Ismail in favour of his son, Tewfik

1881   (February and September) More army mutinies. Colonel Arabi Pasha emerged as the main leader

1881–3   The 'Mahdi' led a successful revolt against Egyptian rule in the Sudan

1882   (11 June) Alexandria massacre. About 50 Europeans were killed in a riot

(11 July) A British fleet bombarded the fortifications of Alexandria; considerable collateral damage was caused in the city

(August–September) A British force, under Sir Garnet Wolseley, entered Egypt, nominally at the request of the Khedive Tewfik to save him from his rebellious army. Won complete victory at Tel-el-Kebir (13 September)

1882–3   Lord Dufferin, the British ambassador in Constantinople, came to Egypt to establish a new representative constitution

1883   (September) Evelyn Baring (Lord Cromer) came to Egypt as Consul-General

(November) An Egyptian force, led by a British officer, William Hicks, was defeated by the Mahdists

1884   British government appointed General Charles Gordon to carry out an evacuation of the Sudan

1885   (January) Gordon was killed at Khartoum. Gordon was a national hero and his death caused a political crisis in England

(March) Convention of London. The troubles in the Sudan had further crippled Egyptian finances. The European Powers agreed to new loans in return for the permanent continuation of the *Caisse de la Dette*. Britain now administered Egypt but with international control of the finances

1887   Sir Henry Drummond Wolfe was sent to Constantinople to negotiate a British withdrawal from Egypt but the mission failed

1895   The British feared that a hostile power in the Sudan could, by controlling the Nile, render Britain's position in Egypt untenable

(September) An Egyptian force under Herbert Kitchener reconquered Dongola

1897–8   Kitchener advanced cautiously into the Sudan, culminating in complete victory at the battle of Omdurman (2 September 1898)

(18 September) Kitchener found small French force under Major Marchand at Fashoda. 'Fashoda incident' brought Britain and France to the brink of war

1899   (January) Britain proclaimed Anglo-Egyptian condominium over the Sudan

(March) Britain and France defined boundaries, which left the Sudan in the British sphere of influence

1904   (April) France agreed to cease to demand a British withdrawal from Egypt and to agree to changes in the Egyptian debt in return for concessions elsewhere

North Africa

1871   Third French Republic established. Reversed Napoleon III's policy of creating an Arab state in Algeria and re-opened it to French settlement. Led to Arab uprisings throughout 1870s and early 1880s

1881   Treaty of Bardo (Kasser-Said) Bey of Tunis reluctantly accepted a French protectorate over his territory

1904   (April) Anglo-French *entente*. British withdrew their opposition to French predominance in Morocco

1906   Algeciras Conference. Germany won some concessions on internationalisation of Morocco

1911   (June–July) Agadir crisis. A new German challenge to French position in Morocco won them a few concessions elsewhere in Africa but strengthened Anglo-French alignment against them

1912   French protectorate established over Morocco

West and Equatorial Africa

1865   Committee of British House of Commons recommended that Britain should reduce her existing commitments in West Africa and should avoid any extension of them

1872   The Dutch, who were the allies of the Ashanti, sold their possessions in West Africa to the British, who were traditionally the allies of the Fanti

1873–4 Britain became involved in a war with the Ashanti. Sir Garnet Wolseley led textbook campaign, covered by many prominent journalists

1874   Britain constituted the coastal strip as the Gold Coast colony

1875–82 Savorgnan de Brazza explored Congo region and concluded unofficial treaties ('Makoko' treaties) with local chiefs

1876   French forces began to advance from existing colony of Senegal towards Upper Niger. Met with strong resistance from the Muslim states of the region

1876   King Leopold II of the Belgians began to manifest interest in the Congo and, in subsequent years, to conclude treaties with chiefs and 'open up' the region to commerce

1878   France gained treaty rights in Cotonou (Dahomey). Also began to intervene in the Ivory Coast

1879 George Taubman Goldie formed United African Company (later National African Company) to combat French competition on the Niger

1882 French, angered by British influence in Egypt, decided to accept Makoko treaties as official

1883 France renewed lapsed protectorate over Porto Novo

1884 French secured promise that Leopold II's interests in the Congo would revert to them, if he wished to relinquish them. Alarmed, Britain secured a treaty with Portugal, (February) defining northern boundaries of Angola and Portugal's historic claims to the Congo. Other Powers' objections to these bilateral agreements led to meeting of Berlin West Africa Conference, 1884–5

(May) The British consul at Fernando Po, Edward Hewitt, sent to sign treaties with Niger chiefs to pre-empt French action

(July) Gustav Nachtigal proclaimed a Protectorate over Cameroons, which had previously been regarded as in the British sphere of influence. Subsequently proclaimed a Protectorate over Togoland

1885 (February) General Act at the end of the Berlin Conference in effect laid down the ground rules for the Scramble, such as the idea of 'effective occupation'

The USA was the first state to recognise the Congo Free State which Leopold had created as a nominally sovereign state, with himself as head

British proclaimed a Protectorate over the 'Oil Rivers', that is the Niger delta, and reached agreement with Germany on the boundary with the Cameroons

1885–91 France made further advances in Equatorial region

1886 National African Company received a royal Charter as the Royal Niger Company and effectively took over the administration of the Niger delta

1887–c.1898 Potentially dangerous quarrels with other Powers about navigation rights on the Niger and 'race' between Britain and France to secure treaties with chiefs on Upper Niger

1892 French completed conquest of Dahomey

1893 French occupy Timbuktu. Struggles with Toaregs of the Sahara begin

1895 French bring Senegal, French Guinea, French Sudan and the Ivory Coast under the jurisdiction of the Governor-General in Dakar (Senegal)

1895–6 War between Britain and Ashanti, as a result Britain established a Protectorate over the lands of the Ashanti confederation

1896 In course of competition with France Britain extended her jurisdiction from existing colony of Sierra Leone to the hinterland (the Protectorate)

1898 Britain extended her protectorate from the lands of the Ashanti Confederation to include the 'Northern Territories'

1898 Britain and France signed treaty defining boundaries in West Africa

1899   Royal Niger Company surrendered its administrative rights to the British government but retained its trading rights

1900   Britain established the Protectorates of Northern and Southern Nigeria

1900–1 'War of Golden Stool' with Ashanti, after which Britain assumed jurisdiction over whole of what later became Ghana

1904   (April) *Entente cordiale* modified some Anglo-French boundaries in West Africa

1906   Scandal of Leopold's exploitation of the Congo became public

1908   Reluctant Belgian parliament assumed responsibility for the Congo as a normal colony

1910   French Equatorial Africa (Gabon, Middle Congo and Ubanghi-Shari) was constituted into an administrative unit, under a Governor-General in Brazzaville

East Africa

1872   A Glasgow ship-owner, William MacKinnon, organised a regular mail service between Britain, India and Zanzibar

1873   Sultan Barghash of Zanzibar signed an anti-slavery treaty with Britain and British influence became politically dominant but was challenged on the commercial level by the Germans

1877   Mackinnon put forward an ambitious scheme to administer large areas of the East African Coast, in the name of the Sultan of Zanzibar, who claimed jurisdiction there. It was deliberately sabotaged by the British government, which wanted no extension of responsibilities there

1884   The German explorer, Karl Peters, concluded treaties with chiefs on the East African mainland, ignoring the Sultan's claims to suzerainty

1885   After the Berlin West Africa Conference. The German government accepted Peters' treaties as official, although he had been previously warned that they had no force

1886   Britain, Germany and France defined their spheres of influence on the East African mainland. Zanzibar remained independent. Uganda, where British and French missionaries had penetrated and clashed in the 1870s, was in the British sphere, as was what became Kenya; Tanganyika was in the German sphere

1888   The Imperial British East Africa Company (associated with William Mackinnon) was chartered and entrusted with the administration of what later became the British protectorates of Kenya and Uganda

1889   Italians secured treaty with claimant to the throne of Abyssinia

1890   Heligoland Treaty between Britain and Germany. Britain ceded the island of Heligoland in the North Sea to Germany, together with some small territorial concessions in Africa, notably the Caprivi Strip connecting German South West Africa with the Zambezi, in return for German recognition of a British protectorate over Zanzibar

1892   British government underwrote the construction of a railway from Mombasa to Lake Victoria

1894   Britain declared formal Protectorate over Uganda

1895   Imperial British East Africa Company surrendered its charter

A Protectorate (the East African Protectorate) was proclaimed over most of what became Kenya

1896   Abyssinians defeated Italians at battle of Adowa (only significant defeat of a European army by an African country in this period). But Italians retained control of Eritrea and Somaliland

1900–14   European settlers began to come to Kenya

Southern Africa

1870–1   Rich diamond field discovered in sensitive area in angle of Orange and Vaal rivers, to which Transvaal, Orange Free State and Cape Colony all had claims

1877   Britain annexed the Transvaal, which was bankrupt and threatened by resurgent Zulu power. Many Boers claimed they had never truly given their consent

1880–1   First Boer War. Boers of Transvaal tried to regain their independence. Subsequent agreements (Convention of Pretoria, 1881, and Convention of London, 1884) were ambiguous on how much control Britain retained over the Transvaal

1882   Boers from the Transvaal set up two small republics, Stellaland and Goschen, in Bechuanaland

1884   The Germans established themselves in Namaqualand and Demaraland (later German South West Africa). Believed to have ambitions to extend control into Bechuanaland

1885   Britain annexed Bechualand south of the Malopo River as a colony and proclaimed larger area north of the river as a Protectorate

1886   Large gold deposits found in Transvaal on Witwatersrand

1887   Two Boers, the Grobler brothers, claimed to have won substantial concessions from Lobengula, the king of the Matabele. Alarmed, the British government persuaded Lobengula to agree not to alienate any of his territory without the agreement of the British High Commissioner in South Africa

1888   Rudd Concession. C.D. Rudd, acting for Cecil Rhodes, persuaded Lobengula to grant mineral rights in his country in return for money and weapons

Who's who

Aberdare (Henry Austin Bruce), 1st Baron (1815–95): British politician. Home Secretary, 1868–73. President of the Royal Geographical Society. First Governor of the Royal Niger Company.

Ampthill (Odo Russell), 1st Baron (1829–84): British diplomat. British ambassador to Germany, 1871–84.

Anderson, Sir Percy (1831–96): British civil servant. Became Head of the Foreign Office Africa Department in 1883. British delegate at Berlin West Africa Conference, 1884–5. Unusual in trying to develop a coherent plan for British policy in Africa.

Arabi Pasha (Colonel Ahmed) (c. 1839–1911): Egyptian nationalist. Son of a peasant family. Became Minister of War in 1882. After British intervention put on trial and exiled to Ceylon. Returned to Egypt in 1901 but took no further part in politics.

Baker, Sir Samuel (1821–93): British explorer. Best known for search for the source of the Nile in the 1860s. Employed by Khedive of Egypt in 1869 to try to suppress slave trade in the Sudan.

Barghash, Ibn Said (c. 1837–88): Sultan of Zanzibar, 1870–88. Claimed jurisdiction on East African mainland, as well as over island of Zanzibar.

Barnato, Barney (Rufus Isaacs) (1852–97): Speculator and diamond merchant. Founded Barnato Diamond Mining Corporation, which merged with De Beers Consolidated in 1888.

Barth, Heinrich (1821–65): German explorer. Published 3 volume account, *Travels and Discoveries in North and Central Africa* in 1857–8.

Beecroft, John (1760–1854): Sailor, explorer, merchant and anti-slavery crusader. British consul 'for the Bights of Benin and Biafra', 1849–54. Established such remarkable personal influence there that Professor Dike calls him 'de facto Governor'.

Beit, Alfred (1853–1906): Financier and diamond merchant. Born in Hamburg but later became naturalised British subject. 1875 went out to Kimberley diamond fields and became close associate of Cecil John Rhodes in De Beers Mining Company and later in the British South Africa Company (1889).

Bismarck, Otto von (1815–98): Chancellor of Germany, 1871–90. Never an enthusiast for a colonial policy he, nevertheless, intervened in the Scramble for Africa on a number of occasions for diplomatic advantage.

Bleichröder, Gerson von (1822–93): German banker, who had influence over Bismarck. Historians have differed in their interpretations of Bleichroder's role in the Scramble.

Blunt, Wilfrid Scawen (1840–1922): English gentleman with entrée to political circles. Traveller and writer. Supported, among many other radical causes, the Egyptian nationalists. Published important book *The Secret History of the English Occupation of Egypt* (1907).

Blyden, Edward Wilmot (1832–1912): Academic and civil servant. Probably of Ibo descent but born in St Thomas in the Virgin Islands. Went to Liberia in 1851. In 1880s became Liberian ambassador to both Britain and France. Chiefly important for trying to make Africans conscious of and proud of their heritage, and also for trying to build bridges between Christianity and Islam.

Brazza, Savorgnan de (1852–1905): French explorer. In 1880 concluded series of unauthorised treaties with African chiefs in Congo region (inaccurately known as the Makoko treaties). In November 1882 the French government accepted these treaties as official.

Bright, John (1811–89): Quaker and radical British politician. He resigned from the government in protest at the British bombardment of Alexandria in 1882.

Burke, Edmund (1729–97): British politician. Famously led proceedings to impeach Warren Hastings for his actions in India. The impeachment failed but Burke had set out a doctrine of 'trusteeship', which permanently influenced British thinking about empire.

Burton, Sir Richard Francis (1821–90): British explorer and writer. Became involved in famous controversy with John Hanning Speke about the source of the Nile. Very able writer, whose low opinion of Africans did them a grave disservice.

Buxton, Thomas Fowell (1781–1845): Anti-slavery campaigner, who succeeded William Wilberforce as the leader of the anti-slavery campaign in

1824. Played an important role in the 'Niger experiment' of 1841–2, which tried to replace slave trading with legitimate commerce in the Niger delta. Although it failed in the short run, it laid the foundations of the later important palm oil trade.

Caillié, René (1799–1838): French explorer. Most famous for reaching Timbuktu in 1820s.

Cameron, Lieutenant Verney Lovett (1844–94): British explorer. Sent out by Royal Geographical Society in 1873 to contact David Livingstone. First European to cross central Africa from east to west. His report of the potential riches of the Congo region inspired others, notably King Leopold II of the Belgians, to try to exploit them.

Campbell-Bannerman, Sir Henry (1836–1908): British Liberal politician. Played minor but important role in British intervention in Egypt in 1882. Prime Minister 1906–8. Had reluctantly supported government in the Boer War and restored autonomy to Transvaal and Orange Free State in 1906.

Cardwell, Edward, Viscount (1813–86): British Liberal politician. Colonial Secretary, 1864–6, Secretary for War, 1868–74. Leading member of parliamentary committee which recommended in 1865 that Britain should disengage as far as possible from West Africa but later member of Colonial Society.

Carnarvon, Henry Howard Molyneux Herbert, 4th Earl of (1831–90): British politician. Colonial Secretary, 1866–7 and 1874–8.

Carnarvon, George Herbert, 5th Earl of (1866–1923): British Egyptologist. Financed excavation of Tutankhamun's tomb in 1920s, which led to explosion of public interest in ancient Egypt.

Cave, Stephen (1820–80): British politician. Paymaster General but not in the Cabinet, 1874–80. Wrote important report on the Egyptian finances in 1876.

Cetewayo (contemporary spelling usually Cetshwayo) (c. 1826–84): Fourth, and last independent, ruler of Zululand. Succeeded his father Mpande in 1872. Defeated British force at Isandlwana in January 1879 but was crushed at battle of Ulundi in July 1879. Allowed to return to govern truncated Zululand in 1882 but died in 1884, following a civil war.

Chaka See **Shaka**.

Chamberlain, Joseph (1836–1914): British politician. President of the Board of Trade, 1880–85. Broke from Gladstone on Irish issue. Became Conservative (technically a Unionist). 1895–1902 Colonial Secretary. Only slowly converted to imperialist cause but came to advocate both imperial federation and imperial preference. The latter split the Unionist party in 1903.

Cherif Pasha (1826–87): Egyptian politician from a Turkish family. Headed moderate ministries, 1879, 1881–2 and again during the British occupation, 1882–4.

Churchill, Lord Randolph (1849–95): British politician. A conservative who frequently disagreed with his own party. One of the few critics who seriously attacked Gladstone's intervention in Egypt in 1882.

Cobden, Richard (1804–65): British politician. Although he died before the Scramble for Africa began, his influence lived on in the Manchester School, which generally stood for retrenchment and no foreign adventures.

Cromer, Lord (Evelyn Baring), 1st Earl (1841–1917): Member of important banking family of Baring. Regarded as one of the great 'Pro-consuls' of the period. Served in Egypt, 1877–80 as the British Commissioner for the Debt and subsequently the Controller of the Revenue. Again served in Egypt, 1883–1907, technically as Consul-General, but with the virtual powers of a Governor. Set about reforming Egyptian finances, which he regarded as first priority. In 1908 published *Modern Egypt*, a defence of British policy in Egypt and became embroiled in famous controversy with W.S. Blunt.

Crowther, Samuel Ajayi (c. 1807–91): Bishop. A Yoruba, rescued from a Portuguese slave ship and educated in Britain and a notable linguist, he became the Anglican bishop of the Niger region in 1843.

Curzon, Lord (1859–1925): British Conservative politician. Viceroy of India, 1898–1905. Foreign Secretary, 1919–23.

Darwin, Charles (1808–1882): Scientist. The theories he advanced in *The Origin of Species* (1859) were later debased by some into what is sometimes called 'Social Darwinism' to argue that the strongest and most aggressive survive not, as Darwin had argued, those best adapted to their environment.

Decoeur, Henri-Alexis, Captain (1855–1900): French soldier. Engaged in race with British Captain (later Lord) Lugard to conclude treaties with African chiefs in the Niger region in the mid-1890s to secure strategic and commercial advantages.

Delcassé, Théophile (1852–1923): French politician. Belonged to group which believed that colonies would enhance French power. Under-Secretary for the Colonies, 1893; Colonial Minister, 1894–5; Foreign Minister, 1898–1905. Had to concede to Britain over Fashoda incident in 1898. Concluded Anglo-French Agreements in 1904 which settled a number of colonial disputes, particularly relating to Egypt and Morocco.

Derby, 15th Earl of (1826–93): British politician. Foreign Secretary in Disraeli's Conservative administration, 1874–6 but joined the Liberals in 1879. Colonial Secretary in Gladstone's Liberal administration, 1882–5.

Devonshire, 9th Duke of (1868–1938): British Conservative politician. Colonial Secretary, 1922–4. Famous for issuing a White Paper which insisted that Kenya was an African territory and that the interests of the Africans must have priority.

Diaz, Bartolomeu (d. 1500): Portuguese navigator. Discovered sea route to Indian Ocean round what became known as Cape of Good Hope. Landed at Mossell Bay on east coast of South Africa in February 1488. Employed in administration of Guinea gold trade until 1894. Portuguese claims in Africa date back to this early period.

Dilke, Sir Charles (1843–1911): British politician. Under Secretary for Foreign Affairs, 1880–2. Played an important role in Egyptian crisis.

Disraeli, Benjamin (Earl of Beaconsfield) (1804–81): British politician. Prime Minister, 1868 and 1874–80. Generally regarded as an advocate of imperialism from the time of his speech at the Crystal Palace in 1872 but his real interest was in India and the route to India. Not an enthusiast for expansion in Africa but took decisions which were to be very important for Africa – the purchase of the Khedive's Suez Canal shares in 1875 and the conclusion of the Cyprus Convention with France in 1882. Probably not personally enthusiastic about the annexation of the Transvaal in 1877.

Enim Pasha See **Schnitzer, Edward**.

Étienne, Eugène-Napoléon (1844–1921): French politician. Leading member of colonial group in Chamber of Deputies. Brought up in Algeria. Interested in railway development in Africa. Under-Secretary for the Colonies, 1887–8, 1889–92.

Fabri, Friedrich (1824–91): German colonial propagandist. Director of Barmen Rhine Missionary Society, 1857–84. Believed colonies could solve Germany's domestic problems. Thought, exaggeratedly, that his 1879 book *Does Germany Need Colonies?* triggered the whole German colonial movement.

Faidherbe, Louis (1818–89): French soldier and administrator. Sent to Senegal in 1852; Governor, 1854–61 and 1863–5. In 1854–8 subdued immediate hinterland in conflict with Al-Hajj Omar. Wished to link Senegal with Niger. Elected to Senate in 1879. Interested in both African archaeology and Islam.

Fauré, François Félix (1841–99): French shipowner from Le Havre. Under Secretary for the Colonies, 1883; Minister of Marine, 1894; President of the Republic, 1895–99.

Ferry, Jules (1832–93): French politician. Prime Minister 1880 and 1883–5. Interested in colonial matters. Mainly associated with French policy in Indo-China, he was also active in advocating developments in Tunisia.

Frere, Sir Henry Bartle (1815–84): British administrator. After distinguished career in India, sent to South Africa in 1877 as Governor of the Cape and High Commissioner. Understood situation much less well there. Arbitrated between Transvaal and Zulus, generally in latter's favour, but his subsequent demand that they disarm, led to war. Recalled in 1880.

Freycinet, Charles Louis de (1828–1923): French politician. Prime Minister and Foreign Minister, 1879–80, 1882 and 1886; Foreign Minister, 1885–6. The British regarded him as weak and indecisive during the Egyptian crisis in 1882 but it is now recognised that Freycinet, a railway engineer by profession, had ambitious plans for French West Africa, including a railway from Senegal to Algiers.

Gambetta, Léon (1838–82): French politician. Regarded as strong man of French politics. Many thought he would have played strong role in Egyptian crisis of 1882 but only briefly Prime Minister, November 1881 to January 1882. Died (possibly assassinated) in December 1882.

Gladstone, William Ewart (1809–98): British politician. Prime Minister, 1868–74, 1880–5, 1886, 1892–4. He was opposed in principle to any territorial expansion of the empire but, ironically, much of Britain's acquisition of further territory in Africa dated from his administrations. In particular, he was responsible for the occupation, intended to be temporary, of Egypt in 1882.

Goldie, George Taubman (1846–1925): British soldier who, by chance, acquired shares in a company with interests on the Niger. Set up the United Africa Company and later the Royal Niger Company. Was the Governor of the latter company, 1895–9.

Gordon, General Charles (1833–85): British soldier. Originally made a name for himself in China in suppression of Taiping rebellion. In 1873 seconded to serve under Khedive of Egypt in the Sudan to suppress the Arab slave trade. Governor of the Sudan (under the Egyptians), 1877–81. In 1884 he was sent back to the Sudan to evacuate the Egyptian forces after the Mahdi's successful revolt. Killed in Khartoum by the Mahdists in January 1885. Gordon was a popular hero. His death was very damaging to the Gladstone government and 'Revenge Gordon' became a potent slogan in Africa.

Goschen, George Joachim, 1st Viscount (1831–1907): British banker and politician. His firm Frühling and Goschen had lent money to the Egyptian Khedives Said and Ismail. In 1876, having renounced any personal financial interest, he went out to represent the British bondholders in an Anglo-French enquiry into the Egyptian finances, which led to the setting up of the Commission of the Public Debt. Originally a Liberal, he became a Unionist and was Chancellor of the Exchequer, 1886–92.

Granville, George Leveson-Gower, 2nd Earl (1815–91): British politician. Colonial Secretary, 1868–70; Foreign Secretary, 1870–4, 1880–5. Prominent Liberal who was, at one time, expected to succeed Gladstone as the leader of the party.

Grey, Albert George, 4th Earl (1851–1917): British politician and administrator. Became closely associated with Cecil John Rhodes. Director of British South Africa Company, 1898–1904. 1896, Administrator of Rhodesia.

Grey, Sir Edward (Lord Grey of Falloden) (1862–1933): British Liberal politician. Under-Secretary for Foreign Affairs, 1892–5. One of group known as 'Liberal Imperialists' who supported the government during the 2nd Boer War. Foreign Secretary, 1905–16.

Hannington, James (1847–85): Anglican Bishop. First went to Uganda as a missionary in 1882. Appointed first bishop of Eastern Equatorial Africa, 1884. In July 1885 he was murdered, with others, on the orders of Mwanga, the ruler of Uganda. Violence against missionaries was very rare but his death convinced many in Britain of the savage nature of African society.

Hanotaux, Gabriel (1853–1944): French politician. Foreign Minister, 1894–5, 1896–8. Favoured a forward policy in Africa and initiated policy which led to the Anglo-French clash at Fashoda in 1898.

Harcourt, Sir William (1827–1904): British politician. Home Secretary, 1880–5; Chancellor of the Exchequer, 1886 and 1892–5, Consistent in his opposition to imperial expansion, notably in East Africa. Among those nick-named 'Little Englander'.

Harrison, Frederic (1831–1923): British lawyer and writer. Strenuous opponent of British intervention in Egypt in 1882.

Hartington, Lord (later 8th Duke of Devonshire) (1833–1908): British politician. Closely associated with Gladstone until he broke with him over Ireland and became a Unionist. Secretary of State for India, 1880–2, Secretary of State for War (Dec) 1882–5.

Henty, George Alfred (1832–1902): British war correspondent and writer. Reported on many wars, including Ashanti campaign of 1873–4, but better remembered as the author of numerous boys' adventure stories, usually set abroad, which influenced a whole generation of young men.

Herbert, R.G.W. (1841–1905): British civil servant. Permanent Under Secretary at the Colonial Office, 1871–92. Generally the Colonial Office officials were unenthusiastic about colonial expansion, unlike some of their colleagues at the Foreign Office.

Hewett, Edward Hyde (1830–91): British consul. Held various posts in West Africa, some connected with the suppression of the slave trade. 1880, consul at Fernando Po. 1885, sent to conclude treaties with Niger chiefs to forestall French. Instructed to do the same in the Cameroons but there forestalled by German Gustav Nachtigal.

Hobson, J.A. (1858–1944): British writer and propagandist. Strong supporter of free trade and opponent of imperialism. Visited the Rand on behalf of the *Manchester Guardian*, just before the 2nd Boer War and published *The War in South Africa* (1900) and *The Psychology of Jingoism* (1901). His best-known book was *Imperialism: a Study* (1902), which influenced Lenin.

Hutton, James, (1826–90): Manchester business man and MP, who had considerable trading interests in Africa. President of Manchester Chamber of Commerce, 1884–5. He worked closely with other interested parties, including George Taubman Goldie, and was a very effective lobbyist.

Ismail, Khedive (1830–95): Appointed Pasha (Governor) of Egypt in succession to his brother, Said, in 1867 but persuaded the Sultan to give him the more exalted title of Khedive (roughly, 'Viceroy'). Did much to modernise Egypt but ran into serious debt. The Sultan, possibly pressurised by European interests, deposed him in favour of his son, Tewfik, in 1879.

Ja Ja of Opobo (c. 1820–91): West African merchant. Important trading partner for Europeans on the Niger.

Jameson, Dr Leander Starr (1853–1917): South African politician. A close associate of Cecil John Rhodes. His 'Raid' into the Transvaal in December 1895 did much to discredit both Rhodes and the British government.

Jauréguiberry, Jean-Bernard (1815–87): French Admiral. Served in various theatres. Governor of Senegal, 1861–3. Minister of Marine and Colonies, 1878–83. His caution led to the French navy pulling out of planned joint Anglo-French action against Egypt in July 1882. But he favoured a forward policy in Indo-China and in West Africa.

Johnson, Sir Frank (1866–1943): British soldier and Rhodesian 'Pioneer'. Went to South Africa as young man. Became manager of Bechuanaland Exploration Company and had grandiose schemes to buy Mozambique from the Portuguese. 1890 volunteered to lead 'Pioneer' column into Mashonaland.

Johnston, H.H. (Sir Harry) (1858–1927): British explorer and consul. Explored Angola and Congo region, 1882–3 and, in 1884, the area round Mount Kilimanjaro, which he recommended for British settlement. Held various consular posts in Africa in 1880s. In 1889 explored area of Lakes Nyasa and Tanganyika and became Commissioner for Central African Protectorate (later Nyasaland) in 1891. Consul-General in Tunis, 1897–9 and Special Commissioner in Uganda, 1899–1901. A strong propagandist for British expansion in Africa.

Joubert, Edmond: French banker. Sent on mission to investigate Egyptian finances with British banker, G.J. Goschen, in 1876 but while Goschen's position was unofficial, Joubert was officially employed by his government. Mission triggered formal European intervention in Egyptian finances.

Kimberley, John Wodehouse, 1st Earl of (1826–1902): British politician. Colonial Secretary, 1870–4, 1880–2; Secretary of State for India, 1882–6, 1892–4; Foreign Secretary, 1894–5. Took important decisions on West Africa in 1873–4 but, generally during the Scramble, the lead role was played by the Foreign, rather than the Colonial, Office.

Kirk, Sir John (1832–1922): British Consul-General and Agent in Zanzibar. Medical doctor. Served in Crimean war and accompanied David Livingstone on his second expedition in 1858. Strong opponent of the slave trade, he was the British plenipotentiary at the Brussels Slave Trade Conference in 1889–90. Arrived in Zanzibar, 1863; Consul-General, 1873; Agent, 1886–7. Played a key role in British expansion in East Africa.

Kitchener, Herbert, 1st Earl (1850–1916): British soldier. Having served in various campaigns, was employed to draw the boundaries between the British and German spheres of influence in East Africa in 1886. Became Commander-in-Chief of the Egyptian army in 1892 and led the campaign to reconquer the Sudan, culminating in the battle of Omdurman in September 1898. Succeeded Lord Roberts in command in South Africa in December 1899. Became Secretary of State for War in 1914 and drowned at sea in June 1916, when on a mission to Russia.

Knutsford, Henry Thurstan Holland, 1st Viscount (1825–1914): British politician. Colonial Secretary, 1887–92.

Kruger, Paul (1825–1904): Boer leader. One of the original Voortrekkers of 1836. Bitterly opposed the British annexation of the Transvaal in 1877. President of the Transvaal Republic, 1883–1902. British suspected him of conspiring with the Germans in the 1890s. Unclear whether he wanted war with the British in 1899 but the Boer defeat lead to Kruger's exile in 1901.

Labouchère, Henry (1831–1912): British radical politician and journalist. Particularly critical of Cecil Rhodes.

Lavigerie, Charles, Cardinal (1825–92): French ecclesiastic. Bishop of Algiers, 1867, and Primate of Africa, 1884. Opposed slave trade and saw it as his mission to convert Africa. Founded White Fathers, 1867, and White Sisters, 1869. Saw conversion and advance of French influence as inextricably mixed.

Lenin, V.I. (1870–1924): Russian politician. Creator of the Soviet state and leading communist thinker. 1917, published *Imperialism: the Highest Stage of Capitalism*. Saw imperialism as the death throes of over-ripe monopoly capitalism.

Leopold II, King of the Belgians (1835–1900): Had travelled widely and when he became king, 1865, dreamt of a colonial empire. Central Africa would not have been his first choice but set up an elaborate international organisation supposedly to end slave trade and open up Africa, which proved to be mere cloak for creation of a personal fief in the Congo. Scandal eventually became so great Belgian parliament had to assume responsibility for the Congo as an ordinary colony in 1908.

Lesseps, Ferdinand de (1805–94): French diplomat and engineer. While consul at Alexandra in 1830s began to dream of canal across isthmus of Suez. Organised Suez Canal Company in 1858. Canal opened 1869.

Lister, Thomas Villiers (1832–1902): British Foreign Office official. Under Secretary with special responsibility for Africa. Became convert to the idea that Britain must intervene to protect its trade.

Livingstone, David (1813–73): British missionary and explorer. First went to Africa in 1840. Explored the Zambezi region in 1853–6 (seeing the Victoria Falls for the first time in November 1855); the Lake Nyasa region in 1858–64. Later searched for sources of the Nile. Became national hero and buried in Westminster Abbey. But, although he campaigned strenuously against the slave trade, his belief that legitimate commerce was the best way to drive it out and raise African standards of living, provided a convenient argument for those who wished to 'open up' Africa for their own purposes.

Lloyd George, David (1863–1945): British Liberal politician. Prime Minister, 1916–22. Incurred great unpopularity by supporting the cause of the Boer Republics during the 2nd Boer War, 1899–1902.

Lobengula, King (c. 1836–1894): Last independent king of Matabele (Ndebele). Succeeded in 1868. Agreed to, but later repudiated, Rudd concession in 1888. Died in rather mysterious circumstances in Matabele war in 1894.

Luderitz, Adolf (1834–86): German trader, who wished to see German expansion in Africa. Associated with negotiations with the Transvaal. Set up trading station at Angra Pequena in 1883, which led to quarrels with British and establishment of German South-West Africa.

Lugard, Frederick John Dealtry, 1st Baron (1858–1945): British soldier and administrator. Served in Afghan war, 1879–80. After being invalided out of the army worked for African Lakes Company and Imperial British East Africa Company, in 1880s, partly in suppression of slavery in East Africa. Strongly in favour of British control of Uganda. But mainly associated with West Africa. Employed by Royal Niger Company from 1894. Actively resisted the French. High Commissioner for Northern Nigeria, 1900–6. Governor of the whole of Nigeria, 1912–19. Pioneered system known as 'Indirect Rule'. In 1922 published very influential book *The Dual Mandate in British Tropical Africa*, arguing that European and African interests should be complementary, not antagonistic. Member of League of Nations Mandate Commission, 1922–36.

McCarthy, Sir Charles (1770–1824): British soldier. 1812, Governor of Sierra Leone with responsibility for Cape Coast Castle. 1824 became involved in war to protect British allies, the Fanti, against the Ashanti. Was killed and, according to legend, his skull was used as a drinking cup by the Ashanti.

Macdonald, Sir Claude Maxwell (1852–1915): British soldier and diplomat. Served in Egypt 1882–4. 1887 Acting Consul-general in Zanzibar. Sent by British government in 1888 to conduct enquiry into complaints against the activities of the Royal Niger Company, by both the Germans and rival Liverpool traders. Produced remarkably forward-looking report, emphasising the rights of the African too. Subsequently British envoy in China at the time of the Boxer rebellion, 1896–1900 and British ambassador to Japan, 1900–12.

MacKinnon, Sir William (1823–93): British merchant and shipowner. Founded shipping line which, in 1862, became British India Steam Navigation Company. 1873 established mail service between Aden and Zanzibar. Early attempts to secure concessions on the African mainland were not supported by the British government but, in 1888, in the face of German threats, Mackinnon secured a royal charter for his Imperial British East Africa Company.

Mahdi See **Muhammad Ahmad ibn Abdullah**.

Malet, Sir Edward (1837–1908): British diplomat. Consul-general in Egypt 1879–83. Sent home rather alarmist despatches, which may have helped to persuade the British government to intervene.

Marchand, Major, Jean Baptiste (1863–1934): French soldier, leading a small force which encountered Kitchener's army at Fashoda after the battle of Omdurman. Part of deliberate French advance from West Africa. Fashoda incident came near to causing Anglo-French war but French government backed down.

Mehemet Ali (1769–49): Albanian soldier. Rose to power in Egypt in 1805. Originally the Pasha (Governor) answerable to the Sultan of Turkey, he obtained more and more independent power. In 1840 secured agreement that the Governorship of Egypt would be hereditary in his family. Conquered much of the Sudan in 1820s. Consciously modelling himself on Napoleon, he set out to reform all aspects of Egyptian society, often employing French experts.

Milner, Alfred, 1st Viscount (1854–1925): British administrator and politician. Worked under Cromer in Egypt. Became committed imperialist and published *Britain in Egypt* in 1894. 1897–1905, British High Commissioner in South Africa. Secretary for War, April 1918; Colonial Secretary, December 1918–21.

Moffat, John (1835–1918): Influential British missionary in southern Africa. In 1887 persuaded Lobengula to sign what became known as Moffat Treaty, undertaking not to enter into agreements with other Powers, without consulting the British High Commissioner.

Morel, E.D. (1873–1924): British radical. Campaigned against brutal policy of Leopold II in the Congo. Published very influential book *Red Rubber* in 1906.

Moshesh (1785–1870): Leader of Basutos, who were harassed first by the Zulus, then by the Boers. In 1868 persuaded British government to take his people under British protection.

Muhammad Ahmad ibn Abdullah (the Mahdi) (c. 1844–85): Sudanese religious leader. Felt called to lead *jihad* against both Turkish and Egyptian influences. Defeated Egyptian force under William Hicks in 1883. His men killed General Gordon in Khartoum in January 1885 but the Mahdi himself died later that year.

Mutesa I, Kabaga (King) of Buganda (c. 1838–84): Did much to make his country prosperous but during his reign encouraged rival Muslim and Christian missionaries, both Catholic and Protestant, to enter the country, which led to conflict.

Mwanga, Kabaka (King) of Buganda (c. 1866–1901): Succeeded Mutesa but insecure and brutal. Shocked opinion by murdering 30 Christian boys in 1885. Deposed by his enemies in 1888.

Mzilikazi (c. 1795–1868): Zulu leader, founder of Matabele (Ndebele) kingdom. Ally of Shaka, 1818–23, but fled after a quarrel. Led his followers into the territory of the Shona people and established his capital at Bulawayo.

Nachtigal, Gustav (1834–85): German explorer. In 1884 concluded protectorate treaties with chiefs in Cameroons.

Palmerston (Henry John Temple), 3rd Viscount (1784–1865): British politician. Foreign Secretary, 1830–4, 1835–41, 1846–51; Prime Minister, 1855–8, 1859–65. Played an important role in Near Eastern crisis of 1840–41, with implications for the future of Egypt. Strong defender of British interests but no interest in expansion in Africa.

Park, Mungo (1771–1806): British surgeon and explorer. Employed in 1795 by the African Association to explore the Niger region. The government commissioned another expedition in 1805. Navigated over 1000 miles by canoe but died in an accident.

Peters, Karl (1856–91): German explorer. Although warned in advance that he had no authority to do so, he concluded a series of treaties with East African chiefs in 1884–5, which were accepted by the German government on his return. Founded German East Africa Company and, in 1891, became Administrator for German East Africa.

Prester John: Legendary Christian king, perhaps based on emperor of Abyssinia, with whom early European explorers hoped to make contact.

Quaque, Philip (1741–1816): A Fanti, educated in England. First African to be ordained in the Church of England. Chaplain at Cape Coast Castle.

Reade, William Winwood (1838–75): British traveller and writer. Wrote a number of books on West Africa and was *The Times'* special correspondent in the Ashanti War of 1873.

Rhodes, Cecil John (1853–1902): Founder of Rhodesia. Went to South Africa in 1869 and made a fortune on the Kimberley diamond fields. 1880, founded De Beers Mining Company. Became convinced imperialist. Wished to see Britain in control of all of southern Africa, south of the Zambezi. 1890, Prime Minister of Cape Colony. 1885, secured Bechuanaland for Britain. 1888 persuaded Lobengula by 'Rudd concession' to grant Britain monopoly over minerals within his territory. 1889, founded British South Africa Company. Secured control of Matabeleland and Mashonaland. Implicated in Jameson Raid and had to resign as Prime Minister of the Cape.

Ripon, 1st Marquis of (1827–1909): British politician. 1880–4, Viceroy of India. 1892–5, Colonial Secretary. Known for liberal views on empire.

Rosebery (Archibald Philip Primrose), 5th Earl of (1847–1929): British politician. Became interested in the empire while on a world tour in 1883–4. Foreign Secretary, 1886, 1892–4; Prime Minister, 1894–5. Played important role in British decision to retain control of Uganda in early 1890s.

Rothschild family: International financiers, who several times played a key role in financing ventures in Africa. Lionel Rothschild, 1808–79, enabled Disraeli to purchase the Khedive's Suez Canal shares in 1875. Nathaniel Rothschild, 1840–1915, helped Cecil Rhodes to buy a substantial stake in the Witwatersrand in 1888.

Rudd, Charles Dunell (1844–1916): British businessman. Went to South Africa in 1865 and became closely associated with Cecil Rhodes. In 1888 persuaded Lobengula to grant the 'Rudd Concession', which gave the signatories monopoly rights over the minerals in Lobengula's lands.

Said Pasha (1822–63): Descendant of Mehemet Ali. Became Pasha (Governor) of Egypt. Gave concession to Ferdinand de Lesseps to build Suez Canal. In modernising Egypt began policy of raising loans from European financiers but it was later that loans got out of control.

Salisbury (Robert Arthur Talbot Gascoigne-Cecil), 3rd Marquis of (1830–1903): British politician. Foreign Secretary, 1878–80. Prime Minister, 1885–6, 1886–92, 1895–1902, combining that office with being Foreign Secretary, 1885–6, 1895–1900. Presided over British empire at its zenith and conscious of need to defend it but not himself an enthusiastic expansionist. More interested in India than in Africa. 1890–1 concluded a number of important boundary agreements in Africa and by the Heligoland Treaty (1890) conceded Heligoland to Germany in return for British acquisition of Zanzibar. 1896 initiated campaign to regain control of the Sudan.

Schnitzer, Edward Carl Oscar (1840–92): German doctor. Acquired nickname Enim Pasha when working for the Ottoman empire in Albania. In 1875 General Gordon appointed him as medical officer in Equatoria. In 1878 became Governor of Equatoria, where he tried to eliminate the slave trade. In 1880s was cut off from Cairo by the Mahdi's forces. H.M. Stanley determined to 'rescue' him, although he wished to stay at his post. The Enim Pasha Relief Expedition was one of the darkest episodes of the time. Badly organised, it led to many deaths and subsequent accounts by various participants confirmed European views of the essential savagery of Equatorial Africa.

Selborne, 1st Earl of (1812–95): British politician and lawyer. Lord Chancellor, 1872–4, 1880–5. Expressed well-founded suspicions about authenticity of treaties concluded with African chiefs.

Shaka (sometimes Chaka) (c. 1787–1828): Founder of the Zulu nation. From 1816 transformed small Nguni clan into formidable fighting force.

When his original patron, Dingiswayo, was murdered in 1818, became paramount chief. Spread terror in the region. 1828, murdered by his half-brother, Dingaan.

Speke, John Hanning (1827–64): British explorer. Engaged in famous controversy with his fellow explorer, Richard Burton, about the true source of the Nile.

Stanley, Henry Morton (original name John Rowlands) (1841–1904): British journalist and explorer. Most famous journalistic exploit was meeting with David Livingstone in 1871. Crossed Central Africa from Zanzibar to the Atlantic in 1874–7. Worked for Leopold of the Belgians in the Congo, 1879–84. Conducted Enim Pasha Relief expedition, 1887–90. Prolific and popular author but did Africans great disservice by representing Africa as dark and savage place. Church authorities refused him burial in Westminster Abbey, not because of his humble origins, but because of dubious activities in Africa.

Tewfik, Khedive of Egypt (1852–92): Eldest son of Khedive Ismail. The Sultan of Turkey deposed his father in his favour in 1879, probably under pressure from European Powers, who wanted more malleable ruler. Tewfik proved too weak to deal with the situation. In theory, Britain intervened in 1882 at his request to save him from his rebellious army.

Thomson, Joseph (1858–95): British explorer. 1878 explored Tanganyika region on behalf of the Royal Geographical Society. Continued to travel in East Africa until 1893.

Van Riebeeck, Johan (1619–77): Official of Dutch East India Company. 1652 established 'refreshment station' at Cape of Good Hope for Dutch ships on their way to East Indies. Encouraged settlement there.

Wilhelm II, Kaiser (Emperor) of Germany (1859–1941): Succeeded to the throne in 1888. Anxious to play world role. Sympathetic to Boer Republics in their disputes with Britain. Caused international incident by sending telegram of support to Paul Kruger at the time of the Jameson Raid in 1896.

Wolff, Sir Henry Drummond (1830–1908): British diplomat. Sent to Constantinople in 1885 to try to arrange British withdrawal from Egypt. Mission failed.

Wolseley, Sir Garnet (1833–1913): British soldier. Served in many theatres and regarded as one of Britain's best generals. Commanded successful campaign against the Ashanti in 1873–4 Conducted what was generally regarded as a textbook campaign in Egypt in 1882. Sent to rescue General Gordon from the Sudan in 1884 but too late. Campaigned hard during his career for reforms in the British army.

Glossary

American Civil War War between Northern and Southern States (1861–5). Although slavery became an issue, the original quarrel was about States' Rights. Created world shortage of raw cotton (normally exported from the Southern States). Played a part in imperialism when alternative sources were sought in Egypt, India and Fiji.

Ashanti A strong and warlike group of African people in West Africa, who came together in the Ashanti Confederation. They oppressed weaker groups like the Fanti and often supplied European slave traders with captives.

autonomy Literally 'self government'. Sometimes applied, as in the Boer Republics, to the right of internal self-government but stopping short of full independence.

Balkanisation A collection of small states, often with ill-defined boundaries, created by the break-up of a larger unit; derived from the situation in the Balkans during the break-up of the Ottoman empire in the nineteenth century.

Bantu In origins a linguistic term, denoting a related family of African languages. It fell into disrepute because of the derogatory way in which it was applied to those who spoke them during the *apartheid* era in South Africa.

Boer Derived from the Dutch for 'farmer', applied to Dutch (and some German and French Huguenot) settlers in South Africa, who spoke Afrikaans, not English, as their first language.

Buganda The largest of the four kingdoms which went to make up Uganda. Its inhabitants were called Baganda.

Bulgarian Horrors Popular term for atrocities committed by the Ottomans after a rising in Bulgaria in 1876. William Gladstone played a prominent role in denouncing them.

Caprivi Strip Strip of land connecting German South West Africa with the Zambezi. Named after the German Chancellor (1890–4), Count Caprivi.

Concert of Europe An informal alignment of the Great Powers of Europe, originating at the end of the Napoleonic Wars, designed to settle disputes by negotiation, not war. Regarded as particularly important in relation to the Eastern Question.

consul-general Senior diplomatic post. An ambassador could only be accredited to an independent state. Egypt at this time was still legally part of the Ottoman empire. British envoys to Cairo (even Lord Cromer, who became for practical purposes the Governor of Egypt during the British occupation) technically bore only the title of Consul-General.

corvée Labour service owed by a peasant, usually as part of his rent.

crown colony Most usual form of British colonial administration, consisting of Governor, Executive Council and Legislative Council. The Legislative Council could be made up of both 'official' and 'unofficial' (sometimes elected) members. Most British acquisitions in Africa started as protectorates but became assimilated to conventional Crown Colonies in the early twentieth century.

Dreyfus affair Political scandal which split French politicians and society in the late nineteenth century. Captain Dreyfus, a Jewish French army officer, was wrongly convicted of spying for the Germans.

Eastern Question The problems caused by the slow break-up of the Ottoman empire in the nineteenth and early twentieth centuries which, several times, seemed likely to cause a general European war. It caused the Crimean war in 1854 and, in the opinion of some historians, the First World War in 1914.

effective occupation Idea adopted by the Berlin West Africa Conference of 1884–5 that a European Power claiming territory in Africa must demonstrate an 'effective' presence on the ground. Although primarily intended to disallow theoretical and historical claims, it had the unintended consequence of increasing European intervention in Africa in areas in which they were interested.

El Dorado Literally 'the golden one'. A land of fabled wealth, originally applied to South America but in the nineteenth century sometimes used of Africa.

entente (entente cordiale) Literally a 'cordial understanding' between nations, stopping short of a formal alliance. Most commonly applied to the Anglo-French agreements of 1904.

Fellah (plural fellahin) An Egyptian peasant.

Great Zimbabwe Remarkable ruins in what became Southern Rhodesia. When they were discovered in 1868, Europeans could not believe that Africans could have built them and attributed them to the Phoenicians, but scientific archaeology has firmly attributed them to local African peoples. Post-independence Southern Rhodesia adopted the name, Zimbabwe.

Hamitic peoples Nineteenth-century anthropologists posited a race, lighter-skinned and more advanced than the African 'Negro', who were probably responsible for any signs of higher civilisation in Black Africa. Modern anthropologists do not believe any such race ever existed.

Huguenots French Protestants who had to flee persecution in their own country after 1685. Most went to other European countries but a significant number went to Cape Colony, where they were quickly assimilated by the Boers.

Kaffir wars A long series of wars on the eastern boundary of Cape Colony, which lasted from 1779 to 1853.

Khoikhoi (sometimes simply *Khoi*) Modern name for people previously called the Hottentots.

Mashona A peaceful pastoral tribe, who lived in what became Southern Rhodesia, and were harassed by the Matabele in the period immediately before the arrival of the Europeans.

Matabele The usual name in the Victorian period for the people now known as the Ndebele. They were an offshoot of the Zulus, who moved into the area that later became Southern Rhodesia.

mfecane A Nguni word, literally meaning 'crushing', applied to the migration of the Nguni peoples and particularly to the expansion of the Zulu kingdom in southern Africa in the first half of the nineteenth century, which destabilised the region.

Ndebele See *Matabele*.

Negro A difficult term as many now see it as offensive and prefer 'Black'. The problem is that 'Black' has no precise meaning. Many people of mixed race and even some Asians call themselves 'Black'. When Victorian anthropologists spoke of Negroes they meant quite specific peoples living in Africa, and their descendants in the Americas. In some contexts it is impossible to avoid.

Niger experiment A well-meaning attempt in the eighteen-forties, by anti-slavery campaigners, to replace the slave trade with legitimate commerce in palm oil in the Niger delta. It failed because so many Europeans died, mainly of malaria.

Orleanist France   France under an Orleanist king, Louis-Philippe, 1830–48. France became deeply involved in Algeria, although the intervention had begun under the previous Bourbon king, Charles X. This was also the period of the first Anglo-French *entente cordiale*.

Ottoman empire   The empire of the Ottoman Turks (see Map 2, p. xxxix) ruled over by the Sultan. Its gradual disintegration in the nineteenth and early twentieth centuries presented European diplomacy with its most dangerous and intractable problem.

Paymaster General   British Treasury Minister.

protectorate (protected state)   Terms recognised in international law, by which a stronger state extended its protection to a smaller state. It normally assumed control of its foreign and defence policies but, in theory, left its internal administration intact. In practice, particularly in Africa in this period, there was often intervention in domestic matters and the distinction between a protectorate and a colony became blurred. In the British empire protectorates came under the Foreign Office, not the Colonial Office. Many African protectorates later became conventional colonies. Protected states tended to continue to enjoy greater autonomy.

res nullius   Latin term, used in international law, to denote a territory which had no apparent owner.

San   Modern term used to denote people known in the nineteenth century as the Bushmen.

Sudan (Soudan)   In its more restricted sense this means the area of the modern state of Sudan, the Upper Nile region, often called in the nineteenth century the Egyptian Sudan. But it can also be applied to a wide swath of territory between the Sahara to the north and the rain forests to the south. This was sometimes called the French Soudan and sometimes spelt Soudan, rather than Sudan. But the usage was not consistent.

Sultan   An Islamic ruler. A number of men were accorded the title, for example, the Sultan of Zanzibar. But in particular it meant the ruler of the Ottoman empire, resident in Constantinople, who had some religious, as well as political, authority, very roughly comparable to the role of the Pope in western Europe in the Middle Ages.

uitlander   Afrikaans term for a foreigner. It was particularly applied to white residents in the Transvaal, who were not Boers and were refused citizenship.

Zulu   A particular group of the Nguni people, who established a powerful kingdom in southern Africa, at much the same time as the Boers were moving north from the Cape.

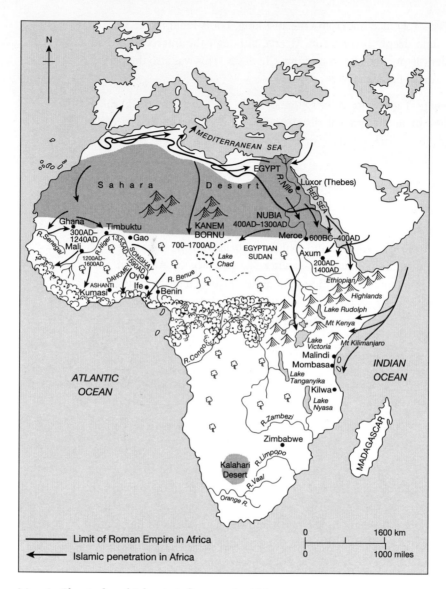

Map 1 Classical and Islamic influences in Africa

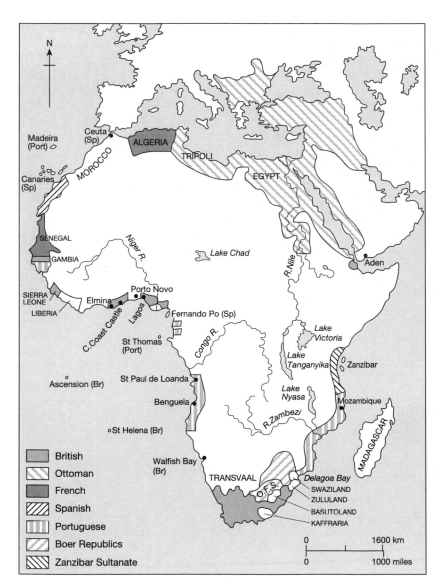

Map 2 Africa and the Ottoman Empire, c. 1870

Map 3 Africa and the Ottoman Empire in 1914

Part 1

THE PROBLEM

1

Introduction

In 1870 barely one tenth of Africa was under European control. By 1914 only about one tenth – Abyssinia (Ethiopia) and Liberia – was not. Most of the partition of Africa, colloquially but accurately described as the 'scramble' or 'grab' for Africa, had taken place during a period of only six years, between the Berlin West Africa Conference of 1884–5 and a series of 'tidying up' agreements in 1890.

To the twenty-first century it seems almost incredible that a whole continent could have been carved up between the European Powers (some of them not even 'Great Powers') in this way, with little or no consultation of the inhabitants. To the nineteenth century, it seemed not only natural but inevitable. One explanation is obvious. Europe had undergone an industrial revolution and Africa had not. For the first time in history there was an enormous gap, economic, technological and military, between the two continents with the balance entirely in Europe's favour. The second explanation is less obvious but equally important – the mindset of the Europeans. Europeans were at the forefront of progress and civilisation; Africans 'primitive' and 'backward'. Naturally, the Europeans would take over. This was sometimes justified by a debased form of 'Social Darwinism', which had little to do with what Charles Darwin had really argued about 'natural selection' in the animal world.

This mindset persisted into the second half of the twentieth century. Reputable scholars could write 'For countless centuries, while all the pageant of history swept by, Africa remained unmoved in primitive savagery' (Davidson, 1970: 20). A distinguished British historian, Hugh Trevor-Roper, could say in 1963, 'Perhaps in the future there will be some African history to teach. But at present there is none: there is only the history of Europeans in Africa. The rest is darkness . . . and darkness is not a subject of history' (Trevor-Roper, 1963:871). In this they were echoing the opinions of their Victorian predecessors. The explorer Sir Samuel Baker told a Victorian audience in 1874:

Central Africa . . . is without a history. In that savage country . . . we find no vestiges of the past – no ancient architecture, neither sculpture, nor even a chiselled stone to prove that the **Negro** savage of this day is inferior to a remote ancestor. . . . We must therefore conclude that the races of man which now inhabit [this region] are unchanged from the prehistoric tribes who were the original inhabitants. (Quoted in Cairns, 1965: 86)

The distinguished colonial administrator Sir Bartle Frere, with a wide experience of India, as well as of Africa, did not disagree, believing:

If you read the history of any part of the Negro population of Africa, you will find nothing but a dreary recurrence of tribal wars, and an absence of anything which forms a stable government, and year after year, generation after generation, century after century, these tribes go on obeying no law but that of force, and consequently never emerging from the state of barbarism in which we find them at present, and in which they have lived, so far as we know, for a period long anterior to our own. (Ibid.)

It seemed not only inevitable that the 'Dark' continent would be conquered and opened up by the enlightened Europeans but that it would be a positive blessing for its benighted inhabitants.

Even at the height of nineteenth-century imperialism, most Europeans were aware that in Asia, in India or China, European control was an episode in the life of those countries. It came after centuries, even millennia, of their own civilisations and most accepted that it would in turn end. No such consciousness pervaded their attitudes to Africa.

Negro: A difficult term as many now see it as offensive and prefer 'Black'. The problem is that 'Black' has no precise meaning. Many people of mixed race and even some Asians call themselves 'Black'. When Victorian anthropologists spoke of Negroes they meant quite specific peoples living in Africa, and their descendants in the Americas. In some contexts it is impossible to avoid.

2

The African background

Only in the 1960s did both Africans and Europeans begin to radically reassess their relationship. It was underpinned by an increasing interest in and understanding of African history, connected with the establishment of new universities in Africa where most European colonies were about to become independent, and with a new interest in such studies in British and American universities. It percolated surprisingly fast to the general public, particularly through the works of Basil Davidson, whose pioneering studies *Old Africa Rediscovered* and *Black Mother* were first published in 1959 and 1961 respectively. People began to realise that relations between Africa and Europe in the late nineteenth century were not the norm, but a strange anomaly. It slowly became apparent that historically Africa had supported societies and civilisations as colourful and sophisticated as those of Europe.

This was hidden from Europeans for a variety of reasons. Europeans were accustomed to study history through written records. For large parts of Africa no such records exist. Where they do exist, they are often in Arabic, and European scholars did not at first pay much attention to them. Only in recent years too have archaeological techniques, the use of oral traditions, and scientific anthropology become sufficiently developed to make possible the reconstruction of the history of societies which kept no written records. Another difficulty bedevilled the European understanding of Africa. Nineteenth-century Europe had become so used to seeing political power embodied in nation states that Europeans found it almost impossible to recognise any other form of political organisation, and came to regard the absence of identifiable states as proof of anarchy.

Even early explorers were impressed by some African art forms. African sculptures, carvings and textiles became known to Europeans at a time when the Romantic movement was taking the place of the eighteenth-century admiration for classical models, and from the beginning their strange and exotic forms attracted some interest. But the most important examples of African art became known to Europeans comparatively late. The beautiful bronzes and ivories of Benin were discovered in 1897 but they showed clear traces of Portuguese influence. The first of the magnificent bronzes of Ife, the earliest of which date from the thirteenth century and owe nothing to Europe, was not found until 1910 and the main collection did not come to light until 1938. Europeans stumbled upon the remains of **Great Zimbabwe** in 1868, but it was long supposed that they could not be the work of indigenous Africans and must be the relics of the Phoenicians who, it was surmised, had mined gold in what in colonial times was called Rhodesia. Radio-carbon tests have yielded dates between the fifth and fifteenth centuries and, combined with other archaeological evidence, leave no doubt that they were an African creation. The European reaction to the discovery of Zimbabwe was just one striking example of the generally held belief that the African had played a passive part in history, occasionally influenced by Phoenicians, Arabs or other outside peoples, but never himself creative.

This picture cannot be sustained in the face of later and more scientific investigations, but men act on the basis of what they believe to be true, and it is instructive to compare the Victorian 'image of Africa' with what painstaking, and still incomplete, enquiries have suggested is nearer to the truth. Archaeologists and palaeontologists in particular have centred much attention on Africa in recent years, for Africa may well have the longest human history of any of the continents. If Asia was the cradle of civilisation, as the word is commonly understood today, Africa was almost certainly the birthplace of man himself. In the words of one historian, 'Africa was the mother of mankind', the place where *homo sapiens* first emerged. In the Stone Age Africa was 'not even relatively backward: it was in the lead' (Oliver and Fage, 1990: 14).

Great Zimbabwe: Remarkable ruins in what became Southern Rhodesia. When they were discovered in 1868, Europeans could not believe that Africans could have built them and attributed them to the Phoenicians, but scientific archaeology has firmly attributed them to local African peoples. Post-independence Southern Rhodesia adopted the name, Zimbabwe.

ENVIRONMENTAL FACTORS

The influence of climate on civilisations has fascinated both modern archaeologists and Victorian scientists. Modern archaeologists would accept that favourable climatic conditions helped the emergence of relatively advanced human groups in Africa. The continent did not suffer the ravages of the Ice Age as Europe and Asia did. Its history was influenced rather by alternating 'wet' and 'dry' periods during which the size of the Sahara desert varied greatly. In the nineteenth century it was fashionable in some quarters to suppose that climatic conditions were decisive in determining relative degrees of civilisation. Early anthropologists thought that all human society developed through three stages: savagery, characterised by hunting and food-gathering; barbarism, characterised by the emergence of settled agriculture; and civilisation, characterised by the development of commerce. To some Victorian observers Africa seemed to have got stuck in the second stage. They sought explanations for this and found it in the doctrine of 'tropical abundance'. The very richness of Africa had helped the progression from the first stage to the second but then tended to stultify progress because a tolerable life could be obtained with comparatively little effort. Advanced civilisations only appeared in temperate regions where a high degree of organisation was necessary to ensure adequate food and shelter. The inhabitants of all tropical regions, not just Africa, were likely to remain in the stage of 'barbarism'. This was often coupled with the stock charge that black people were naturally 'lazy' and always did the minimum of work. This seems to have arisen partly because the picture of the black man was drawn from the (often unfavourable) view that was held of the American slave, partly because of a failure on the part of early observers to appreciate the natural rhythms of work of any agrarian community.

Despite the gratuitous charge of laziness, it should be remembered that those who argued this way were essentially environmentalists, not racialists; that is to say, they contended that a particular combination of geographical and climatic factors had produced a particular, rather backward, society, not that the genetic endowment of the inhabitants would have caused them to fall behind the rest of mankind no matter how favourable their environment had been. Many modern commentators are perhaps not so far removed from this thesis as might appear at first. Few modern anthropologists or archae-ologists would care to use the crude classification of 'savagery, barbarism and civilisation'. 'Barbarism' is a loaded word (and a relative one: the great art historian Bernard Berenson could refer to Italian paintings of the thirteenth century as 'barbaric'); it is plainly better avoided. But Victorian observers were attempting to describe what modern writers would prefer to call a 'high' or 'mature' Iron Age civilisation. For those who approached it from an environmental point of view, the outlook for the African was necessarily much more favourable than for the racialist. With Victorian confidence in the mastery of man over nature, they believed that the environment could be drastically changed.

Environment obviously did play a crucial role in the development of Africa. The Sahara desert was the great divide. The North African littoral looked towards Europe and the Near East. Despite links through the valley of the Nile and the routes across the Sahara itself, in historic times its develop-ment has been very different from that of Africa south of the Sahara. The savanna belt immediately south of the Sahara, or the highlands of East Africa, provided a quite different environment from that of the rain forests of West Africa or the Congo. In the extreme south of the continent were temperate lands which demanded a quite different form of economy from the tropical regions further north. Deserts and forests formed natural barriers to free communications in some parts of Africa. Africa was also unfortunate in having few easily navigable rivers. The presence of the tsetse fly over large areas of the continent precluded the use of draught animals and meant that goods had to be carried by human porters. All these factors were a severe check to rapid developments.

Geographical factors affected the very complex distribution of races in modern Africa. North of the Sahara the earliest known peoples were the ancestors of modern Berbers but, in historic times, there has been a considerable admixture of Arab blood. South of the Sahara the **San** and the **Khoikhoi** (who used to be called the Bushmen and the Hottentots respectively) are probably derived from the aboriginal stock – so far as that can be guessed at. The origin of the peoples who are today the most numerous race in Africa, whom the Victorians would have called the 'Negro', is not known with certainty, although it may well have been in the equatorial forests of West Africa. The term 'Negro' has fallen out of favour because it has been used in a derogatory sense, especially in America. But the preferred modern term 'Black' is not very satisfactory in this context because it is used much more widely than the Victorian anthropologists' definition of the 'true Negro' in Africa. In northern and eastern Africa there was some immigration of other peoples from western Asia whom the Victorians referred to as '**Hamitic**'. The Victorians believed that these people were 'white' and so, by definition, superior to the 'Negro', which led to the theory that wherever a more advanced culture appeared in black Africa, it must be due to some infusion of 'Hamitic' blood. Modern anthropologists would dismiss the idea of the existence of any group which could be defined as 'Hamitic'.

Linguistic divisions are sometimes more useful, and meaningful, than racial ones. The most widespread family of languages in Africa are the **Bantu** ones. Unfortunately, because of misuse, the term 'Bantu' is also offensive to many, but it is in origin a purely linguistic term. These languages are not always mutually intelligible but they clearly derive from some common original, as Spanish and Italian derive from Latin. Their original heartland has been variously placed in the Great Lakes region and in the Congo but as those who spoke them migrated southwards, they became dominant over most of Africa south of the Sahara. The most likely explanation of the beginning of this expansion is an improvement in food supplies consequent on the arrival of new crops – different kinds of bananas and yams – from Asia, about the beginning of the Christian era. Numbers increased rapidly and extensive movements of population followed. These movements, arising from developments within African societies, were to have significant consequences for Europeans when they first began to venture into the interior of Africa in the nineteenth century, but the Europeans themselves were almost totally ignorant of them.

San: Modern term used to denote people known in the nineteenth century as the Bushmen.

Khoikhoi: (sometimes simply *Khoi*) Modern name for people previously called the Hottentots.

Hamitic   peoples: Nineteenth-century anthropologists posited a race, lighter-skinned and more advanced than the African 'Negro', who were probably responsible for any signs of higher civilisation in Black Africa. Modern anthropologists do not believe any such race ever existed.

Bantu: In origins a linguistic term, denoting a related family of African languages. It fell into disrepute because of the derogatory way in which it was applied to those who spoke them during the *apartheid* era in South Africa.

EGYPT

Nineteenth-century Europe knew that Africa had produced one of the great civilisations of the ancient world, that of Egypt, the longest lasting of all high civilisations, its history stretching from the fourth to the first millennium BC. Egypt derived some of its ideas and technology from western Asia, some from Black Africa to its south and perhaps some from a hypothetical 'Saharan-Sudanese' culture embracing a wide of variety of peoples and stretching from the Atlantic to the Red Sea during the 'wet' Makalian phase (c. 5500–2500 BC), when much of the Sahara was fertile. But essentially Egyptian civilisation was an indigenous product created in the Nile Valley at astonishing speed. Within a thousand years the Egyptians had developed a state characterised by divine kingship, a highly developed bureaucracy and a hardworking and skilled artisan force. Egypt's great age was over by the first millennium BC but for some centuries it formed part of what western Europe was later to think of as the classical world of Greece and Rome. Egypt was conquered by the Arabs in the seventh century AD and by the Ottoman Turks in the sixteenth. Egypt virtually disappeared from the gaze of Europe. Eighteenth-century Europe knew little about it. When Napoleon's troops first set eyes on the monuments of Luxor (the ancient Thebes) in 1799 they are said to have spontaneously grounded their arms and stared in amazement.

From the time of the Napoleonic invasion of Egypt the new science of Egyptology was born. Its earliest exponents were mainly Frenchmen and Italians. The Louvre in Paris became full of Egyptian antiquities. Later, particularly after the British occupation of Egypt in 1882, Englishmen also became prominent in the field. The whole cult reached its climax with the discovery of Tutankhamun's tomb by Howard Carter and the Earl of Carnarvon in the 1920s. Egyptology reinforced the European sense of the mystery and richness of Africa. 'From Africa always something new.' Strangely enough it did not increase Europeans' respect for the inhabitants of Africa. They did not really identify the Egyptian **fellahin** they knew with the authors of the ancient civilisation which fascinated them, even though Victorian anthropologists believed that the Egyptian peasants, both Coptic Christians and Muslims, were direct descendants of the ancient Egyptians with comparatively little admixture of Arab blood. The Egyptians themselves were occasionally sufficiently conscious of their past to remind the British during the long British occupation of Egypt that their ancestors had built the pyramids while their conquerors' ancestors were still dressed in woad, but this was the exception not the rule. The European attitude at its extreme was represented by Lord Curzon who could stand in the shadow of the pyramids and ponder seriously on the possibility of 'civilising' the Egyptians.

Fellah (plural fellahin): An Egyptian peasant.

Sudan (Soudan): In its more restricted sense this means the area of the modern state of Sudan, the Upper Nile region, often called in the nineteenth century the Egyptian Sudan. But it can also be applied to a wide swath of territory between the Sahara to the north and the rain forests to the south. This was sometimes called the French Soudan and sometimes spelt Soudan, rather than Sudan. But the usage was not consistent.

The history of Egypt is often not treated as part of the history of Africa and certainly Egypt had vital links with the Mediterranean world and with Asia but it also interacted in important ways with Black Africa to its south. At the greatest extent of its power dynastic Egypt had governed what later ages called the Egyptian **Sudan**, the biblical land of Kush. When Egypt proper succumbed to foreign invaders in the first millennium BC, Egyptian civilisation continued in Kush. As Professors Oliver and Fage point out, a development which western historians have seen simply as the slow decline of Egypt was 'according to the very different perspectives of African history . . . ancient Egypt moving nearer to black Africa, at a period when at least part of black Africa was more capable than it had ever been before of experiencing the influence of an urban civilisation' (1990: 40). Kush itself became increasingly a Black kingdom. It stood at important trade crossroads. It proved to have such resources of iron ore that the often quoted archaeologist Sayce, standing amid the slag heaps of its ancient capital Meroe, christened it 'the Birmingham of Africa'. Meroe itself declined in the early centuries of the Christian era before the rising power of Axum, which had its centre in the Ethiopian highlands. But it passed on many ideas of Egyptian civilisation, and probably some metal-working techniques as well, to the Black kingdoms of tropical Africa. These ideas seem to have spread along two main axes, one westwards through the savanna belt lying between the Sahara desert and the equatorial forests, where important states were to rise a few centuries later; another, more problematic, southwards along the highlands of east Africa to the area of the modern Zimbabwe.

ISLAM

A few centuries later, in the seventh century AD, Africa suffered the first of the great alien invasions of historic times, that of the Arabs. They swiftly overran the whole of Africa north of the Sahara and by the second decade of the eighth century had reached the Atlantic coast of Morocco and had begun the invasion of Spain. Farther south they were checked by the Christian kingdom of Nubia, the heir of Kush, which did not finally collapse until the fourteenth century. Another Christian kingdom, Abyssinia, the successor to Axum, never surrendered and remained an isolated island of Christianity in the surrounding sea of Islam. Faint memories of Abyssinia, the fabled land of Prester John, remained in Europe. Apart from that, Europeans had little idea of what was happening in Africa. A few centuries later another wave of Arab invaders passed south of the Sahara along the Sudanic belt. Physically the Arab presence was always a limited one in this region but the ideas of Islam made rapid headway. The adoption of Islam involved far less of a 'culture shock' for many of the existing inhabitants than Christianity was to be later. In particular it required no fundamental upheaval of family structure, since polygamy was permitted. The adoption of Islam had certain distinct advantages. It brought people into the great diplomatic and trading world which stretched from the Atlantic to China.

The savanna belt supported a number of states, or 'empires', in the period which corresponded to the Middle Ages in Europe. They attained a high degree of organisation and urban civilisation. Among these empires one of the earliest and most interesting was that of Ghana. Geographically, it lay well to the north of the present state of Ghana, but a tradition, accepted by some modern scholars but rejected by others, traced a major migration of peoples from ancient to modern Ghana. Unquestionably the adoption of the ancient name by the citizens of what, in colonial times, had been known as the Gold Coast, represented a desire to identify themselves with what they felt to be their own past, before it had been rudely interrupted by foreign invasions. Historic Ghana was, according to tradition, founded about AD 300. It was a great iron-working centre. It also stood at a most important trade crossroads. Gold came from the mines to the south and was exchanged for the salt of the Sahara. Ghana was essentially a Black creation, although there may have been some diffusion of culture from the Berbers across the Sahara. When the Arabs arrived in force in the eleventh century, their writers testified to its military strength and the splendour of its capital.

Another great savanna empire was that of Mali (its name too has been adopted by a modern African state) which flourished between the thirteenth and fourteenth centuries, probably reaching its height in the fourteenth. Mali burst on the attention of an astonished world in the 1320s when its ruler, Kankan Musa, went on pilgrimage to Mecca. Arab writers recorded the splendour of his entourage. He took so much gold to Cairo that the Egyptian currency was undermined and had to be revalued. Not surprisingly he became known as the 'King of the Gold Mines'. This was not strictly true. Mali, like Ghana, was essentially a trading state, but its economy was highly developed and its chief city, Timbuktu, was already a legend. Modern writers have compared it to the cities of medieval Italy as a centre of learning and commerce.

Slightly younger than Mali was Songhay, another trading state with its capital at Gao, which included the Hausa states of what later became Northern Nigeria, and which seems to have succeeded to Mali's position when the latter declined. Apart from these three, the history of which is becoming increasingly clear, there was the more obscure empire of 'Kanem-Bornu', which seems really to have been a blanket term to cover a series of states which flourished from the eighth to the sixteenth centuries in an area through which migrants and ideas passed steadily. Archaeological evidence suggests that it attained a high degree of technical skill and there may have been important cultural interaction with Christian Nubia.

The savanna belt was a great highway of trade from the Nile to the Niger and beyond. It also lay athwart the trade routes from the North African littoral, across the Sahara to the great mineral riches of the Guinea coast. Lake Chad was at the centre of many of these routes, earning from one writer the all too memorable soubriquet of the 'Clapham Junction' of West Africa. These routes were determined by permanent geographical facts and when, in the late nineteenth century, the European powers tried to open the region to their own commerce they found themselves contending for the same strategic advantages as many generations of their African predecessors, although playing in the process a curious game of 'blind man's bluff', since they rarely had adequate information.

One problem exercised European commentators when, in modern times, they first gained some understanding of these savanna empires. Were they 'African' or 'Arab' civilisations? A later generation of writers has come to see this question as essentially meaningless. Some of these states, notably Ghana, antedated the coming of Islam. Others do seem to have reached their greatest prosperity after their ruling classes were converted to Islam, but only a limited number of Arabs penetrated the region. They intermarried freely with, and were absorbed by, the indigenous population. Undoubtedly they derived many ideas from the common stock of Islam, just as the nations of northern Europe derived many of their ideas from the common stock of Christianity which came originally from the Mediterranean, but they adapted and modified them to their own requirements and created their own culture in so doing. This fruitful contact continued until the seventeenth century, when a series of events seems to have cut off these savanna empires from the heartland of Islam in the Near East. This fortuitous severing of links may have had disastrous consequences for West African development. As Basil Davidson put it, 'never isolated from the medieval world – the world of Arab greatness – the Sudan became isolated from the post-medieval world, the world of technical advance and industrial revolution' (1970: 113).

How much did medieval or renaissance Europe know of these contemporary African empires? Clearly, a certain amount. The Arab conquest of the North African coast had severed older European trade links with West Africa across the Sahara which had existed in classical times. But a few Arabs, for one reason or another, passed information on to Europeans, and Jews had a degree of freedom of travel in both societies. Some important Arabic accounts, notably those of the geographer al-Bakri and the traveller Ibn Battuti, were available in the West but were virtually unused because of the language difficulty. Al-Idrisi, who lived for some time at the court of Roger of Sicily in the eleventh century, also wrote in Arabic but his writings became available in Latin in the seventeenth century. But the best known account was the *Description of Africa*, written by Leo Africanus, an Arab from the Maghrib who had travelled extensively in Africa before he became a Christian prisoner of war. This was published in Italian in the middle of the sixteenth century and translated into English in 1600. Something of the history of North Africa was known from the work of Luis del Marmol Carvajel, who wrote in Spanish using Arab sources in the sixteenth century. The Catalan map of 1375, emanating from a Jewish school of cartographers on Mallorca, showed Timbuktu, Mali and Gao in roughly the correct places. It is possible that Henry the Navigator was inspired to send Portuguese sailors to explore the coasts of Africa in the fifteenth century, not only to find a route to the spice islands of the East but also to make contact with those African kingdoms. Nothing new of much significance was published after the sixteenth century, but memories still coloured European observations of West Africa as late as the eighteenth century. They were not greatly impressed by the African peoples they met on the coast, but legend still spoke of great kingdoms in the interior, and writers were forced to posit 'degenerate' peoples on the coast and purer survivals inland.

Another part of Africa which was deeply affected by Islam was the east coast. Just as North Africa traditionally looked across the Mediterranean to Europe, so East Africa looked across the Red Sea and the Indian Ocean to Arabia, India and even China. There is ample archaeological evidence that a great Indian Ocean trading complex involving East Africa long antedated Arab conquests. But the incorporation of the East African coast into the Islamic system in the thirteenth century gave a new impetus to trade. Great cities – Kilwa, Mombasa and Malindi – were built on the coast. Here, as in the Sudan, it is sterile to ask whether this was an Arab or an African civilisation. The predominant racial type was Black, but Blacks who had adopted Arab dress and names along with the Islamic religion. Davidson suggests that the relationship between East Africa and Arabia was not unlike that between England and Renaissance Italy. Ideas and culture flowed from the one but were adapted by the native genius of the other. The trading cities of the coast were the intermediaries between the African hinterland (although apparently without exercising any political control there) and the ocean trading routes. Africa imported textiles and other goods from India. It exported gold and ivory. Slavery always formed a minor item in this trade, but in the late eighteenth-century there was a great expansion in the Arab slave trade and, for the first time, raiding parties penetrated deep into the interior of Africa to obtain slaves in large numbers, disrupting the life of many communities in the period immediately before the arrival of Europeans in the interior.

THE SLAVE TRADE

If the Arab slave trade disrupted East Africa, on the west coast there had been the long drawn-out agony of the Atlantic slave trade. Almost all the maritime nations of western Europe participated. Estimates of the numbers thus transported vary greatly. Modern research would suggest a figure between 11 and 13 millions (3 millions of whom were carried in British ships). Slavery of a limited and domestic kind was already an established institution in African society when the Europeans arrived, but this represented a drain of healthy young men and women of a totally different order. Apart from those actually transported, an unknown number died as the result of the intertribal conflicts which the trade provoked.

But it is as well to remember that, if the Europeans were the buyers, Africans were the sellers. Europeans did not venture inland to capture their slaves as the Arabs did, but bought what the Africans brought to the coast to await shipment. It used to be believed that Europeans were so slow to penetrate into Africa because of climatic and geographical difficulties. It is now generally accepted that these were no greater than those the Europeans encountered and overcame in Central America. It was the strength of African political organisation, at least in West Africa, which kept the Europeans on the coast so long. The Africans supplied the goods the Europeans wanted, whether it was slaves or gold. The Europeans knew that the gold mines lay a bare hundred miles from the coast but they never saw them. Between the Europeans and the African merchants conditions of equal trading partners prevailed. Some commentators have suggested that the slave trade, morally repugnant though it was, did act as an important stimulus as well as an instrument of destruction on the West Coast. The slave trade period saw the rise of Benin, Oyo, Dahomey and the Ashanti Confederation. The appearance of European ships along the Guinea coast certainly altered the direction of trade. Previously the mineral wealth of the coast had gone north to the trading cities of the savanna belt and even across the Sahara to North Africa; now it went south to the sea.

SOUTHERN AFRICA

The southern tip of Africa presented an entirely different picture from East or West Africa. Here there were no obstacles to European penetration. The climate was temperate and the hinterland accessible: above all, the region was uninhabited apart from some wandering groups of **San** and Khoikhoi. Bartholomew Diaz landed near the Cape of Good Hope in 1488, but the Portuguese never made much use of the Cape region as a staging post to the

San: Modern term used to denote people known in the nineteenth century as the Bushmen.

East. They preferred to call at East African ports like Mozambique. It was their successors, the Dutch, who established a base at Table Bay in 1652. This was intended only as a service station for ships of the Dutch East India Company going to and from the East, but a few company employees remained at the Cape after their discharge and began to farm. A number of settlers, many of them French **Huguenots**, came out. By the middle of the eighteenth century settlement stretched 300 miles east of Cape Town. They met with no serious resistance from the Khoikhoi. The Company neither encouraged nor restricted their actions and the land was in practice free. In the 1770s the eastward expansion reached the Great Fish River. For the first time the Boer settlers encountered stiff resistance. Quite unknowingly, they had bumped into another stream of settlers coming south. These were the vanguard of the **Bantu**-speaking Africans. In the words of one historian, 'The free land had run out and Africa was no longer endless. . . . The contact now was between two well-organised societies both of which were based on cattle and both of which required ever-broadening lands in order to survive' (Morris, 1968: 23–4), or as another put it, even more pungently, 'When the gap filled by this race was at last closed, strong-armed cattle-rustlers on each side of the border at last met their match' (Keppel-Jones, 1963: 53)

The advance of the Bantu-speaking peoples had already gone on for over a thousand years. Some historians have suggested that the 'Dark Ages' of the East African coast, between the fourth and the tenth centuries, when little is known of its history, mark the period when these invaders settled along the coastline of modern Kenya and Tanzania. The scanty sources seem to suggest a change in the racial composition of the people of the coast. The migrants had passed the Zambezi by the fourteenth century and settled in the Transvaal by the sixteenth. By the early eighteenth century different groups had passed east and west of the Drakensberg Range and had settled in what became Natal and in the area east of the Great Fish River.

They were a highly organised, essentially warlike, people. They treated the Khoikhoi whom they found in their path as cavalierly as the **Boers** did. Even now it is difficult to follow either their movements or their politics in detail, but from time to time they threw up leaders of exceptional talent. The first of these to make an impression on European observers was Shaka, a splendid military tactician, who earned the nickname 'the Black Napoleon'. Under Shaka, the **Zulus**, who were in origin only one clan of the Nguni, who had occupied the Transvaal region in the sixteenth century, became one of the most formidable fighting forces in southern Africa. A quarrel between Shaka and one of his lieutenants, Mzilikazi, led to the latter leading his followers, who became known to Europeans as the **Matabele**, northwards out of Shaka's domains into the land of the **Mashona** in the modern Zimbabwe. Possibly Mzilikazi turned northwards only because it was the most convenient

Huguenots: French Protestants who had to flee persecution in their own country after 1685. Most went to other European countries but a significant number went to Cape Colony, where they were quickly assimilated by the Boers.

Bantu: In origins a linguistic term, denoting a related family of African languages. It fell into disrepute because of the derogatory way in which it was applied to those who spoke them during the *apartheid* era in South Africa.

Boer: Derived from the Dutch for 'farmer', applied to Dutch (and some German and French Huguenot) settlers in South Africa, who spoke Afrikaans, not English, as their first language.

Zulu: A particular group of the Nguni people, who established a powerful kingdom in southern Africa, at much the same time as the Boers were moving north from the Cape.

Matabele: The usual name in the Victorian period for the people now known as the Ndebele. They were an offshoot of the Zulus, who moved into the area that later became Southern Rhodesia.

Mashona: A peaceful pastoral tribe, who lived in what became Southern Rhodesia, and were harassed by the Matabele in the period immediately before the arrival of the Europeans direction to take to escape the wrathful Shaka. Northward movements were not unprecedented in the long saga of these migrants' wanderings. But it may also have reflected a realisation that the southern frontier was closing. Donald Morris summed up the situation dramatically:

> History had offered them a continent . . . and they had dallied a little too long. When Van Riebeeck landed at the Cape in 1652, the nearest Bantu were 500 miles to the north and 1,000 miles to the [east] and in this generous toehold the newcomers flourished, so that when the two civilisations finally met . . . the Bantu encountered not an artificial colonial outpost but a fully-fledged vigorous folk, rooted and growing, with a vested interest in its hinterlands. Because they did not know that they were in a race with a continent for a prize, the Bantu lost it. The hare in a twinkling of a century, had outstripped the tortoise. (Morris, 1968: 26)

Kaffir wars: A long series of wars on the eastern boundary of Cape Colony, which lasted from 1779 to 1853.

The result was an endless and dreary succession of **'Kaffir' wars** on the border where the two peoples met. These in turn had a profound effect on Boer psychology for they continued to see the 'Bantu' as something alien to their society, the enemy beyond the frontier even when economic pressures had compelled them to draw their rivals into their own society as a labour force – in the striking metaphor of De Kiewiet, 'the pressures of white colonization pumped them [the Bantu] into every artery and limb of South Africa's social body, until they could not be drained from it safely' (De Kiewiet, 1937: 2).

3

The Victorian image of Africa

The misunderstandings that bedevilled race relations in southern Africa were no doubt aggravated by the peculiarly introspective and self-sufficient nature of Boer society, but they found echoes all over the continent. Europeans in the nineteenth century were almost totally ignorant of all but a few small corners of Africa. Until late in the century they knew practically nothing of the geography or the peoples of its interior. When they spoke – as they frequently did – of the 'Dark Continent', they properly meant a continent which was dark to them, about which they knew little. But this idea merged imperceptibly with another more sinister idea of 'Darkest Africa', Negro Africa, a place of savagery and brutality. Circumstances seemed to conspire to increase misunderstandings.

When Europeans first penetrated into Africa south of the Sahara a number of African communities were in decline. The Atlantic slave trade in the west and the Arab slave trade in the east accounted for some of this, but other African states, like the savanna empires, seem to have declined for purely local reasons. It is possible that the '**Balkanisation**' of Africa was more extreme in the middle of the nineteenth century than it had been for centuries. If it is true that it was African strength which had kept the Europeans on the coast in the past, this may itself be a contributory factor in the timing of the European 'opening up' of Africa. Probably, though this was secondary to another factor, the enormous technological gap which had appeared between European and African civilisations. When the Portuguese first reached the Congo in the late fifteenth century they found a powerful and well-organised state. In the sixteenth century cordial relations developed between the two powers. Congolese came to Europe. Portuguese experts, including even printers, went to the Congo to instruct the inhabitants. Clearly, even then, the Congolese admired European skills but, equally clearly, no unbridgeable gap was felt to exist between the two cultures. This fruitful relationship continued until the Portuguese became more interested in their Brazilian colony and largely lost interest in Africa except as a source of slaves. A few centuries later such

Balkanisation: A collection of small states, often with ill-defined boundaries, created by the break-up of a larger unit; derived from the situation in the Balkans during the break-up of the Ottoman empire in the nineteenth century.

a relationship would have been almost unthinkable. The peasant communities of medieval Europe, even perhaps the towns of Renaissance Europe, were not impossibly far removed from their African counterparts. But Africa had nothing remotely like the urban civilisation of Europe in the period after the industrial revolution. Psychologically the two cultures had moved very far apart, the more so because of the great stress nineteenth-century Europeans were prone to put upon technological advance. To them it became almost a badge of 'civilisation'.

But Europe had changed at incredible and unprecedented speed in more ways than in technological advance in the centuries after the Renaissance and, perhaps still more, after the scientific revolution of the eighteenth century. Whole ways of thinking had been revolutionised. Rationalism and humanitarianism had made Europe turn its back on much of its own past. Many things which nineteenth-century Europeans found shocking in Africa – public executions, torture, mutilating punishments such as lopping off the hand of a thief, a prevailing fear of witchcraft – would have been part of the fabric of life to their own recent ancestors. At no moment in time perhaps were Europeans less able to understand African society than at a period of breakneck change in their own in the nineteenth century.

THE INFLUENCE OF THE SLAVE TRADE

European views of Black Africa were originally formed during the slave trade era and related particularly to the coast of West Africa. In the eighteenth century West Africa was particularly important to Britain. Britain sent manufactured goods to West Africa to exchange for slaves who were shipped to the West Indies in return for sugar and similar tropical products. Although there are difficulties in accepting, in its simple form, Dr Eric Williams' famous thesis (*Capitalism and Slavery*, 1944) that the profits of this 'triangular' trade provided the capital to support the industrial revolution in Britain – not least because there are other demonstrable sources for that capital – it was certainly central to the British economy in a way that West African trade never was to be again.

West Africa therefore naturally attracted some popular attention. The slave trade itself was necessarily brutalising for all who participated in it. Most Europeans were shocked by their first contact with it. Dealing with human beings as merchandise in this way almost compelled those concerned not to see them as human beings at all. Paradoxically, however, since they also dealt with African merchants who sold the slaves, the slavers were among those most able to think of Africans as individuals and not just see them as a stereotype 'Negro'.

The agitation for the abolition of the trade in the late eighteenth century cut both ways in forming the image. Some defenders of the trade, and in the next generation those who opposed the abolition of slavery itself in the British empire, argued that the Negro was not fully human, or was such a degenerate form of humanity that slavery was a desirable condition for him. Arguments raged between those who supported the theory of 'polygenesis', that is that the different races of mankind were created separately and were therefore technically different 'species', and the more orthodox believers in 'mono-genesis', that the whole human race sprang from a single pair, Adam and Eve, whatever might have happened to its different branches since. It was notice-able, though, that even those who argued for abolition tended to condemn the cruelty of the trade and of the condition of slavery, or to emphasise the spiritual equality of mankind which derived from the fatherhood of God, and to slide over the difficult question of the temporal equality of the Negro to the white man. Indeed, many abolitionists inclined to take a paternalistic line and to suggest that the Negro must be defended because he could not defend himself, to see him as a child in an adult world. [**Doc. 1, p. 98**]

There were a few correctives to the general 'slave' stereotype. There was the literary tradition of the 'noble savage' which had a considerable vogue in the eighteenth century. This was usually applied to the American 'Indian' or the Polynesian, but the African Negro occasionally benefited from it. Indeed the first African hero in English literature (leaving aside the difficult question of Othello's colour) was Oroonoko who appeared in 1688. More important than this, real Africans were not totally unknown in England in the eight-eenth century. First, there were several thousand personal servants of one kind or another. Some of them had originally been slaves brought from the West Indies, but the famous judgment of Lord Mansfield in Somersett's case in 1772 laid down that no man could be a slave in England, whatever his sta-tus elsewhere. There were also, perhaps more surprisingly, some fifty African 'trainees' in Liverpool in the 1780s direct from West Africa, learning English and English commercial practices. The scanty information available suggests that the relations of these people with the indigenous population were nei-ther better nor worse than those of any other group of foreigners, generally amicable but prone to occasional friction arising from dislike of strange customs or competition for jobs or girls.

EIGHTEENTH CENTURY SCIENTIFIC INTEREST

If slavery forced men to formulate an attitude towards the Negro, the late eighteenth century also saw an unprecedented flowering of scientific interest. Both geographical and biological enquiries were the fashion. Captain Cook's voyages had solved many long-standing problems concerning the Pacific. A number of men longed to do the same for Africa. The African Association (strictly the 'Association for Promoting the Discovery of the Interior Parts of Africa') was founded in 1788, largely under the inspiration of Joseph Banks, the President of the Royal Society, who had accompanied Cook to the Pacific in 1768, with the support of a few personal friends. They were principally interested in the interior of West Africa. Although nothing new had emerged since the accounts, mainly Arabic, of the tenth to the sixteenth centuries (see above pp. 12–13), these had become widely available in English for the first time in a number of famous collected works in which the eighteenth century excelled. The greatest triumph of the African Association was the despatch of Mungo Park's first expedition, that of 1795–7, which finally established the general direction of the river Niger which had long mystified Europeans.

There was also some British government interest in this period when it was looking for possible compensation for the material and prestige losses of the American War of Independence and for strategic positions during the French revolutionary and Napoleonic wars. Mungo Park's second expedition to the Niger, that of 1805, was government-financed. This interest survived into the early nineteenth century. In 1817 a mission was despatched to the king of the **Ashanti** in his capital at Kumasi, to sign a political and commercial treaty. A member of the expedition, T.E. Bowdich, published a book about it, *Mission from Cape Coast Castle to Ashantee*, two years later. This was a meticulous account of Ashanti culture, including beautifully illustrated sections on subjects like architecture and musical instruments. Bowdich did not attempt to disguise the harsh side of Ashanti life, including public executions and the human sacrifices demanded on the death of the king and on certain other occasions, but they were seen in their context as part of a highly organised society.

Ashanti: A strong and warlike group of African people in West Africa, who came together in the Ashanti Confederation. They oppressed weaker groups like the Fanti and often supplied European slave traders with captives.

Generally, however, British interest in West Africa declined during the first thirty or forty years of the nineteenth century, although the Sierra Leone experiment continued. This was the nearest approach to a colony that Britain maintained on the coast at that time, although there were small communities of merchants resident on the Gold Coast and at the mouth of the river Gambia. The Sierra Leone colony was founded in 1787 as a home for freed slaves and was the forerunner of the better-known American experiment in Liberia. Sierra Leone had a chequered early career and played a paradoxical role in the development of British thinking about Black Africa. It was under frequent attack from the indigenous population of the area, and while it convinced many that, given time, Africans could adopt a European form of civilisation successfully, it also led to increasingly hostile comparisons being drawn between westernised Africans and their still 'primitive' brethren who had been a danger to the colony.

SLAVE TRADE VERSUS LEGITIMATE TRADE

Interest in the West Coast revived with the ill-fated 'Niger experiment' of 1841–2. This is always associated with the name of the anti-slavery campaigner Thomas Fowell Buxton, although he took many of his ideas from James MacQueen, an earlier writer, better known in his own day than in ours. Although Britain and the United States had outlawed the slave trade in 1807 and other European countries had committed themselves, at least nominally, to the same position in 1815, Britain alone of the European powers had made serious attempts to police the West Coast and stamp out the trade. Its success had been limited. As long as slavery continued in the United States and Brazil, slavers of various nationalities would try to carry on the contraband trade, and as long as there were customers, Africans would sell slaves. A growing body of opinion in Britain believed that only legitimate commerce would stamp out the trade. The African middlemen must have commodities other than human beings to sell to European traders. In West Africa a promising beginning had been made in palm oil, much in demand for soap and for the lubrication of the new machinery now employed in industrial Britain. The Niger experiment was an attempt to expand this. It failed because of the heavy mortality suffered by the expedition, mainly from malaria.

Niger experiment: A well-meaning attempt in the eighteen-forties, by anti-slavery campaigners, to replace the slave trade with legitimate commerce in palm oil in the Niger delta. It failed because so many Europeans died, mainly of malaria.

But the principle was of wider application than the Niger. That legitimate trade would drive out the slave trade became a generally held maxim to be applied to the Arab slave trade of the East Coast as well as to the Atlantic trade, which died a natural death with the abolition of slavery in the United States in the 1860s. (Although slavery was not abolished in Brazil until the 1880s it alone was not sufficient to maintain the trade.) But the argument went further. Commerce, it was held, would raise the African standard of life. It was the natural transition from 'barbarism' to civilisation. It was necessary for the advance of Africa, and Europeans were increasingly beginning to feel responsible for bringing about such an advance. [**Doc. 2, p. 98**] It also, of course, promised rewards to European traders and investors, but a historian very sympathetic to Africa, P.D. Curtin (1965), rightly warns against the crude simplification of seeing this philosophy simply as a cover for immediate economic self-interest. Among the many theories advanced in the middle of the century there were even some forerunners of Lugard's famous *Dual Mandate*, the hypothesis that the interests of the Europeans and the Africans were essentially complementary. 'Europe benefited by the wonderful increase in the amenities of life for the mass of her people which followed the opening up of Africa at the end of the nineteenth century. Africa benefited by the influx of manufactured goods, and the substitution of law and order for the methods of barbarism' (Lugard, 1922: 615).

'BACKWARD' AFRICA

Despite its ill-success, the Niger experiment temporarily revived British interest in Black Africa, especially West Africa, but it was at a much lower intellectual level than the scientific enquiries of Park or Bowdich. The 1840s saw a rash of ephemeral publications, mainly travellers' tales. Curtin remarks that the only excuse for yet another book seemed to be a story of personal adventure and the accounts became steadily more subjective and more sensational. The nadir was perhaps reached with J. Smith's *Trade and Travel in the Gulph of Guinea* (1851) with chapters such as 'Human Sacrifice, Nailing Prisoners, Jack Ketch, Decapitation, Cooking and eating human flesh, King Pepple eats King Amacree's heart . . .'. But saturation point was eventually reached. Interest fell off in the 1850s. *Blackwood's* Magazine, which had carried much on West Africa in earlier decades, published nothing at all in the 1850s. The noted traveller, Richard Burton, wrote in 1845 that people were bored with 'ugly savages' and 'with the monotonous recital of rapine, treachery and murder'. Unfortunately this boredom also extended to much more serious studies. The great compendium of information about Africa gathered by the German Heinrich Barth, first published in English in 1875, sold so badly that the print of 2,250 copies for the first three volumes was reduced to 1000 for the later volumes.

This dismissal of African societies as savage and uninteresting coincided with other developments. The period 1829 to 1859 saw a complete rethinking of biological concepts. This reappraisal went back earlier, in fact to Linnaeus's work in 1734, and was to culminate in Darwin's *Origin of Species* (1859). Men were fascinated by the 'classification' of natural phenomena; the definition of species and ideas of natural selection and even of evolution were in the air long before Darwin gave them a coherent form. It was natural that the study of human races should play a part in these enquiries. Old disputes about polygenesis and monogenesis were revived, given special impetus by the arguments about the abolition of slavery in the United States. It was understandable that European scholars should conclude that the white or 'Caucasian' races were the most highly developed. All men are prejudiced in favour of their own kind and the superior technology of Europe gave the proposition a good deal of plausibility in the nineteenth century. It was easy enough then to rank other races according to their resemblance to Europeans, and physically 'Negroes' were the least like Europeans in their external appearance. (No one, of course, could know in the nineteenth century that blood groups and 'tissue typing' would cut across all racial groups.) This comforting thesis seemed to receive reinforcement from the fact that the Chinese and other Asians, who were more like Europeans, had achieved some degree of civilisation. The Africans at the bottom of the heap seemed to be sunk in savagery.

As ideas of evolution gained a hold on the public imagination, men increasingly saw African societies as examples of what their own societies had been in earlier eras, 'contemporary ancestors' in H.A.C. Cairns' phrase. This theory at least held out hope that the Africans could improve. Even in the nineteenth century it was attacked from two different sides. First, there were the objections of a man of African descent, the West Indian Edward Blyden, an important figure, who has belatedly become the subject of serious study. Writing in 1887, he rejected the idea that 'the Negro is the European in embryo . . . and that when, by and by, he shall enjoy the advantages of civilisation and culture, he will become like the Europeans; in other words, that the Negro is on the same line of progress, in the same groove, with the Europeans, but infinitely in the rear' (Cairns, 1965: 89). A more common type of objection to trying to change the African was that expressed by a correspondent to *John Bull* in 1823: 'We are expending our thousands and tens of thousands a year: to do what, Sir? To wash the Blackamoor white – monstrous absurdity!' (Curtin, 1965: 261).

In fact the British taxpayer had little reason to complain for most of the century that his money was being spent in Africa. The upkeep of the Africa squadron to thwart the remaining slavers cost a certain amount until the 1860s. So did the upkeep of the four British stations on the West African coast, the Gambia, Sierra Leone, the Gold Coast (Cape Coast Castle) and, after 1862, Lagos, but in 1865 a Select Committee of the House of Commons reported that Britain would be well-advised to relinquish all her holdings on the West Coast, except perhaps Freetown in Sierra Leone, which had possibilities as a naval base. Although the recommendations of the Committee were never carried out, they faithfully reflected the lack of official interest in Africa in the period immediately preceding the Scramble.

The new interest in Africa in the late nineteenth century was a private, not an official, matter. It is interesting to see both how it differed from, and how it built on, earlier precedents. Many British attitudes to Africa were formed during their long slaving and trading connections with the Guinea coast. What is surprising is how many of these attitudes were set and hardened, rather than modified and corrected, during the decades which saw the great European exploration of the African continent. Many of the basic elements in the eighteenth-century connection between Europe and Africa emerge strengthened and reinforced in the late nineteenth century. There is an increasing awareness of the economic possibilities of Africa, a genuine scientific interest, an equally genuine humanitarian interest, but arising from this melange, a deep and inexorable misunderstanding growing between Europeans and Africans.

THE MISSIONARIES

The heirs of the eighteenth-century humanitarians were the missionary societies. Missionary endeavour came to most of Africa comparatively late. The great era for the foundation of missionary societies in Britain was the late eighteenth century, but not all of them were at first interested in Africa. Even in Sierra Leone the Church Missionary Society (Anglican) did not begin work until 1806 and the Wesleyan Methodist Mission until 1811. The Wesleyans began work in Ashantiland in 1842. In what later became Nigeria the first permanent mission was established in 1844 by the Church Missionary Society. It is worthy of note that during the early days of the missions on the Guinea coast, Africans played a more prominent part than they were to be allowed to do again for several generations. Philip Quaque, a Fante who had been educated in England, was the chaplain at Cape Coast Castle in the late eighteenth and early nineteenth centuries. Rather later Samuel Crowther, a Yoruba who had been rescued from a slave ship and also educated in Britain, became the first Anglican bishop on the Niger. In South Africa the Boers had tended to avoid missionary activity among the Africans because of the tattered remnants of the doctrine that a baptised Christian had a claim to civil rights, irrespective of his nationality, but the London Missionary Society (inter-denominational Protestant) was active there by 1800. The Church Missionary Society had a small station at Mombasa on the East Coast, staffed by German Lutherans, in the middle of the century. Two of these Germans, Johann Krapf and Johann Rebmann, were the first Europeans to set eyes on Mount Kenya and Mount Kilimanjaro in 1847. But the classic missionary penetration into the interior of Africa was a phenomenon of the 1880s. The missionary societies, almost without exception, had very effective propaganda machines and the picture they drew of Africa gained very wide acceptance.

Unfortunately, in the opinion of Cairns (1965), the missionaries bore a special responsibility for the increasing 'cultural arrogance' of the British public and misrepresenting African society in a way calculated to give rise also to racial arrogance. The reasons are not difficult to discern. The missionaries were entirely dependent on public support and subscriptions to carry on their work. Missionaries were urged to send home detailed reports of their activities and of the conditions they found. These reports were then given a very wide circulation. The breadth of the range they covered may be judged by the fact that the societies found it worthwhile to run special publications for children and for 'working class' readers. To gain public sympathy missionaries were inevitably tempted to stress the temporal as well as the spiritual aspects of their work and to represent the life of the unconverted African here on earth as brutal and barbarous. Some reverted to a kind of 'before and after' vignette, representing the converted African as in a much happier condition. This form of propaganda (like the theories of the evolutionists) did at least portray the African as capable of improvement, but it also of necessity denigrated his indigenous culture. African religion was often ill-served by missionary observation. Few tried to penetrate below the surface and ask what rituals and apparent crudities meant to the believer. It was easier to assume that Africans worshipped monkeys and serpents, although one wit did comment that an observer from another planet might, on much the same evidence, come to the conclusion that Christians worshipped lambs and doves in their churches. Against this, however, must be set valuable pioneering work by the missionaries in the study of African languages and, where their prejudices were not too deeply engaged, some of the earliest attempts at scientific anthropology.

EXPLORATION AND ITS CONSEQUENCES

If humanitarian impulses produced ambiguous results in nineteenth-century Africa, so did science. Many motives drove men into Africa during the great age of exploration: a hope of gain, a love of adventure and just plain curiosity. The last should not be underestimated. The Victorians had intensely enquiring minds. The interior of Africa held the most tantalising mysteries left in the world after the exploration of the Americas, Australia and much of Asia. The public at home shared the thrill of discovery of the man on the spot. The Victorians loved heroes. R.C.K. Ensor once suggested that Victorian politicians were gladiatorial figures to the public, fulfilling a role that in the twentieth century was taken over by sporting personalities. Explorers and quarrelsome scientists seem to have filled something of the same role. Sometimes national competition entered into it, as in the race between Henry Morton Stanley and Savorgnan de Brazza to reach Stanley Pool in 1880, or of Lugard and Decoeur to reach Borgu in 1894. But at other times it seems to have been simply a love of a good scrap, as in the eager public anticipation of the expected confrontation between Richard Burton and John Hanning Speke at the British Association meeting in Bath in 1864 to defend their rival views of the source of the Nile – a confrontation prevented by Speke's death by shooting (probably accidental, although the suspicion of suicide has never been completely laid) on the very morning of the meeting.

The exploration of the interior of Africa centred on the four great river systems, the Niger, the Zambezi, the Nile and the Congo. The pioneering work on the Niger had been done long ago by Mungo Park. He was followed by Hugh Clapperton, the Lander brothers, William Bailkie, René Caillié, the

consul-general: Senior diplomatic post. An ambassador could only be accredited to an independent state. Egypt at this time was still legally part of the Ottoman empire. British envoys to Cairo (even Lord Cromer, who became for practical purposes the Governor of Egypt during the British occupation) technically bore only the title of Consul-General.

Frenchman who reached Timbuktu in the late 1820s, and the great German explorer Heinrich Barth. The Zambezi was, above all, the territory of David Livingstone who explored much of the course of the river between 1851 and 1856. In another great journey, 1858–64, with John Kirk, subsequently the British **consul-general** at Zanzibar, Livingstone explored the river Shire and discovered Lake Nyasa. His later years were taken up with his almost obsessive search for the headwaters of the Nile. Livingstone was rivalled in his search for the Nile by Richard Burton, who had already made a name for himself by his travels in Arabia and the Horn of Africa, and a young officer, John Hanning Speke, who accompanied Burton on his expedition in 1857–9. Speke returned alone in 1860 and met Samuel Baker and his young Hungarian wife who were travelling up the Nile, also searching for its source. Livingstone's activities also drew in two other men. Henry Morton Stanley and Lieutenant Lovett Cameron. Stanley was at this time a journalist on the staff of the *New York Herald* and he was sent to look for Livingstone who was believed to be missing near Lake Tanganyika in 1871. He met Livingstone and brought the story out for the world. Livingstone died in 1873, before Cameron, who had been sent out by the Royal Geographical Society, could make contact with him. Cameron carried on with his scientific mission, crossing central Africa from east to west (the first European to do so) and emerging in Portuguese Angola in 1875. Cameron had not attempted to follow the river Congo all the way and, when he heard of Livingstone's death, Stanley determined to do so and to settle once and for all whether the river 'Lualaba' which Livingstone had sighted was the Congo or the Nile. The result was Stanley's east–west crossing of the African continent between 1874 and 1877. The Germans Gerhard Rohlfs and Georg Schweinfurth, the Portuguese Serpa Pinto and the Frenchman de Brazza also contributed much to the exploration of Central Africa in this period.

All these men wrote long, and often vivid, accounts of their experiences for their public at home. [**Docs 1, 3, 4, 5, pp. 98, 99, 100, 101**] Read more than a century later, they exhibit some curious features. Most of them wrote as if they were the first men to penetrate to unknown regions. The African inhabitants were regarded as mere background, 'part of the local fauna'. At the same time they were very conscious of the possibilities of these 'new' regions. Africa was once again coming to seem an **El Dorado**. There had always been stories of the wealth of Africa, the legendary kingdom of Prester John or the fabled city of Timbuktu. Africa had been known as a source of gold for centuries – Edward II had struck his coins from African gold. Now the careful reports of men like Lieutenant Cameron [**Doc. 3, p. 99**] seemed to confirm this. Many of these 'prospectuses' that came out of Africa in this period proved false, but the diamonds of Kimberley, which burst on an astonished world in the early 1870s, and the gold of the Witwatersrand,

El Dorado: Literally 'the golden one'. A land of fabled wealth, originally applied to South America but in the nineteenth century sometimes used of Africa.

discovered in 1886, were real enough. Men did grow rich in Africa: Cecil Rhodes [**Doc. 19, p. 122**] for example, or Leopold II of the Belgians.

The possibilities seemed unlimited and, behind it all, stood the new Victorian technology, the steamship, the telegraph and, above all, the railway, which for the first time seemed to promise the real opening up of the interior of Africa, defeating the limitations imposed by the tsetse fly. Men began to 'think big'. It was not coincidental that Africa began to be opened up on a large scale just as the American frontier was 'closing'. Men meant it when they spoke of Africa as the 'new America'. Planning was on a continental scale. The Cape-to-Cairo railway did not seem an extravagant project to those who had seen the Canadian Pacific or the Union Pacific take shape.

Livingstone himself had been an enthusiast for 'progress'. [**Doc. 2, p. 98**] But Livingstone's enthusiasms had always been tempered, indeed in part forged, by his concern for the Africans. A few men of the next generation, notably Joseph Thomson, shared Livingstone's regard for the African and even, in Thomson's case, questioned whether this kind of progress would be good for the average African. But this was very much the exception. A new sense of racial superiority had emerged in which the Europeans' sense that they had the right to do what they liked with Africa was only one manifestation.

The European explorers of Africa were unquestionably brave men venturing into a situation totally unknown to them. They seldom had men of their own race with them, and they often found their African hosts strange and unpredictable, and feared their hostility. In this situation they created their own image of themselves. They must be wise – sometimes they even resorted to fireworks, musical boxes or electric batteries to overawe surprised tribes and establish their reputation as near-magicians. They must be strong, always keeping their word and never showing any physical weakness. They must maintain that British tradition of the 'stiff upper lip' and never show emotion – this may well be the real explanation of Stanley's strange greeting to Livingstone: 'Dr Livingstone, I presume'. This 'white man's burden' that they created for themselves was not altogether without a good side. Sometimes it involved trivialities, like Harry Johnston's insistence on dressing for dinner in the jungle, but the concept of a 'gentleman', whose word was his bond and who was chivalrous to those weaker than himself, especially towards women, was a very meaningful one to many Victorians and may explain why the British were often far from being the worst 'aliens' with whom the Africans found themselves dealing.

But there was a much darker side to this growing sense of the gap between the black and the white races. If the white man had a position to maintain, respect for the black man sank lower and lower. There had always been those who preferred the sensational to the objective. Smith's *Trade and Travel in the Gulph of Guinea* has already been noted. A much greater writer than Smith,

Richard Burton also did his share, notably in his *Mission to Gelele, the King of Dahomey* (1864), which had chapter headings very similar to those of Smith. Burton also discussed 'the Negro's place in Nature', which he placed very low, contending that, although a Negro child might be intelligent, he became stupid at puberty, like the great apes. He was also an exponent of the 'Hamitic' theory, believing that there had only been progress in Africa where more advanced peoples had penetrated. Burton's theories demonstrably influenced certain politicians, including Lord Derby and even the liberal and enlightened Lord Ripon.

But the man who reached by far the widest public was Henry Morton Stanley. It was no accident that Stanley's greeting to Livingstone on the shores of Lake Tanganyika became a Victorian catchphrase. All Stanley's activities took place in a blaze of publicity. He usually had massive press backing. His expedition to find Livingstone was undertaken for the *New York Herald*, his trans-continental journey was financed by the *New York Herald* and the *Daily Telegraph* jointly. His best-known books, *How I Found Livingstone*, *Through the Dark Continent* and *In Darkest Africa* (the very titles give the flavour), ran through numerous editions, including cheap 3s 6d. ones. *In Darkest Africa* [**Doc. 5, p. 101**] sold 150,000 copies in the English edition alone (like Stanley's other works it was translated into many other languages), and one reviewer commented that 'it has been read more universally and with deeper interest than any other publication of the present year'.

Stanley lectured all over the world, in America and Australia, as well as on the continent of Europe. He was a natural showman. Even his worst public quarrels at the British Association or the Royal Geographical Society only served to focus more public attention on him. Fate could hardly have chosen a worse interpreter of Africa to Europe. Stanley's childhood experiences – he was illegitimate, rejected by his family, brought up in a workhouse of Dickensian horror – were enough to sour any man. His own character and judgement seem to have undergone a progressive degeneration as a result of years of loneliness, anxiety and malarial fever. There is a great difference between the tone of the first book he wrote describing the British Abyssinia expedition of 1868, in which he posed as a disinterested American observer (he had emigrated from Wales to the United States as a boy) prepared to criticise both the Europeans and the Abyssinians, and his last book describing the Enim Pasha Relief Expedition in which he almost exalted in atrocities. [**Doc. 5, p. 101**] Not everyone admired Stanley. The authorities of Westminster Abbey refused to bury him in the Abbey near Livingstone as Stanley himself wished, not because of his humble origins – he was by this time a celebrity and an MP – but because of his tainted reputation. But, although the discriminating might criticise him, he undoubtedly had the ear of the new literate public, which enjoyed sensationalism, especially if it was laced with jingoism. J.A. Hobson, the most cogent of the contemporary critics of the new imperialism, exclaimed in disgust: 'Popular education, instead of serving as a defence, is an incitement towards Imperialism; it has opened up a panorama of vulgar pride and crude sensationalism to a great inert mass who see current history and the tangled maze of world movements with dim bewildered eyes . . .' (Hobson, 1938: 101).

Stereotypes are always dangerous, whether of one's own people or of others. Cairns reminds us of Dean Inge's remark, 'If you marry the Spirit of your generation you will be a widow in the next' (Cairns, 1965: xiii). Nineteenth-century Englishmen frequently saw Africa through what Curtin calls 'a haze of cross-cultural misunderstanding' (Curtin, 1965: xiii) which led to 'the acceptance of views of Africa more prejudicial than factual'. Nevertheless, there is an opposite danger, namely that 'the pull of contemporary liberal opinion, opposed to the policies of imperialism and racial hegemony, may incline the researcher to select his material in favour of the non-white races' (Cairns, 1965: xiii). To slide over criticisms of other cultures which one would apply to one's own, can be as patronising as any Victorian attitude. Even exaggerated feelings of guilt may be a final fling of Victorian arrogance, for it is to take the white men who ventured into Africa at their own valuation, as masters of their own and Africa's destinies. Often, as the sad tale of the 'Scramble' developed, both individual Europeans and Africans seemed to be at the mercy of forces which they neither understood nor controlled.

Part 2

ANALYSIS

4

The British occupation of Egypt, 1882

'It is a nasty business, and we have been much out of luck', the British Foreign Secretary, Lord Granville, wrote to a colleague, Lord Spencer, in June 1882, referring to the tangled situation in Egypt. Few have doubted that the last thing which a British Liberal government, under William Gladstone and pledged to reverse the 'forward' foreign policy of the previous Conservative administration of Benjamin Disraeli, wanted was a military intervention in Egypt in 1882, followed by a prolonged occupation. It has been generally agreed by contemporaries and most historians that the British cabinet 'muddled' into the Egyptian occupation. How then did they get into this situation? A number of very different factors must be taken into account: Egypt's role as part of the collapsing Ottoman empire, the newly built Suez Canal and its significance for British communications with India, the investment of European financiers in Egypt and the diplomatic alignments of Europe at this time. [**Docs 6, 7. 8. 9, pp. 102, 103, 105, 107**]

Although Egypt had been conquered by the Ottoman Turks in 1517, it had always retained some degree of **autonomy**. Nevertheless, a Turkish ruling class had been introduced into the country and the Turks virtually monopolised the higher administrative and, in particular, army appointments. This was naturally resented by the Egyptians, and the Egyptian nationalist movement of the nineteenth century was anti-Turkish before it was anti-European.

autonomy: Literally 'self government'. Sometimes applied, as in the Boer Republics, to the right of internal self-government but stopping short of full independence.

The attention of Europe was first directed towards Egypt by the Napoleonic campaign of 1798–99. The reasons for the campaign were complicated, but one motive was certainly to strike at Britain by posing a threat to her comparatively newly acquired Indian empire. From a military point of view the campaign was a disaster but it had far-reaching consequences. It caused a change of government in Egypt and it established the French, despite the military *débacle*, as the dominant European influence in Egypt. The Albanian Mehemet Ali, who consciously modelled himself on Napoleon, was able to seize power. Mehemet Ali remained a vassal of the Sultan of Turkey but he was an ambitious man who was determined to gain the maximum possible independence for Egypt. He embarked on a campaign of conquest and took much of the (Egyptian) Sudan and Syria. It is possible that he hoped one day to become Sultan. In his attempts to 'modernise' Egypt, Mehemet Ali made extensive use of French experts, military, agricultural, educational and others. The Egyptian educational system, which was more advanced than that of many parts of Europe, was modelled on the French system and Egyptian law was codified according to Napoleonic practice. Some Egyptians became interested in French philosophy and political thought. The leader of the 1882 rising, Colonel Arabi Pasha, although no scholar, was surprisingly familiar with the precedents of the 'Great Revolution' of 1789. At first those Egyptians who wanted to change their country were by no means hostile to European influence. On the contrary they saw Europeans as allies against the obscurantist elements in their own society.

Unfortunately for the Egyptian reformers their country was so placed strategically that it could hardly avoid becoming a bone of contention to the European powers, especially Britain and France. The Napoleonic campaign had alerted Britain to a possible threat to her Indian empire. Mehemet Ali was known to be a French *protégé*, and in 1840 Palmerston, the British Foreign Secretary, joined with Russia, Prussia and Austria to curb Mehemet Ali's ambitious campaigns against the Sultan, even at the expense of destroying the diplomatic **entente** between Britain and **Orleanist France**. When the Tsar Nicholas I put forward contingency partition plans for the **Ottoman empire** before the Crimean War, he recognised that the area Britain would wish to acquire would be Egypt. Britain, however, at this time and for many years afterwards, was committed to a policy of preserving the decrepit Ottoman empire intact to avoid the worse international complications which would follow its dissolution.

The next great threat to the Ottoman empire came with the Russo-Turkish War of 1877–8. Once again there was talk of a possible partition of the empire. For the first time the debate was known and discussed among the newly educated classes in Egypt, and it has been suggested that it was an important stimulus to the development of national feeling and created the beginning of a demand for what a later generation would call 'self-determination'. The Ottoman empire survived the crisis but Britain leased the island of Cyprus from the Sultan, thus providing itself with a base in the eastern Mediterranean, in return for a guarantee of Asiatic Turkey against Russian expansion. During the 'behind the scenes' negotiations at the time of the Congress of Berlin in 1878, France secured a promise from Britain and Germany that they would not oppose a French occupation of Tunis. France was concerned about the fate of Tunis because it bordered her existing colony of Algeria, the occupation of which had begun as long ago as 1830. France did not take up its option on Tunis until 1881, but the French occupation of Tunis mortally offended

entente (entente cordiale): Literally a 'cordial understanding' between nations, stopping short of a formal alliance. Most commonly applied to the Anglo-French agreements of 1904.

Orleanist France: France under an Orleanist king, Louis-Philippe, 1830–48. France became deeply involved in Algeria, although the intervention had begun under the previous Bourbon king, Charles X. This was also the period of the first Anglo-French *entente cordiale*.

Ottoman empire: The empire of the Ottoman Turks (see Map 2, p. xxxix) ruled over by the Sultan. Its gradual disintegration in the nineteenth and early twentieth centuries presented European diplomacy with its most dangerous and intractable problem.

the Sultan (Tunis was still nominally part of his empire) and made cooperation between France and Turkey impossible during the Egyptian crisis of the
following year.

THE SUEZ CANAL

The completion of the Suez Canal in 1869 introduced a new element into the
situation. Egypt had had a strategic importance to Britain before, especially
since the 1840s when the 'overland route' began to be used extensively. This
involved going to Alexandria by mail boat, crossing Egypt to Suez and picking
up another mail boat for India and the East there. The journey was facilitated
when a railway was built (by George Stephenson) from Alexandria to Cairo
in the 1850s. The route was too complicated for bulk cargoes but for despatches
it was invaluable. It was much used during the Indian 'Mutiny' of 1857. The
idea of a canal to connect the Red Sea and the Mediterranean went back
to Ptolomaic times but it was only in the middle of the nineteenth century
that a Frenchman, Ferdinand de Lesseps, provided the right combination of
enthusiasm, technical competence and political influence to get the job done.

   From the first the British opposed the building of the Suez Canal. For them,
any advantage of a more convenient route to India was heavily outweighed
by the fact that the Canal might fall into the hands of an enemy. The security
of British India depended largely on British command of the seas, but as
Lord Palmerston, one of the shrewdest of British Foreign Secretaries, pointed
out, control of the high seas was something very different from control of a
200-foot 'ditch' through someone else's territory. The only result of British
opposition, however, was that the Canal was finally built by French enterprise
and capital, although by Egyptian labour. The British contended, almost up
to the actual opening of the Canal, that it was technically impossible to build
it. Even when it was open, leading men in Britain, including Gladstone
himself, continued to believe that in time of war the Canal would probably
be closed and that the vital British route to India was still round the Cape of
Good Hope. [**Doc. 6, p. 102**]

   The Suez Canal, however, soon began to assume a crucial commercial as
well as a military importance. There was an element of coincidence in
this. If the age of sail had continued, the usefulness of the Canal would have
been limited by the uncertainty of the winds in the Red Sea. But about this
time important technical developments – the triple marine engine and water
condensers – greatly increased the freight-carrying capacity of steam ships and,
for the first time, made them economic competitors of sailing ships on long
voyages. For steam ships the Canal was an unalloyed advantage. In 1870 the

shipping tonnage passing through the Canal was 436,609: by 1882 it had grown to 5,074,809 tons. Before the First World War it had reached over 20 million tons a year. In 1882 over 80 per cent of this traffic was British. [**Doc. 6a, p. 102**]

Britain plainly could not remain indifferent to the fate of Egypt, but there was a long step between an interest in an area and military occupation. Palmerston, who could hardly be accused of indifference to British interests, never wished for the occupation of Egypt. He famously said:

> We do not want Egypt or wish it for ourselves, any more than any rational man with an estate in the north of England and a residence in the south would have wished to possess the inns on the north road. All he could want would have been that the inns should be well-kept, always accessible, and furnishing him, when he came, with mutton-chops and post-horses. (Quoted in Mansfield, 1971: 4)

Put less picturesquely, this is the 'informal influence' which Professors Robinson and Gallagher contended was the British ideal in dealing with Africa (and many other parts of the world) in the nineteenth century. The difficulty was that, in British eyes, Egypt was ceasing to be 'well-kept' and 'always accessible' in the 1880s.

Mehemet Ali had died in 1849. Neither of his immediate successors, Abbas or Said, showed any great ability, but Said took a number of decisions of critical importance for the future of Egypt. Above all, he gave Ferdinand de Lesseps permission to go ahead with the building of the Suez Canal on terms very unfavourable to Egypt. The Canal was not in itself likely to be to Egypt's advantage since it would kill the lucrative 'overland' trade. Nevertheless, Said agreed to take 45 per cent of the shares in de Lesseps company, to lease the land de Lesseps required and to provide labour by an extension of the **corvée** system, which compelled the Egyptian *fellah* (peasant) to work for the government for a period each year on projects such as irrigation. Said took another decision which was to have unforeseen consequences. He promoted a number of native Egyptians, including a certain Ahmed Arabi, to the rank of colonel in the army.

corvée: Labour service owed by a peasant, usually as part of his rent.

FINANCIAL PROBLEMS

When Said died in 1863, Egypt appeared tranquil and prosperous enough, although Said had had to raise a modest loan of over £3 million from Frühling and Goschen. Said was succeeded by his nephew, Ismail, who has always attracted both critics and defenders. During his reign from 1863 to 1879 Egypt's foreign debt increased from £3 million to over £100 million. Some dismissed him as a mere irresponsible spendthrift but as the British government minister, Stephen Cave, who investigated the situation in 1876 demonstrated [**Doc. 7, p. 103**], the truth was much more complex than that. A contemporary journalist, J.C. McCoan, was almost certainly right when he observed that Ismail had tried by diplomatic and financial means to accomplish what his predecessor, Mehemet Ali, had tried unsuccessfully to do by the sword, to transform Egypt into a powerful state, practically independent of the Sultan. He employed American officers, redundant after the Civil War, to pacify the Sudan, conquered by Mehemet Ali. He spent great sums in Constantinople to alter the normal Islamic law of succession so that he might be succeeded by his son, Tewfik, instead of by his brother and dangerous political rival, Halim. But a high proportion of his expenditure was accounted for by his attempts to turn Egypt into a 'modern' country. In some ways he was unlucky. There was an enormous boom in Egyptian cotton at the beginning of his reign because the **American Civil War** interrupted normal supplies of raw cotton to Europe but the bubble burst as soon as the war ended. Ismail turned to sugar production to replace cotton, but some bad planning mistakes were made; refineries, for example, being sited in the wrong places. Nevertheless, as Stephen Cave pointed out [**Doc. 7, p. 103**] worse mistakes were made during the English industrial revolution but, whereas England could afford such mistakes, Egypt could not.

American Civil War: War between Northern and Southern States (1861–5). Although slavery became an issue, the original quarrel was about States' Rights. Created world shortage of raw cotton (normally exported from the Southern States). Played a part in imperialism when alternative sources were sought in Egypt, India and Fiji.

All the evidence is that Egypt's fundamental economy was sound enough. During the fifteen years of Ismail's reign the country's exports boomed. The cultivable area of Egypt increased by one-third, largely thanks to the new irrigation canals Ismail had built. Over 1,000 miles of railways were built: proportionately Egypt had more miles of railways than Austria or Spain. Alexandria was steadily transformed into a great Mediterranean port. The trouble was that Egypt did not have the capital to undertake these works itself. At first Ismail had no difficulty in raising capital in Europe; rather the contrary, for the low interest rates prevailing in Europe (at one time bank rates in Britain fell to 2 per cent) meant that investors were glad to consider loans to Egypt at a nominal rate of 7 per cent. He raised his first loan in 1864, intending to clear the debt left by Said and use the surplus for public works. Thereafter loan followed loan at almost annual intervals. The amount actually received by the Egyptian treasury, after the expense of raising the loan in Europe, was often far less than the nominal amount. One observer calculated that the Egyptian treasury only received £35 million from five loans with a nominal value of over £55 million. Since interest was calculated on the nominal value, this raised apparent rates of about 7 per cent to over 20 per cent in some cases. It was said that by 1875, having repaid over £29 million in interest and a sinking fund (on the £35 million actually received), the Egyptian government still owed over £46 million. Plainly, financially, Ismail was having to run to stand still. Moreover, whereas the earlier loans had been raised from highly respectable banking firms like Frühling and Goschen, and Oppenheim and Company, Ismail was eventually reduced to the desperate expedients of either accepting short-term loans from very dubious financial groups, mainly French, or issuing 'treasury bonds' to cover debts immediately due.

By 1875 bankruptcy was staring him in the face. It was in these circumstances that the British Prime Minister, Benjamin Disraeli, learning privately that Ismail was considering selling his Suez Canal shares to a French group, carried out his great coup, with the help of the Rothschilds, and bought the shares for the British government. Disraeli's hyperbolic phrase to the Queen, 'You have it [the Canal], Ma'am', was, of course, untrue. He had only secured 45 per cent of the shares and since Ismail had mortgaged the interest on these at an earlier stage in his financial embarrassment, they did not even carry voting rights. Nevertheless, the whole transaction entered into the mythology of British imperialism. The British public, and perhaps some British politicians, became convinced that, in some peculiar sense, the Suez Canal was 'theirs'.

The following year Ismail asked for the assistance of two British Treasury officials to help him sort out his finances. Instead Disraeli despatched his **Paymaster General** Stephen Cave to investigate the situation. There were some, unproven, suspicions that this was intended as a prelude to a British seizure of Egypt. If any such thought did pass through Disraeli's mind, the inevitable international complications provided a sufficient deterrent. Cave reported that the Egyptian situation was far from hopeless, but he did recommend the introduction of a stronger European element, which he regarded as both more efficient and less corrupt. [**Doc. 7, p. 103**]

Cave's mission was followed by that of Goschen and Joubert. Joubert officially represented the French government, Goschen technically represented only a consortium of British bondholders. Goschen was a member of the banking firm which had raised the original loans for Said and Ismail – indeed, he said that that was why he felt under an obligation to undertake the mission – but he had personally renounced any financial interest some time before. Goschen and Joubert produced an elaborate scheme to bring some order to the Egyptian finances. There were to be two high officials, an Englishman to be Controller-General of the Revenue, and a Frenchman to be Controller-General of the Expenditure. They were to ensure that certain revenues which had been assigned to the servicing of the foreign debts were paid over to a Commission of the Public Debt, consisting of representatives of the bondholders. Once again, the French government had no objection to appearing as a principal in the transaction and appointed a representative on the Debt Commission. The British government, adhering to the traditional

Paymaster General: British Treasury Minister.

view that they would not accept responsibility for private investments made abroad by British citizens, refused an official nomination, but privately agreed that Evelyn Baring, later Lord Cromer, who had recently been acting as private secretary to Lord Northbrook, the Viceroy of India, should act for the British bondholders. Baring was a member of the great banking family of that name, although he himself had been a soldier and had no previous financial experience.

The Anglo-French 'Dual' financial control lasted (apart from the brief abortive experiment of the 'European ministry' in 1878–9) until the British occupation in 1882. It had considerable success in reducing the Egyptian finances to order. In 1880 the Law of Liquidation was agreed, which had the effect of dividing the revenues of Egypt into two parts. The 'assigned revenues', such as the receipts of the railway, telegraph and customs departments and the port dues of Alexandria, were to be used to pay the charges on the foreign loans, with the interest on these fixed more modestly at 4 or 5 per cent. The 'non-assigned' revenues, in effect all the rest, were to be used for the ordinary administrative purposes of the Egyptian government. If, however, the assigned revenues proved insufficient, the loan charges were to be the first charges on the non-assigned revenues, but if there was a surplus in the assigned revenues, this was not to be transferred to the administration but used to pay off the loans more quickly. The basic health of the Egyptian economy meant that these charges were not crippling but, before the Dual Control began to work, the ordinary Egyptian had been reduced to straits of great misery. His plight was aggravated by the natural disaster of a 'low Nile' in 1876 and 1877 with resultant bad harvests. Egyptian methods of tax collection had always been brutal and the peasants fell into the hands of moneylenders, while in Upper Egypt hundreds actually starved to death. Politically more dangerous for the government was the disaffection in the army, where pay was in arrears. The Egyptian officers were also discontented because Ismail had not continued Said's policy of promoting them rather than Turks.

The first army mutiny, that of February 1879, was almost certainly arranged by Ismail himself to get rid of the 'European ministry', but the soldiers quickly learnt their power. In June 1879 Ismail was deposed by his overlord, the **Sultan**, acting under German pressure. The British Foreign Secretary, Lord Salisbury, suspected that Bismarck had been persuaded to take this action by Bleichroder and the German bankers, who were angered by the neglect of German interests in Egypt. Fritz Stern's detailed study (1977) suggests that Bleichroder himself, although influential in Constantinople, had little interest in Egypt at this time, but the matter remains unproven. Ismail was succeeded by his son, Tewfik. Tewfik was acceptable to the Powers because he was believed to be much more amenable to influence than Ismail. The Powers soon had every reason to regret placing a weak man in such a crucial position.

Sultan: An Islamic ruler. A number of men were accorded the title, for example, the Sultan of Zanzibar. But in particular it meant the ruler of the Ottoman empire, resident in Constantinople, who had some religious, as well as political, authority, very roughly comparable to the role of the Pope in western Europe in the Middle Ages.

Most historians have come to accept that what developed in Egypt in the late 1870s and early 1880s was a genuine national movement. Lord Cromer, who was virtually governor of Egypt from 1883 to 1907, eventually reached that conclusion himself. For many British Liberals, however, the situation was genuinely obscured by the prominent role of the Egyptian army. [**Doc. 8, p. 105**] Nevertheless, at first the British government was not altogether unsympathetic. Lord Granville, the Foreign Secretary, wrote a despatch in November 1881 at the request of Sir Edward Malet, the British Consul-General in Egypt – he had the title 'consul-general', not 'ambassador', because Egypt being part of the Ottoman empire, was not a sovereign state – expressing cautious approval of the reformers. This policy was reversed, at least in Egyptian eyes, by the Anglo-French Joint Note of 8 January 1882. On the face of it, this was a restrained document simply expressing support for the Khedive against anyone who might disturb the peace. The British government meant that and no more, but it was Gambetta's government in Paris which had been the initiator of the Note, and the Egyptians immediately linked it with the French invasion of Tunis the previous year, and feared that it was a prelude to intervention. There is little doubt that Gambetta was moved by his desire to protect the French bondholders. Gladstone's government, on the other hand, was deeply embarrassed by an association with the bondholders.

Lord Cromer later said that the Note was like lighting a candle in a mine full of fire damp. From then on Britain and France on the one hand, and the Egyptian national movement on the other, were on a collision course. Possibly a confrontation could have been avoided if there had been a sufficient states-man in any of the three countries principally concerned. There was not. In France Freycinet replaced Gambetta and allowed matters to drift. In Britain, Lord Granville was elderly and indecisive. The Prime Minister, Gladstone, regarded Egypt as an irritating distraction from his real business at home and in Ireland. In Egypt Tewfik, in the aftermath of the excitement about the Joint Note, allowed the ministry of Cherif Pasha to retire. Opinions of Cherif differ, but in British eyes the educated and polished Cherif represented a moderate and comprehensible reform movement. [**Doc. 8a, p. 105**] They felt much less able to get on with his successor, Mahmoud Pasha Sami, an avowed nationalist, who included in his cabinet Arabi Pasha, one of the leaders of the army mutinies of February and September 1881.

MILITARY ACTION BEGINS

The situation deteriorated rapidly. Sir Edward Malet sent home somewhat alarmist reports of the dangers to European lives and property in Egypt. Late in May Britain and France sent a small squadron of warships to Alexandria, nominally to evacuate refugees, but in part to try to overawe the Egyptians and ensure that there would be no violent outbreaks – a tactic that had occasionally worked in other parts of the world. This time, however, it did not. On Sunday, 11 June 1882, there was a riot in Alexandria in which about fifty Europeans, including an officer and two sailors from the British fleet, were killed. The British government believed, almost certainly wrongly, that Arabi Pasha and the nationalists had been behind the riot. Negotiations between the two sides became virtually impossible. A month later, on 11 July, the British fleet bombarded the fortifications which were in process of erection at Alexandria. Militarily there was a valid excuse for doing so – work had been resumed after the Egyptians had promised to stop – but even Gladstone in the House of Commons admitted that there was an element of revenge in the action, for he feared that if the massacre of 11 June remained unavenged, all the scattered British communities in distant places would be at risk.

After the bombardment of 11 July there was no real alternative to military intervention. Arabi's army camped outside Alexandria and cut off water supplies to the town. The Suez Canal was probably in real danger – certainly the British government believed it to be so. They now felt that the Canal would only be safe if 'anarchy' were put down in Cairo. The Quaker John Bright had resigned from the cabinet rather than agree to the bombardment, arguing that if it would endanger the Canal it had better not be undertaken. But no one went with him. Gladstone and his colleagues were puzzled and unhappy but committed.

They still hoped to avoid a unilateral intervention. Technically the Sultan, as suzerain, had the strongest legal right to intervene and, despite the embarrassment of calling on the 'abominable' Turk after Gladstone's denunciation of the '**Bulgarian Horrors**' four years earlier, the British tried to persuade him to act. The Sultan, however, had no intention of being the cat's paw of Britain and France and determinedly procrastinated. Gladstone hoped that Britain and France might intervene jointly as the 'mandatories' of Europe, preserving his ideal of the **Concert of Europe** acting on the **Eastern Question**. The Freycinet government, however, failed to secure the necessary vote of credit in the Chambers at the end of July and fell. The British even tried to secure a joint intervention with Italy. But the most influential man in Europe was the German Chancellor, Otto von Bismarck. Germany, Austria and Italy kept closely in step (this was the year of the signing of the Triple Alliance). Privately, Bismarck encouraged Britain to intervene swiftly, if necessary alone. Possibly he hoped for a diplomatic breach between England and France: possibly he simply hoped to end this dangerous reopening of the Eastern Question as quickly as possible. [**Doc. 9, p. 107**]

The British military intervention in August 1882, nominally undertaken with the approval of Tewfik against a rebellious army, was a textbook success.

Bulgarian Horrors: Popular term for atrocities committed by the Ottomans after a rising in Bulgaria in 1876. William Gladstone played a prominent role in denouncing them.

Concert of Europe: An informal alignment of the Great Powers of Europe, originating at the end of the Napoleonic Wars, designed to settle disputes by negotiation, not war. Regarded as particularly important in relation to the Eastern Question.

Eastern Question: The problems caused by the slow break-up of the Ottoman empire in the nineteenth and early twentieth centuries which, several times, seemed likely to cause a general European war. It caused the Crimean war in 1854 and, in the opinion of some historians, the First World War in 1914.

Sir Garnet Wolseley, who had done all the previous contingency planning at the War Office (with the help of the Under-Secretary, Sir Henry Campbell-Bannerman) commanded the expedition. After a feint at Aboukir, he made straight for the Canal. It was captured in three days. The Egyptian army was finally defeated at Tel-el-Kebir on 13 September 1882. Arabi and some of his associates were put on trial and eventually exiled to Ceylon.

The Gladstone government had every intention of withdrawing their forces immediately Arabi had been defeated, but they soon found that government had apparently collapsed in Egypt. Withdrawal was not easy. Gladstone himself said bitterly, 'We have done our Egyptian business, and we are an Egyptian government' (Morley, 1903: III, 119).

Moreover, the Sudan had risen under its own leader, the Mahdi, and was threatening the security of Egypt proper. The British government put pressure on the Egyptians to cut their losses and evacuate the Sudan. General Charles Gordon, who had been Governor of the Sudan for a time under Ismail and was believed still to have a fund of goodwill among the Sudanese where he had tried to suppress the slave trade, was sent to carry out the evacuation. Gordon's name, however, was no match for the magic of the Mahdi. Gordon was a strange and wilful man, who put his own interpretation upon his instructions. He was already a national hero and his death at Khartoum in January 1885 made him a martyr in the eyes of the British people. His death became one of the great legends of British imperialism. The idea of 'avenging Gordon' was immensely popular in some quarters. [**Doc. 10, p. 109**]

THE DEBATE BEGINS

But the tragedy also started a torrent of criticism about the whole British involvement in Egypt. This had been strangely muted until then. Only a few independents, like Frederic Harrison, had suggested that the British invasion of 1882 had been a complete reversal of the whole 'Midlothian' programme of non-intervention and the rights of small nations on which Gladstone had fought the 1880 election. [**Doc. 8c, p. 105**] Most of the critics had been dissident conservatives, like the eccentric Wilfrid Scawen Blunt, with his dream of a resurgent pan-Arab empire, independent of Constantinople. Blunt was closely in touch with the Egyptian nationalists, and such were the workings of the British political system at this time that he was able, through his personal friendship with Edward Hamilton, Gladstone's private secretary, to get the ear of Gladstone himself and come very close to persuading Gladstone that he had misunderstood the whole Egyptian situation. The campaign was later taken up by Lord Randolph Churchill, who had been ill in 1882, but who in 1883 was one of the most strenuous denouncers of the whole intervention as a 'bondholders' war'. [**Doc. 8d, p. 106**] But liberal opinion in general was held for a time in uneasy silence by Gladstone's own great prestige.

When the denunciations began it lasted for a generation. Egypt came to be regarded as the classic case of financial imperialism. Capitalists invested in foreign countries, sometimes on usurious terms, then demanded the protection of their government, by military force if necessary. Against this it has been argued that Britain intervened in Egypt for strategic reasons, because of the vital importance of the Suez Canal. But for the Canal, British investors would have been told, as they had been told in other cases, that risky foreign speculations were their responsibility, not the government's. But the situation is not quite as simple as that. The British government intervened in August 1882 because they believed, rightly or wrongly, that the Suez Canal was in immediate danger. But the Canal would never have been in any sort of danger but for the situation which had developed in Cairo and Alexandria, and it is more difficult to argue that that was not directly connected with the foreign financial and political pressures to which Egypt had been subjected for the previous twenty years.

The British occupation of Egypt ended Anglo-French understanding there and caused difficulties in the relations between the two countries until the Agreements of 1904. The French were irritated, not so much by the actual intervention, from which they realised they had withdrawn by their own act, but by the subsequent British actions in remaining in Egypt and ending the Anglo-French Dual Control as part of their general 'tidying up' of the tangled Egyptian situation. It has been contended by some historians, and strenuously denied by others, that the Anglo-French estrangement over Egypt had repercussions all over Africa, that indeed it was the trigger that began an unexpected and unintended chain reaction which resulted in the partition of tropical Africa among the European Powers.

The Egyptian case attracted immense attention from later imperial theorists. To some, J.A. Hobson among them, it went far to prove that the whole imperialist movement was financial in origin, a fraud on the whole nation by a sectional interest. If this were the case then the insights gained from an analysis of the Egyptian example would be generally applicable and would provide a general theory of imperialism. Some writers have held that this was so. Others, however, have questioned it, pointing out that the financial motives so obvious in Egypt are by no means so easily proven in tropical Africa. If the latter school of thought is correct, Egypt must be regarded as a special case, a unique combination of strategic and financial interests, not a general explanation of imperialism, and other cases must be investigated to see what pattern, if any, emerges from them.

5

West Africa

In 1865 an all-party Select Committee of the House of Commons recommended that, ideally, Britain should relinquish all its possessions on the west coast of Africa with the possible exception of the harbour of Freetown in Sierra Leone. [**Doc. 11, p. 110**] If this were not immediately practicable, Britain should be careful not to extend its commitments and should prepare the Africans already under its rule for speedy independence. The proposals were generally welcomed.

Forty years later the small colony of Sierra Leone, centred on Freetown, with a total area of about 250 square miles, had been extended to include the hinterland of the Sierra Leone protectorate of 27,000 square miles. The small Gold Coast colony, centred on Cape Coast Castle, had come to include the great Ashanti Confederation and the extensive 'Northern Territories'. The tiny colony of Lagos had been linked up with a British protectorate over the Niger delta (where Britain had had commercial but no political interests in 1865) and had expanded northwards to include the whole of modern Nigeria, the second largest state in modern Africa. Only the Gambia, the oldest British colony in West Africa, had been unable to expand significantly, because it was almost entirely surrounded by the expanding French colony of Senegal. What had brought about this dramatic change of government policy? Had there, indeed, been any deliberate change of government policy or had British governments, Conservative and Liberal alike, been overtaken by forces they could not control?

Britain's interest in Egypt had traditionally been strategic; in the 1870s financial interests were added to this. Britain's traditional connection with West Africa had always been trade. The Guinea coast had been one corner of the important 'triangular trade' with the West Indies (see p. 18). When the slave trade was forbidden in 1807, new trades grew up slowly to replace it. The most important of these was the trade in palm oil carried on between British merchants, mainly from Liverpool, and the chiefs of the Niger delta, the so-called 'Oil Rivers'. In return for the oil the British merchants supplied cheap textiles, mainly from Manchester, some hardware from Sheffield and Birmingham, firearms also from Birmingham, and spirits mostly imported from Holland. The trade of the Oil Rivers was opened up by British capital and enterprise, as indignant merchants were later to remind their government [**Doc. 12, p. 111**], and for many years Britain was alone in the field. Britain, however, undertook no formal political responsibilities in the Niger delta during the first three-quarters of the century. Only in 1849 did it appoint a British consul 'for the Bights of Benin and Biafra'. This was John Beecroft, sailor, explorer, merchant and anti-slavery crusader. Beecroft was a very remarkable man. Professor Dike calls him 'something of an institution in the Bight of Biafra' (Dike, 1956: 94) He had no authority except that of an ordinary consul but, such was the respect he commanded among Europeans and Africans alike, that he became a kind of general arbiter. Dike concluded:

> In time Africans came to look on the British Consul as the de facto Governor of the Bights of Benin and Biafra. This position of power which Beecroft won for himself passed on to his successors and enabled Britain to enjoy the authority of a protecting power before the Berlin West Africa Conference had legalised the status in international diplomacy. (Dike, 1956: 128)

With 'moral suasion', to use Professor Robinson and Gallagher's convenient phrase, so satisfactorily established on that part of the Guinea coast, the British government had no desire for any more costly or demanding kind of influence there, unless or until they should be directly challenged.

QUARRELS WITH THE ASHANTI

The challenge in fact came first in other areas. The British had long maintained a few forts in the region of Cape Coast on the Gold Coast. In 1850 and 1872 respectively they bought the remaining Danish and Dutch forts in the region. Although this might seem strange at a time when the British were wondering whether it was worth maintaining their presence on the Gold Coast at all, the explanation is that they hoped the additional stations might make the colony financially self-sufficient. British governments in the middle of the nineteenth century had no objections to mercantile stations in distant places so long as they were neither a political nor a financial liability. The Gold Coast, however, soon came to be both. British commercial relations were with the Fanti people on the coast, but the Fanti enjoyed very precarious relations with their powerful inland neighbours, the Ashanti Confederation. The Ashanti Confederation, which had originally been formed by a few small tribes to defend themselves against aggressive neighbours, had grown on the profits of the slave trade into one of the strongest states in West Africa. The head of the Confederation, the Asantehene, had his capital at Kumasi and the symbol of his authority was the famous 'golden stool' which, legend said, had come straight from heaven. Throughout the nineteenth century the Ashanti were anxious to extend their authority to the coast, and after 1807 they were resentful of the British influence which was used against their slaving activities. The first serious clash occurred in the 1820s. In 1823 they defeated Sir Charles McCarthy and a small British army. (McCarthy was killed and his skull seized as a trophy and made into a drinking cup.) The British defeated the Ashanti in 1826 but made no attempt to penetrate inland. After 1830 a young army officer, George Maclean, established an influence on the Gold Coast similar to that which Beecroft had achieved in the Oil Rivers, and in 1844 the British government signed treaties with a number of Fanti chiefs which entitled them to some degree of British protection. The situation again became critical in 1863 when the British government refused to return a fugitive slave to the Ashanti. The Ashanti invaded the 'protectorate'. The campaign became a stalemate but there were a significant number of British casualties. Revulsion against the futility of the Ashanti War formed the background to the Report of the Select Committee quoted at the beginning of this chapter.

Yet another Ashanti war broke out in 1873. The immediate cause was another Ashanti invasion of the protectorate provoked by the transfer of the Dutch possessions (the Dutch had been on good terms with the Ashanti) to their enemies, the British. This war attracted a good deal more publicity than its predecessors. It was conducted with vigour and success by one of the ablest man in the British army, Garnet Wolseley, who defeated the Ashanti and temporarily occupied their capital. It was reported by a remarkable band of war correspondents, including H.M. Stanley, G.A. Henty and Winwood Reade. After Wolseley's victory, Disraeli's government decided in July 1874 to constitute the vague Fanti protectorate into a **crown colony**. At first glance this might appear to be an example of the more 'forward' policy of Disraeli's new Conservative administration, but McIntyre (1967) demonstrated that all the critical decisions had been taken at the end of the previous Liberal administration, when Gladstone was still Prime Minister and Lord Kimberley, Colonial Secretary. The policy of the 1865 committee, the so-called 'Cardwell policy' (Cardwell had been a leading member of the committee), had been virtually abandoned. On the Gold Coast the challenge had come from an African power, but this was unusual in the situation that was now developing on the west coast.

crown colony: Most usual form of British colonial administration, consisting of Governor, Executive Council and Legislative Council. The Legislative Council could be made up of both 'official' and 'unofficial' (sometimes elected) members. Most British acquisitions in Africa started as protectorates but became assimilated to conventional Crown Colonies in the early twentieth century.

THE CHALLENGE FROM THE FRENCH

In the 1850s the French colony of Senegal began to expand in area under the vigorous leadership of General Faidherbe, who first became governor in 1854. Senegal expanded until it virtually engulfed the old British colony of the Gambia. The Gambia was of little real use to Britain, but to the French it now began to assume some importance as a possible trade route. The idea of exchanging the Gambia for some other part of West Africa more immediately valuable to the British was first mooted in 1861. It was seriously discussed in 1865–6 and on several occasions in the 1870s but, by now, a remarkably powerful 'Gambia lobby' had emerged, partly commercial, partly missionary, which was strongly opposed to any cession of British territory there. The project was to be revived at intervals – it was discussed as late as the Anglo-French agreements of 1904 – but the idea of ceding territory once British had now become quite repugnant. The British attitude to colonies was very slowly but surely changing.

Two new factors entered into the situation in the late 1870s. One was a great increase in French interest in the area, partly military, partly commercial. The other was a challenge by a new group of British merchants to the Liverpool merchants who had so long traded with the chiefs of the Niger Delta. These chiefs were only middlemen. The palm oil in which they traded was produced further up the Niger. It occurred to some British traders that it might be profitable to by-pass them and to deal directly with the primary producers on the middle Niger. The moving spirit in this was a Manxman, George Taubman Goldie. [**Docs 12a, 15, pp. 111, 115**] Goldie, originally an officer in the Royal Engineers, had been left some shares in a small company trading on the Niger by an uncle. He decided to go out to the Niger and assess the situation for himself. In 1879 he persuaded a number of small companies to join together in what was originally known as the United Africa Company. In 1882 this was changed into the National African Company. Goldie had considerable luck in persuading a South Wales industrialist, Lord Aberdare, who was also President of the Royal Geographical Society and a former Liberal Home Secretary, to become Chairman of the new company. Aberdare, although he had left high political office for good in 1874, still had the ear of Gladstone and of Lord Granville, the Foreign Secretary, 1880–5, in a way that no outsider could have had. Goldie also secured the support of James Hutton, a Manchester MP, and President of the Manchester Chamber of Commerce, 1884–5. Hutton was an extremely influential man who had a finger in most African pies at this time. [**Docs. 12c, 17, pp. 112, 119**] Goldie needed all the support he could get, for his plans for the Niger were far-reaching. In 1881 the British government had revived the old device of a Royal Chartered Company for the North Borneo Company. This once-favoured form of organisation (the great East India Company was the classic example) had been generally regarded as obsolete since 1857, but now Goldie began to study the precedents with interest. Nevertheless, it is unlikely that the British government would have regarded the new ambitions of the Niger traders very sympathetically but for the sudden challenge from France in the area.

Faidherbe had finally left Senegal in 1865 and his ambitious plans went into cold storage. In 1871 Napoleon III was defeated at Sedan and the Second Empire collapsed. Most Frenchmen under the Third Republic had their eyes fixed on the 'blue line of the Vosges' and the lost provinces of Alsace and Lorraine, but a powerful lobby eventually developed which saw colonial success as some measure of compensation for defeat in Europe and a new source of both prestige and economic strength. The French statesman most usually associated with this is Jules Ferry, who was responsible for the French forward moves in both Tunis and Indo-China in the early 1880s, but Kanya-Forstner (1969) showed that Charles Freycinet, who is usually remembered for his weak policy on Egypt, had ambitious plans for West Africa. He was ably supported by Admiral Jauréguiberry, a former Governor of Senegal, who became Minister of Marine in February 1879. These plans turned on building a great railway network (Freycinet was himself a former railway engineer) which would link Senegal, Algeria and the Upper Niger.

THE NIGER

The British merchants on the Lower and Middle Niger were generally resigned to the fact that the Upper Niger was destined to pass into the French sphere, and in 1883 Goldie and Aberdare urged the British government to strike a bargain with France which would leave the river below Timbuktu under British influence. The traders were alarmed by the new French challenge which seemed to be being mounted to British interests all round the coast from Sierra Leone to the Congo. To the north of Sierra Leone, the disputed area concerned what were then generally called the Southern Rivers, which Sierra Leone believed to be within its sphere of influence but which the French saw as a possible outlet for their Sudanese trade. Between 1877 and 1882, when an agreement was finally signed, the British and the French continually manoeuvred for position in the region. On the stretch of coast between the Gold Coast and Lagos, the French revived an old protectorate over Porto Novo in 1883. Porto Novo had complicated relations with the powerful inland state of Dahomey (both were successor states of the once-important state of Ardra.) In 1861 Britain annexed Lagos, which was one of the last surviving slaving centres on the coast, most of its victims being prisoners of war from the disintegrating Yoruba empire in what later became western Nigeria. As part of the same sequence of events the French had briefly exercised a protectorate over Porto Novo in 1863–5. Professors Robinson and Gallagher in their *Africa and the Victorians* (1961) put forward the hypothesis that the French resumption of the protectorate in 1883 was a deliberate tit-for-tat for the British occupation of Egypt. Newbury (1962), however, was able to show beyond reasonable doubt that the French decision had been taken before the British invasion of Egypt. Nevertheless, it does seem that the Porto Novo protectorate was a deliberate French attempt to prevent the British from securing an unbroken sphere of influence on the coast from Lagos to the Gold Coast. Robinson and Gallagher also suggested that the French probing of the British position on the Niger was another manifestation of the breakdown of the unspoken 'gentleman's agreement' which, they posited, had restrained the British and the French from encroaching upon each other's spheres in West Africa but which was abandoned after the Egyptian fiasco. Again, however, the balance of the evidence seems to be clearly that the reasons for the French action are to be found in West Africa. The French were anxious to secure, if possible, a route from the Bight of Benin to the Upper Niger which by-passed, not challenged, the existing British influence in the Niger Delta. Nevertheless, the British did feel challenged. [**Doc. 12, p. 111**]

Two French companies, the *Compagnie Fransaise de l'Afrique Équatoriale* and the *Compagnie du Sénégal et de la Côte Occidentale de l'Afrique*, began operating on the Niger. The British identified as their most formidable opponent a certain Lieutenant Mattei, a man not unlike Goldie himself, an army officer who had obtained leave to come to the coast. The French gave Mattei a consular appointment and the British believed – wrongly in fact – that the French government was giving Mattei substantial financial backing. Mattei tried to conclude a treaty with the chiefs at Bonny which, in the opinion of local observers, would have amounted to a French protectorate. The British traders also became alarmed by the activities of French warships on the coast and eventually induced the (usually rather sceptical) British Admiralty to call for urgent reports. The National African Company, however, decided, correctly, that its best hope was to buy out its potential rivals. After undercutting the French prices, at considerable cost to its own profits, it induced the French to sell out in 1884. Lord Granville, hardly the most jingoistic of English Foreign Secretaries, was sufficiently carried away to write 'Hurrah' on the back of the letter informing him of this.

The new danger to British trade on the Niger seemed likely to be paralleled on the Congo. While Britain had fewer commercial interests on the Congo, where the principal traders were Dutch, than on the Niger, a number of Liverpool firms had a foothold there. [**Doc. 12b, p. 111**] The Portuguese still had some shadowy claims to sovereignty at the mouth of the Congo, based on their old connection with the area. The British government, however, had consistently refused to recognise these, notably in a despatch from the then Foreign Secretary, Lord Clarendon, in 1853. The British reluctance to recognise Portuguese jurisdiction anywhere on the coast of Africa where it could be avoided was due to two considerations: first, the bad Portuguese record in tolerating the continuance of the slave trade; and second, the high tariffs which the Portuguese habitually charged on foreign goods. The situation, however, rapidly changed in the early 1880s.

KING LEOPOLD OF THE BELGIANS INTERVENES

A new factor appeared with the sudden entry on the scene of Leopold II, King of the Belgians. Leopold had dreamed of a colonial empire since he had been Crown Prince in the 1860s. Central Africa was not his first choice but his earlier schemes came to nothing, and when first Lovett Cameron [**Doc. 3, p. 99**] and then H.M. Stanley returned with glowing tales of the possibilities of the Congo Basin, which the British government ignored, Leopold acted quickly. He had little or no backing from the Belgian Parliament and he played a remarkable lone hand. In 1876 he invited an extremely distinguished array of geographers and explorers to Brussels to a conference. There were precedents, notably the Paris Conference of 1875, but Leopold had made exceptionally careful preparations. As he intended, the result of the conference was the setting up of the *Association Internationale Africaine* (AIA) for the suppression of the slave trade and the opening up of Central Africa, with Leopold as President, and prestigious 'national committees' – the chairman of the British committee was the Prince of Wales. The British government initially seems to have accepted that Leopold's motives were entirely scientific and humanitarian. It was only in 1884 that strange private reports began to filter into the Foreign Office of questionable activities in the Congo. Different opinions about Leopold's sincerity are possible. The Congo eventually provided the greatest scandal of the whole colonial era in Africa, when E.D. Morel (1906) and others revealed to the world the cruel exploitation that had accompanied the development of the rubber industry there. It could be that Leopold was genuinely ignorant of the excesses of his dubious agents there, but he was one of the few men to make a great personal fortune out of Africa in this period, and most men perhaps came to agree with Lord Rosebery, who had once said that he would be better able to believe in Leopold's sincerity if he looked less like Fagin (Rosebery Papers, National Library of Scotland:Box 109). Some historians have contended that it was Leopold's activities, more than any other single factor, that set off the 'Scramble' in West Africa. The International Association began to conclude treaties with African chiefs in the Congo. It now seems to be established that the initial treaties were commercial ones, but that when Leopold revealed them to the world in 1884 he represented them as political treaties, transferring sovereignty. The deception was probably attributable to Leopold's fear, by 1884, of French competition.

The French had a colony, Gabon, to the north of the mouth of the Congo, founded in 1841. Some Frenchmen believed that the way to tap the great potential wealth of the Congo basin was not by the river Congo itself, which was badly obstructed by rapids near its mouth, but by the river Ogoué which would channel the trade into Gabon. One of the men who believed this was the French explorer, Savorgnan de Brazza. Nominally employed by the French 'national committee', which had been set up in 1876, he undertook an expedition up the Ogoué to the vicinity of Stanley Pool. Indeed the whole expedition became a sort of race with Stanley himself, now in the employ of Leopold. De Brazza concluded a series of treaties in October 1880 with an African chief he knew as the Makoko (a title not, as many supposed at the time, a proper name). These treaties purported to cede large territories to De Brazza as the representative of France, but they were vague and, legally, highly irregular. The French government's original reaction was to pigeon-hole them, much as the British government had done with some earlier treaties which Lovett Cameron had concluded six years earlier. The Makoko treaty was, however, finally accepted as valid by the French government in November 1882. Indirectly this seems to have been the result of the Egyptian crisis. It was not that the French government saw the Makoko treaty as an attack on Britain – on the contrary they were still trying to conciliate Britain in the hope of saving something from the wreck in Egypt – but the French public, angered by the weak role their country had played in Egypt, was peculiarly susceptible to the powerful press campaign that De Brazza and his associates now mounted in favour of a forward policy on the Congo. The government dared not resist.

PORTUGAL'S CLAIMS

The British government was in turn alarmed by the new French interest. Since 1879 they had been engaged in often rather desultory negotiations with Portugal to settle certain colonial questions concerning Goa, Mozambique and the Congo. Those concerning the Congo were now taken up with renewed vigour and resulted in the Anglo-Portuguese treaty of February 1884, by which the British government recognised Portugal's ancient claims to jurisdiction over the mouth of the Congo. They also agreed, against their own better judgement, that the navigation of the Congo should be regulated by an Anglo-Portuguese commission – Britain would have preferred an international commission.

The treaty was signed but not yet ratified and there was an immediate outcry from commercial interests in Britain. [**Doc. 12c, p. 111**] The outcry was not entirely spontaneous. It was clearly organised from Manchester, mainly by James Hutton, who was himself in touch with Leopold of the Belgians. (The evidence for this is in the Mackinnon Papers, School of Oriental and African Studies, University of London.) But it gained wide support. British merchants had lost none of their suspicions of Portuguese protectionist policies and the British government had demonstrably been careless in the terms they had negotiated. They had, for example, agreed that the new 'Mozambique tariff' should be applied to the Congo, believing it to be a liberal one, but they had failed to notice that the duties levied under it on textiles were calculated by weight, not by value: 2 3/4d to 4 3/4d per pound on the high-grade Indian textiles that made up most of Mozambique's imports was moderate; the same rate on the very cheap Manchester goods that went to the Congo would be the equivalent of about 30 per cent on the value, and crippling. The government began to fear that they would be defeated in Parliament on the issue. They were not sorry to find a way to avoid ratification.

This was just as well because other European powers were angered by the prospect of a private Anglo-Portuguese settlement of what they regarded as an international question. In Germany the Chancellor, Otto von Bismarck, saw an opportunity for a diplomatic coup. Alsace-Lorraine had made it impossible for Bismarck to effect a reconciliation with France after 1871, as he had done so successfully with Austria after 1866. Ideally, he would almost certainly have preferred a restoration of good relations with France. The French Prime Minister, Jules Ferry, was known to be interested in colonial questions. Bismarck, who was beginning to be interested in colonial questions himself and considered that he had reason to be annoyed with Britain for the latter's cavalier treatment of German claims (see below, pp. 56–9) seized the chance to suggest to France that they might act together to put pressure on Britain over the Congo. The Franco-German *entente* was short-lived – the Germans as the newcomers in the colonial field soon found that they had more in common with free-trade Britain than with protectionist France – but, while it lasted, it had extremely important consequences.

THE BERLIN WEST AFRICA CONFERENCE

The French and the Germans persuaded the Portuguese to put the question of the Congo to an international conference of all the interested parties, including the United States of America. The conference was held in Berlin from November 1884 to February 1885, the main item on the agenda being the Congo, but the Niger and 'new occupations' of the coast of Africa were also discussed. It really laid down the rules under which the 'Scramble' for Africa was conducted during the next six years.

Britain's motive in concluding the Anglo-Portuguese treaty had been to prevent the French from securing a dominant position in the Congo, and she was quite happy to see the question 'internationalised'. The settlement of the Congo by the Berlin Act of February 1885 was unprecedented in international law. The provisions concerning the river itself, promising freedom of navigation for all, had some precedents in the very successful clauses of the Treaty of Vienna of 1815 concerning the international rivers of Europe. Gladstone himself had been very interested in this aspect and hoped that similar provisions might be applied to all international waterways, including the Suez Canal. But the Act went much further than this and laid down that in a vast area of Central Africa, the 'Conventional Basin' of the Congo, much larger than the geographical basin, there was to be freedom of commerce for all without discrimination of nationality. The Basin was also to be neutralised in time of war, and a number of humanitarian clauses tried to secure religious toleration, the protection of native rights and the end of the slave trade. [**Doc. 14, p. 114**] Most of these clauses became a dead letter. Administrative control of a large part of the area passed to Leopold's Congo Free State, which was recognised as a sovereign state by the leading powers during or after the conference.

The British government was not at first unwilling to consider the possibility of allowing the conference to lay down similar conditions on the Niger to those proposed for the Congo, but more cautious counsels prevailed. They decided that Britain must appear at the conference as '*the* Niger power'. Considering Britain's apparently weak diplomatic position at the beginning of the conference, with Germany and France united to put on pressure over the Congo, Britain emerged with remarkable success: the Congo settlement was not unacceptable, the Niger one was very favourable, Britain's predominant position on the Lower and Middle Niger was internationally recognised. In return Britain agreed to observe freedom of navigation on the Niger similar to that laid down on the Congo.

It was the third 'basis' of the conference negotiations – the one regulating 'new occupations' on the coast of Africa and laying down the doctrine of

effective occupation: Idea adopted by the Berlin West Africa Conference of 1884–5 that a European Power claiming territory in Africa must demonstrate an 'effective' presence on the ground. Although primarily intended to disallow theoretical and historical claims, it had the unintended consequence of increasing European intervention in Africa in areas in which they were interested.

'effective occupation' [Doc. 14, p. 114] – that in some ways caused the British government the most anxiety. They wanted, and received, assurances that it would apply only to future, not to recent, acquisitions. The whole idea of establishing 'effective occupation' of an area was a departure from the traditional British policy of trying to secure only a degree of influence which would ensure that their interests were not discriminated against in favour of any other power. Other countries too were affected by these new definitions. The Berlin Conference was, perhaps, primarily a manoeuvre in European diplomacy with Bismarck using the Congo question as a pawn. It was called to settle only certain specified questions. The insistence on 'effective occupation' was probably only intended to abrogate Portugal's ancient but shadowy claims to half the coast line of Africa. But its consequences were far-reaching. Claims that had been left vague were now clearly defined, and the European Powers now felt compelled to assert their presence on the ground as never before.

THE ROYAL NIGER COMPANY

Even before the conference met, the British traders on the Niger had set out to consolidate their position. The National African Company, through its agent David MacIntosh, had begun to sign treaties with local chiefs, purporting to transfer sovereign rights to the Company. When he saw them subsequently, the Lord Chancellor, Lord Selborne, could not conceal his scepticism. Would any body of men, he asked, sign away their rights for such vague benefits as the Company promised them? The treaties were mostly on printed forms and in English only, although they had supposedly been translated and explained to the signatories. [Doc. 15b, p. 117]. There seems little doubt that the signatures (or, more usually, witnessed marks) were genuine enough, but it is likely that the chiefs thought they were signing treaties of trade and amity, similar to others which had been concluded in the past, and had no suspicion of the very different construction which was about to be put upon such treaties by all the European Powers.

Treaties with a commercial company, however, would have only limited status in international law. The Niger traders were convinced that they must get government backing for their position. The argument went on for a long time in Gladstone's cabinet. The forces of the Colonial Office and the Treasury were firmly ranged against any extension of British responsibilities. The Foreign Office was divided in its counsels. Some permanent officials, like Thomas Villiers Lister, the assistant under-secretary with special responsibility for Africa, became converts to the idea that Britain must act to protect British trade. The government tried, briefly, to put forward the doctrine that the traders who desired protection must be prepared to pay for it, for example, by paying for British consuls on the coast. The traders soon scotched that one. Hutton and Goldie told the Foreign Office, 'To keep France back is a national necessity.' Lord Aberdare demonstrated that British trade with the Niger was greater than with Greece or Japan, where the government paid for consular services without question. The Foreign Office acquiesced. In the last resort it acknowledged that the defence of British trade was a government responsibility. [**Doc. 13, p. 113**]

The British Consul at Fernando Po, Edward Hewett, was instructed to conclude treaties with the Niger chiefs which would virtually establish a British **protectorate** in the region. These treaties, concluded in the summer of 1884, were much more carefully explained to the signatories than were the Company's 'treaties' – in many instances the chiefs insisted on detailed changes in certain clauses (F.O. Confidential Prints 5021, 5063; Granville Papers, PRO 30/29/270, National Archives). They were an important factor in allowing Britain to appear at Berlin as 'the Niger power'. The Company, however, did its share by hastily extending its activities to the important tributary of the Niger, the Benue, to comply with the new ideas about 'effective occupation'. Almost immediately after the Conference in 1885, Britain was able to reach agreement with Germany about the British sphere of influence in the region and in June 1885 a formal notice was inserted in the *London Gazette* proclaiming a British protectorate. The British government was now faced with the problem of exercising its jurisdiction. Goldie was still ready with his suggestion of a chartered company. The matter was argued at length. The Liberal government fell in June 1885 and was succeeded by Lord Salisbury's first Conservative government, which held office until February 1886. It is interesting that there is no discernible difference in the attitude of the two parties to Goldie's proposals. The matter was settled eventually for the reasons which T.V. Lister had spelt out in a memorandum as early as January 1885. If the British government discharged its new responsibilities directly, it would have to face the expense of establishing a colonial government and a river fleet. The Company was on the spot with agents and steamers.

> It is [said Lister] perfectly able and willing to discharge the duties of administration . . . and unless it should be considered necessary that this country should go to the great expense of setting up the machinery of Government upon the two rivers where the Company now rules supreme, there seems to be no other course open, and certainly no better one, than that of legalizing and affirming the position of the Company and placing the business of administration into its hands.

protectorate (protected state): Terms recognised in international law, by which a stronger state extended its protection to a smaller state. It normally assumed control of its foreign and defence policies but, in theory, left its internal administration intact. In practice, particularly in Africa in this period, there was often intervention in domestic matters and the distinction between a protectorate and a colony became blurred. In the British empire protectorates came under the Foreign Office, not the Colonial Office. Many African protectorates later became conventional colonies. Protected states tended to continue to enjoy greater autonomy.

In 1886 the National African Company became the Royal Niger Company [**Doc. 15a, p. 115**]. So was born the first of the great African chartered companies by which Britain ruled vast tracts of Africa in the late nineteenth century.

THE GERMAN CHALLENGE

The agreement of 1885 about the British sphere on the Lower Niger had been reached with Germany, not with the old rival, France. This was symptomatic of a rapidly changing situation. Germany had now appeared as a major factor in Africa. The first Anglo-German clash had centred on the region between Cape Colony and the Portuguese colony of Angola, the region which subsequently became German South West Africa. In 1878 Britain had annexed a small station there, Walfisch Bay, but generally no one had previously paid much attention to this barren and unpromising stretch of coast line. The only resident Europeans were the missionaries from the Barmen Rhine Society, who had originally gone to southern Africa under the auspices of the London Missionary Society. When the German government enquired, in February 1883, whether Britain claimed to exercise any jurisdiction in the area, the British thought that they were seeking protection for their missionaries and returned a polite but evasive reply. It only very slowly dawned on the British that the Germans, who had previously insisted that they had no colonial interests in Africa, wanted to take control of the region themselves. In fact, the Germans may only have reached that conclusion themselves in the course of the negotiations. The German government too was under pressure from its traders to protect their overseas interests. A certain Herr Lüderitz, who had previously been associated with several of his countrymen in ambitious plans for the Transvaal, had set up a trading station at Angra Pequena near Walfisch Bay in April 1883. The British government had no strong objection to a German presence there, since so far Britain had no significant colonial quarrels with Germany. But there was another party to the question. In 1872 Cape Colony had finally attained 'responsible government', in effect complete internal autonomy. The Cape colonists were naturally very interested in what happened on their northern frontier. The British government felt compelled to consult them. The consultation involved long delays, and the Germans, who had little understanding of or sympathy with the very complex constitutional relationships that were evolving within the British empire, regarded it as a mere time-wasting device on the part of the British. The Cape government came out very strongly in favour of refusing to recognise the presence of any other Power between the Cape and Angola. The British government, however, were exasperated by what they saw as a growing tendency of their colonies

Plate 1 Two Africans carrying a European in a hammock

© Wikipedia/GNU Free Documentation license

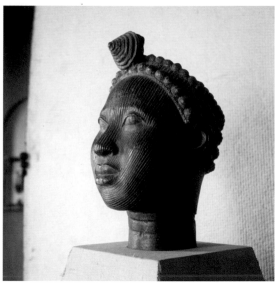

Plate 2 Bronze head from lfe

© Corbis/Paul Almasy

Plate 3 British administrator interviews a native chief in the Gambia

© Mary Evans Picture Library

Plate 4 The Kimberley diamond mines in South Africa, to which thousands flocked in the 1870s after the discovery of diamonds on the nearby De Beers farm 1871

© Getty Images/Hulton Archive

Plate 5 Cecil Rhodes, statesman, entrepreneur and imperialist in South Africa, before the South Africa Committee, London

© Mary Evans Picture Library

Plate 6 The Inauguration Procession of the Suez Canal at El-Guisr in 1865
© The Bridgeman Art Library/Bibliothèque des Arts Décoratifs, Paris

Plate 7 Alexandria after the naval bombardment, July 1882
© Royal Commonwealth Society/L Firolli

Plate 8 Charge of the 21st Lancers at Omdurman, 2 September 1898
© The Bridgeman Art Library/Private Collection

Plate 9 Cartoon depicting 'German efficiency comes to Africa', 1896
© E M Clements

Plate 10 Ahmed Arabi Pasha, Al-Misri
Egyptian nationalist, leader of the
insurrection against foreign interference
in Egyptian affairs
© Mary Evans Picture Library

Plate 11 Loben-Gula and his
favourite wife
© Topfoto/Topham Picturepoint 2000

Plate 12 Portrait of German
explorer Karl Peters (1856–1918)
© Getty Images/Hulton Archive

Plate 13 Leopold II (1835–1909)
King of the Belgians, 1865–1909
© The Granger Collection/Topfoto

Plate 14 Portrait of General Louis Faidherbe
(1818–89), 1884

© The Bridgeman Art Library/Musée de l'Armée, Paris

Plate 15 Sir George Dashwood Taubman
Goldie, 1898

© National Portrait Gallery, London

Plate 16 Henry Morton Stanley (1841–1904), 1870–1904
© The Bridgeman Art Library/Royal Geographical Society, London

Plate 17 Sir Garnet Wolseley, 1884

© The Bridgeman Art Library/National
Army Museum, London

Plate 18 General Gordon's
Last Stand

© The Bridgeman Art Library/Leeds
Museums and Galleries (City Art
Gallery) UK

(the Australians felt much as South Africans did about their neighbouring territories) to proclaim 'a kind of Monroe doctrine' over their region – a Monroe doctrine which the British navy and therefore the British taxpayer, would be compelled to uphold. When the German government announced in April 1884 that they would protect Lüderitz's settlement, and when it was made clear later in the summer of 1884 that this was a territorial and not merely a 'consular' form of protection, the British government acquiesced without many misgivings, although they were irritated by what they saw as Germany's unnecessarily discourteous treatment of a traditionally friendly Power.

The Germans challenged the British much more directly over the Cameroons. The Cameroons, lying between the Oil Rivers and Gabon, were regarded as a desirable region because they were healthier than most of the neighbouring territories. Britain had old-established commercial interests there and the local chiefs had several times asked for British protection in the 1870s. The British government, which was still trying to avoid any extension of its African responsibilities, had refused. Two German firms were established in the Cameroons in 1880 but the British government was not alarmed. Nevertheless, when the British government decided, in May 1884, to order Consul Hewett to strengthen its position on the Niger by concluding treaties with the African chiefs, it was decided to adopt the same policy in the Cameroons. It was still the French, not the Germans, they feared, and Hewett was instructed to go first to the Niger because the greater danger was apprehended there. So little did the British government fear the Germans that when the latter asked the British to assist a German agent, the well-known explorer Gustav Nachtigal, to go to the Cameroons for scientific and commercial purposes, they readily agreed. Only in July 1884 did they learn that Nachtigal had used his visit to the Cameroons to sign treaties with the local chiefs, establishing a German protectorate. There was an understandable outcry from the British commercial interests involved. It is interesting, however, that at first they felt able only to ask that the British government would ensure that their trade was not discriminated against. Only later did they ask for direct British intervention and annexation to protect their trade. [**Docs 12d, 13, p. 112, 113**]

In the middle of 1884 annexation and the assumption of direct political responsibilities were quite foreign to the British tradition in tropical Africa. Britons had previously done very well under a system of 'informal influence'. The situation was quite altered by the sudden new activity of France and Germany and the new 'rules of the game' laid down by the Berlin Conference.

Despite the link with the Egyptian imbroglio suggested by Professors Robinson and Gallagher (1961) and accepted in a restricted form by other writers, including Professors Stengers (1962) and Hargreaves (1963), the 'Scramble' proper seems to have begun in West Africa. Various explanations have been offered – the entry of a maverick individual, Leopold II, into the game, or Bismarck's sudden decision to use Africa as a pawn in his European diplomacy. That there was an important diplomatic dimension to the struggle is undeniable. It is also true, as Robinson and Gallagher insisted, that in the last resort decisions were government decisions taken by cabinets and foreign offices. But what moved a reluctant British government to act was the recognition that British trade was in danger and that, in the last resort, the government had a duty to protect that trade, even if it meant an unwelcome extension of political responsibility. At home, it would seem, pressure was exerted on the government by traders, rather than as Marxist historians would have argued by bankers and financiers, although as Professors Cain and Hopkins contended (1993) the latter should not be entirely forgotten.

The traders who organised themselves to protect their interests are an identifiable group. The same names reappear time and time again on petitions and deputations, supported by MPs who sat for the great manufacturing areas. Manchester was the centre of the movement. Manchester was the capital of the great cotton industry, Britain's leading export industry of the nineteenth century; 80 per cent of Britain's cotton manufactures were exported and it held more than 80 per cent of the world trade in cotton goods. African markets, although they accounted for only a small part of the whole (6 per cent in the 1880s) were important to the Manchester men. West African markets appeared to be growing rapidly. The Board of Trade prepared some figures for the Foreign Office in November 1884 which showed that British exports to British possessions in West Africa had increased from £340,366 in 1860 to £855,486 in 1883. Cotton manufactures accounted for £558,770 worth of this; 'apparel and haberdashery' for a further £39,605. The other important items were hardware and cutlery – £23,400; metals, including iron, £20,550; arms £10,462 and ammunition £9,438. These last figures help to explain why Manchester could usually rely on Sheffield and Birmingham to second its campaigns. Despite some internecine quarrels they could also usually command the support of the great ports, Liverpool, Glasgow and Bristol, with their ancient connections with the African trade. [**Doc. 12, p. 111**]

British participation in the Scramble in West Africa was largely defensive, to protect existing interests against new competition. But both the new challenge from the continental Powers and the strength of the British response may have had their roots in more general economic factors. Whereas during the greater part of the nineteenth century there had only been one highly industrialised Power, Britain, which had supplied a large part of the world with its manufacturing requirements, there were now a number of competing industrial Powers. The United States was getting into its stride again after the Civil War. Germany, united in 1871 and helped by the huge indemnity extracted from the defeated French, was industrialising at a rate that left Britain standing still. Even the France of the Third Republic, although slower off the mark than Germany, was modernising quickly. As a natural result of competitive conditions, nations were once again turning to protective tariff policies. Only Britain had committed itself completely to a free trade policy in the middle of the century. For many Britons, free trade had indeed become almost a religious doctrine, a necessary precondition of peace, prosperity and international cooperation. In these circumstances Britain could hardly abandon it as an obsolete economic theory, but other nations had no such inhibitions. The United States never really relaxed the high tariffs they put on during the abnormal circumstances of the Civil War. Germany reintroduced a protectionist tariff in 1879 – partly, it is true, for domestic and revenue reasons. France, which had never been a whole-hearted convert to free trade, reverted to traditional protectionist duties in 1882. British traders protested time and time again that their real objection to foreign protectorates was that they meant damage to British trade arising from discriminatory duties. [**Doc. 12, p. 111**]

THE GREAT DEPRESSION

A shrill note was added to the complaints of the traders, German and French as well as British, by the background fact of the 'Great Depression'. This depression, about which economic historians still argue vigorously, was marked by low prices, low profits, low interest rates, overproduction of certain commodities and, irregularly, high unemployment. It affected most of western Europe. It began with a financial crisis in 1873 and lasted, with varying degrees of intensity, until 1896. Germany and Britain were badly affected in the 1870s. In France the main effect was not felt until the 1880s. In Germany the French indemnity had proved a two-edged weapon. After an initial boom, hundreds of companies had gone bankrupt in 1873. By 1879 both British and German economists were seriously alarmed. The depression had already lasted longer than was normal and there seemed no way out of it. Some men in both countries began to think in terms of colonial solutions. A few bold men in Britain began to ask for 'fair trade', a euphemism for the taboo word 'protection'. They also began to ask for a parliamentary enquiry. This was eventually set up in 1885 and issued a massive report at the end of 1886. It was one of the most thorough enquiries ever conducted into the state of British industry in the nineteenth century. The Commission called for evidence, not only from government experts but also from chambers of commerce and employers' and working men's associations. The evidence revealed deep and widespread anxieties. There was a great division of opinion as to how the crisis should be met but many spoke of the need for new markets and a few spoke specifically of the existing colonies and of the new possibilities of Africa. [**Doc. 16, p. 118**]

It would be wrong to see a massive or articulate public demand for imperial expansion in the mid-1880s, but the climate of opinion had undoubtedly changed. Britain's industrial position was now challenged and with it the prosperity of all classes of the population, Lancashire cotton workers as much as city businessmen, and this was widely realised. There was a distinct disposition to hang on to everything Britain had and not to shrink from new acquisitions, if this kept them out of the hands of a rival. The government was affected by this as well as the public. There was little logic about Britain's large acquisitions of territory in tropical Africa in the mid-1880s. They were essentially an anxious, even panicky, reaction to new challenges in an already worrying situation.

6

East Africa

Britain gained large areas in West Africa, including the whole of the modern Nigeria, as a direct result of the Scramble. She also acquired vast tracts of East Africa. The simplest and most likely explanation of the West African acquisitions is defence of trade. But Britain had nothing like such an old and well-established trading connection with East Africa as with the West. Can the same explanation hold good there? Some authorities have suggested that it cannot; that, although trade may have been the dominant motive in West Africa, in the East strategy was more important. This was powerfully argued by Professors Robinson and Gallagher who went further and contended: 'The concentration on east Africa shows the preoccupation with supreme strategic interests. . . . Trade prospects had always seemed better in western than in eastern regions. . . . Yet . . . the late Victorians . . . preferred to make the empire safer in the poorer east Africa than to make it wealthier in the richer west' (1961: 393).

There is much that is attractive in this thesis. The east coast had always had close links with India. The British Consulate at Zanzibar was under the jurisdiction of the Government of India until 1883 – although it should be noted that this was a recognition of the importance of British Indian subjects in the trade of Zanzibar (an importance that continued well into the period of the Scramble) as well as of the possible significance of East African ports lying on the Cape route to India. [**Doc. 17d, p. 121**] Until 1869 the Cape route was the main sea route to India. Even after the opening of the Suez Canal, many regarded it as the safer route in times of crisis. [**Docs 6d, e, p. 102**] It was natural therefore that Britain should be reluctant to see a rival great Power installed on the east coast of Africa. The British reaction to the French acquisition of Madagascar in 1883–5 leads one to doubt, however, whether this motive was as central to British policy as is sometimes suggested. The French not only forcibly installed a protectorate on that island, which lay much more athwart the route to India than did the ports of East Africa, but also roughly handled British missionary and other interests in the process.

The British government, however, embarrassed by other problems in Egypt, decided 'to put no difficulties in the way of the French' (Gwynn and Tuckwell, 1917: I, 539). The Admiralty, when asked in 1886 how much importance they attached to the harbour of Mombasa, replied that that it would be of little use to them in wartime. In the last resort, the safety of the Cape route to India depended upon Britain's maintenance of control of the high seas. If it lost that, additional bases would be of no use; so long as control was retained, new bases were on the whole unnecessary.

For many years Britain was content with the informal influence it exercised over the Sultan of Zanzibar. In 1873 it was strengthened by the appointment as Consul General of Sir John Kirk, who attained a degree of influence which has been compared to that which Stratford Canning once exercised at Constantinople. The British persuaded Sultan Barghash to sign a treaty suppressing the slave trade. They supported the Sultan diplomatically when the Khedive Ismail supplemented his expansionist policy in the Sudan by occupying certain East African ports over which the Sultan claimed jurisdiction. A British naval officer, Lloyd Williams Mathews, built up an efficient army for the Sultan. By 1877 the Sultan was prepared to consider placing himself under British protection. The British, however, were not alone at Zanzibar. German firms, first Herz and Sons, later Hansing and O'Swald, had been active there since the 1840s. It was only a matter of time before the Sultan learned that it was possible to play the two Powers off against each other.

A NEW AUSTRALIA

Buganda: The largest of the four kingdoms which went to make up Uganda. Its inhabitants were called Baganda.

In 1877–8, however, British influence was dominant. The explorations of the previous twenty years had begun to make men realise that the interior of Africa might be valuable for its own sake. The populous African kingdom of **Buganda** on Lake Victoria seemed to offer considerable trading possibilities. The highlands, particularly the area round Mount Kilimanjaro, might even be suitable for extensive European settlement. Enthusiasts began to suggest that East Africa might be not only the new India but a new Australia. [**Doc. 17c, p. 120**] A group of Britons, led by the Scottish shipowner Sir William Mackinnon, who in 1872 had organised the first regular mail service between Britain, India and Zanzibar, put forward an ambitious scheme in 1877, under which they would administer the whole vast area from the coast to Lake Victoria in the name of the Sultan. The failure of the scheme is one of the most extraordinary stories in the history of the Scramble for Africa, indeed in the history of British diplomacy. The Foreign Secretary, Lord Salisbury, while pretending to approve the project, sent out an eccentric orientalist, G.P. Badger, ostensibly to help with legal forms but in reality with secret instructions to wreck the scheme. Badger so irritated and offended the Sultan that the latter refused to give his consent. (Oliver and Mathew, 1966: 361)

Salisbury had been determined that there should be no extension of British responsibilities in East Africa. His views were shared by William Gladstone, who a few years later was to lament that his cabinet colleagues could become so excited about the fate of the 'mountain with an unrememberable name [Kilimanjaro]' (Gwynn and Tuckwell, 1917: II 83–4). But in East Africa, as in the West, the situation had changed. There was now a German challenge, and the pressure from British commercial interests had built up to a new level.

One of the strongest advocates of the establishment of an English colony in the region of Mount Kilimanjaro was H.H. Johnston. 'Here is a land', he wrote 'eminently suited for European colonisation, situated midway between the Equatorial lakes and the coast. Within a few years it must be either English, French or German.' If a road could be made into the interior, 'trade will flow entirely into English hands; the ivory, wax, iron, hides of the interior will come to our markets.' He was fortunate in obtaining the whole-hearted support of the British consul at Zanzibar, Frederick Holmwood. Holmwood communicated directly with the Manchester merchants, led by James Hutton. Hutton in turn enlisted the support of Lord Aberdare and others who were contemporaneously supporting him on West Africa. These arguments impressed a number of individuals both in the Foreign Office and in the Cabinet, but Gladstone set his face firmly against a forward policy in East Africa and, for a time, his views prevailed. [**Docs 17a–d, p. 119**]

THE GERMAN CHALLENGE

It was German activity that changed the situation. In 1884 the German explorer Karl Peters went to East Africa. He had been warned before he set out that he had no official status and could not look to his government for support. Despite this, he concluded a number of treaties with chiefs who swore that they were independent of the Sultan of Zanzibar in the general area of what later became Tanganyika. Peters returned to Berlin in February 1885, and on 3 March, the day after the Berlin West Africa Conference dispersed, the German government publicly proclaimed that it would take the territories secured by Peters under its protection.

The British merchants and their supporters redoubled their pressure on the Foreign Office, and suggested taking up the Mackinnon scheme of 1877. The Liberal government fell from office in June 1885 but, as in the Niger region, it is interesting that there is no significant difference in the way in which the Conservatives and the Liberals proposed to deal with the situation. Britain, Germany and France agreed to the setting up, in November 1885, of a Boundary Commission to determine the legal limits of the Sultan's domain. As for the inland areas, which would probably be judged to lie beyond the Sultan's territories, both Conservatives and Liberals felt that a modified version of the Mackinnon scheme would now be the best solution if an agreement could be reached with Germany. An agreement was finally reached in October 1886 which left the coast under the jurisdiction of the Sultan but allocated what became Kenya and Uganda to Britain, and Tanganyika to Germany. So far as the administration of the British sphere was concerned, the British government resorted to the same device as on the Niger, a chartered company. In 1888 the Imperial British East Africa Company, headed by Sir William Mackinnon, was chartered. James Hutton was on its board of directors.

STRATEGY VERSUS COMMERCE

On the east coast of Africa there were undoubtedly strategic considerations which did not apply on the west coast, but so far as the division of the hinterland in 1886 was concerned, exactly the same factors seem to have operated as operated on the Niger. British merchants, centred on, although not confined to, Manchester, with a number of supporters in public life, had fought a fierce battle to prevent a region which might one day be important to British commerce passing under the control of another great Power. [**Docs 17a–c, p. 119**] No one claimed that the commercial benefits would be immediate. They were, as Lord Rosebery was to say, in mining language, 'pegging out claims'. A great inflow of capital was necessary before any return could be seen; in particular a railway from Mombasa to Lake Victoria, the famous 'Uganda Railway', was essential. Moreover it slowly became clear that the economic development of East Africa would be different from that of West Africa. In West Africa the economy was essentially that of peasant proprietors. In the East the development of cash crops meant a plantation economy to grow cotton and coffee. Neither the capital nor the settlers were quickly forthcoming. Even in 1902 there were fewer than a dozen European families farming in Kenya. The lack of capital, above all for railway development, was crippling to the Imperial British East Africa Company. By the early 1890s it was virtually bankrupt. The history of the British East Africa Company, and that of the German chartered companies which suffered similar financial difficulties, seems almost sufficient in itself to demolish the theory that it was 'surplus capital' seeking foreign outlets that caused the annexations of the late nineteenth century. Far from capital fighting to get out, it was almost impossible to persuade it to go.

Naturally disillusionment set in. Vast tracts of Africa had been acquired in a moment of panic in the mid-1880s. Salisbury himself commented on the extraordinary nature of the phenomenon. When he left the Foreign Office in 1880, he said, no one thought of Africa; when he returned in 1885 the whole of Europe was quarrelling about it. Once the moment of panic and 'grab' had passed some men began to return to their earlier views that colonies were expensive and vulnerable and that caution should be exercised in acquiring them. Bismarck himself commented wryly, 'I am not a colonial man.' New factors had, however, now come into play. As the British had found over the Gambia, it was surprisingly difficult to relinquish territory (see above p. 47). Some interest group was bound to be offended and there was an irrational, but none the less powerful, reluctance to abandon a country over which one's flag had once flown. Central Africa was no longer *terra incognita*. European ambitions and interests were established there. New strategic considerations now developed, connected with Africa itself. Colonies had been established. They must be protected and their boundaries and communication routes made as rational as possible. The year 1890 saw a whole series of agreements between Britain and other European Powers. There were essentially 'tidying up' agreements, arising from the hasty arrangements of 1884–6. They have, however, a different quality about them from the earlier negotiations. In Britain this is probably partly only a reflection of the different 'styles' of Salisbury and Granville. Granville was pushed into almost all the decisions he made in 1884–5 by unexpected circumstances. Salisbury, possibly in 1886, certainly by 1889–90, was beginning to play something like the 'Great Game' of Central Asia, transferred to an African context, and to enjoy it. This is very far from saying that Salisbury had become converted to a forward imperialist policy in Africa; probably he never was. But he had had time to assess the situation, to determine what objectives were worth pursuing and even to make Africa play a part in European diplomacy.

The most important of the agreements Britain made in 1890 was with Germany. Bismarck may have been feeling his way towards a more general understanding with Britain but he fell from power before the agreement was finally reached. By it Germany recognised a British protectorate over the dominions of the Sultan of Zanzibar. In return the Germans got some small concessions in West Africa: the famous **Caprivi Strip** – a corridor of land connecting German South West Africa with the Zambezi – and the island of Heligoland in the North Sea, which had been in British hands since the Napoleonic Wars but which was important to Germany because it commanded the entrance to the Kiel Canal. France also recognised the British protectorate over Zanzibar in return for a British recognition of the French position in Madagascar. Portugal acknowledged the British position in Mashonaland and Nyasaland (see below p. 77) in return for the British acceptance of other boundary claims on behalf of Portuguese East Africa.

Caprivi Strip: Strip of land connecting German South West Africa with the Zambezi. Named after the German Chancellor (1890–4), Count Caprivi.

A little ironically the final decision about a British retention of Uganda had to be made by a Liberal government, once again headed by William Gladstone. By this time the question had been complicated by religious strife and new strategic considerations. Until the 1860s the Baganda had been pagans, but traders from Zanzibar brought the Islamic faith with them. The Kabaka (king), Mutesa, was interested and, from 1867, adopted at least some Muslim observances. Henry Morton Stanley, however, on his visit in 1875, drew attention to the rival claims of Christianity. Mutesa, perhaps for political reasons, again expressed interest. In 1877 representatives of the Anglican Church Missionary Society arrived. In 1879 the Roman Catholic White Fathers, sent by the 'Apostle of Africa', Cardinal Lavigerie, came. Soon there were three rival parties: Muslim, English Protestant and French Catholic. Mutesa died in 1884 and his successor, Mwanga, did not share his sympathy for Christian missionaries. In 1885–6 European attention was attracted to Uganda; first, by the murder on Mwanga's orders, of an Anglican bishop, James Hannington; and, second, by the massacre of thirty of Mwanga's pages, Catholic converts who refused to recant. By the late 1880s Uganda was in a state of civil war.

In 1890 the British East Africa Company sent a man later to be famous as the Governor of Nigeria, Captain Lugard, to try to establish the Company's authority in Buganda. A subsequent British Chancellor of the Exchequer, Sir William Harcourt, later blamed the Company for rushing into Uganda, instead of building up their sphere slowly from the coast. The Company in turn protested that they had no wish to go to Uganda so soon, but had been pushed into it by the government who wished to make sure that the area would not slip into German hands, despite the preliminary division of 1886. They had reason to worry. Karl Peters himself had been active in the region, signing treaties with chiefs early in 1890. But the Anglo-German agreement, concluded later that year, meant that the German government never accepted the treaties.

The British East Africa Company, however, had reached its financial limit. In December 1890 Mackinnon asked the government to guarantee the interest on the capital they wished to raise to build the railway from Mombasa to Lake Victoria. Salisbury himself was well disposed, but the strength of parliamentary opposition was such that the proposal was dropped in July 1891. When the Conservatives left office in August 1892 the future of Uganda was still unresolved although the East Africa Company was insisting that, unless they received a substantial subvention, total evacuation was inevitable. Evacuation would have been entirely acceptable to some members of the Liberal cabinet, including Harcourt, John Morley and Gladstone himself. [**Doc. 18, p. 121**] They attached little importance to Uganda, they disliked Lugard's forward policy there, and they lived in mortal dread of a new 'Gordon incident' (see page 42). Against them, however, were ranged very powerful missionary interests, which had already contributed substantial sums to keep a British presence in Uganda, and which feared a new massacre of Christian converts if Britain withdrew. The East Africa Company, despite its precarious financial position, managed to rally significant support from Chambers of Commerce and trading organisations. But the decisive fact was undoubtedly that the new Foreign Secretary, Lord Rosebery, committed himself completely to a retentionist policy. R.R. James (1964) suggested that there was a considerable element of domestic political manoeuvring in this. Rosebery wished to worst Harcourt and demonstrate to the Cabinet that he was the only possible successor to the aged Gladstone. Martel's detailed study (1986) accepts that this was a consideration but also links Rosebery's actions with his determination to impress the Germans. It is also true that Rosebery was a man of the younger generation, an imperialist at least in the sense of believing that colonies were valuable and should be defended, a world apart from Gladstone or his own predecessor at the Foreign Office, Granville. Rosebery prevailed. Uganda was retained and a formal protectorate proclaimed there in 1894.

Uganda now had a strategic importance that it had never had in the past. Until 1887 British governments, both Liberal and Conservative, had been sincere in their avowed intention to end the occupation of Egypt as soon as possible. The muddled events of 1882 had left them in Egypt without any proper status in international law. It had strained their relations with France. The new Egyptian financial crisis of 1885, resulting partly from events in the Sudan, had meant a new international loan and the involvement of still more Powers, Russia and Italy among them, in control of Egyptian finances. Britain was in effect administering Egypt without controlling the purse strings. Foreign Powers, and Liberals at home, could and did taunt British governments with their failure to carry out their earlier promises of evacuation, and foreign Powers could always apply diplomatic pressure in Egypt. It became, as a later Foreign Secretary Sir Edward Grey said, a noose round Britain's neck that other Powers could tighten at will. In these circumstances Sir Henry Drummond Wolff's mission to Constantinople in 1885 to try to secure a British withdrawal upon conditions that would still protect British interests, was entirely sincere. A convention was in fact signed with the Turks in May 1887 providing for a British evacuation within three years but, since it also allowed for re-entry in some circumstances, the Sultan eventually decided not to ratify it. From 1887 onwards Salisbury's policy (and Rosebery's) was determined by the fact that Britain was in Egypt for the foreseeable future and that that position must be protected. Potentially hostile Powers must be kept away from the sources and upper reaches of the Nile. The exact effect of this on British diplomacy has been much debated but the general influence is clear.

Britain was in Egypt because it could not find a safe way of getting out, but it was also beginning to adopt a quite different attitude towards its position there. The administration of Egypt had been undertaken in the autumn of 1882 because there was no alternative. By the late 1880s it was becoming the showpiece of beneficent British imperialism in action. The Egyptian economy was fundamentally sound. Well administered and with a government much better placed than the Khedive's had been to resist international pressures, the country was now very prosperous. In 1883 Cromer had been strongly in favour of early evacuation. [**Doc. 8b, p. 105**] By 1886 he had changed his mind. Joseph Chamberlain, who had so many misgivings about the occupation [**Doc. 8a, p. 105**], visited Egypt and, in the words of his official biographer, J.L. Garvin, 'became whole as an imperialist'. In 1892 one of Cromer's assistants, Alfred Milner, published his *England in Egypt,* praising the British achievements there. The British began to acquire a comfortable conviction that they were a naturally 'governing race', with a mission to bring good government and liberal ideas to the whole world. [**Doc. 26, p. 129**]

Egypt also lay at one end of the famous Cape-to-Cairo railway project, which was beginning to receive serious attention in 1889. It is probably true that neither Salisbury nor his principal Foreign Office advisers, such as Lister's successor, Sir Percy Anderson, ever took it altogether seriously. In any case the final recognition of the German sphere in Tanganyika in 1890 seemed to cut across any hope of an all-red route from north to south but the possibility of a line through Katanga with the consent of Leopold of the Belgians remained. When Kitchener began to lay a railway into the Sudan in 1896 in the course of the reconquest of that region (see p. 82), he chose the same gauge as that in use at the Cape. By the 1890s planning was on a continental scale. Men like Salisbury were playing diplomatic chess with the whole of Africa.

7

South Africa

I n southern Africa the one man who could undoubtedly 'think big' was Cecil John Rhodes. [**Doc. 19, p. 122**] Rhodes had arrived in South Africa in 1870, a thin, tubercular young man, sent to regain his health on his brother's cotton farm in Natal. He spent most of the next few years not in Natal, but on the new diamond diggings at Kimberley. The first diamond had been found there in 1867. For some time the children of a Boer farmer had played with the 'pretty marble' before its value was discovered. Kimberley, perhaps more than anywhere else, symbolised the El Dorado element in the new Africa. Griqualand West, where the diamond diggings were, quickly attracted an overflowing population, old prospectors from America and Australia, petty crooks from the East End of London, the whole choir, according to one report, of the cathedral of Grahamstown. It was a tough society but Rhodes quickly made his mark. His first big *coup* was to corner the market in pumping equipment when the workings were threatened with disastrous flooding. But Rhodes was a great deal more than a smart operator. Otherwise he would have finished up merely as a rich man like some of his rivals on the diamond fields, Alfred Beit or Barney Barnato. Rhodes was always a dreamer too. He spent long nights on the veldt philosophising to anyone who would listen, and he commuted from Kimberley to Oxford intermittently between 1873 and 1881 to obtain a degree. Rhodes retained an almost mystic faith in the powers of education, which was later to bear fruit in his endowment of 'Rhodes scholarships' to take young men from the Empire, the United States and Germany to Oxford.

Rhodes's dream was of the British empire. He became convinced of the peculiar destiny of the Anglo-Saxon people to govern the world beneficently. He regarded the American War of Independence as the greatest tragedy that had occurred in modern times and hoped that one day the United States would reunite with the other English-speaking countries in a new federal empire. Rhodes had an odd habit of expressing his political views in a series of 'Last Wills and Testaments' which he compiled throughout his life. One of the strangest was that of 1877, in which he envisaged the incorporation into the empire of the whole of Africa, much of the Middle East, including the Holy Land, the whole of South America, the islands of the Pacific, Malaya and the seaboard of China and Japan. He considered the founding of a secret society, a 'secular order of Jesuits', to further the interests of the empire. [**Doc. 19b, p. 123**] The dreams sounded too extravagant to be taken seriously but Rhodes was above all a 'doer' – the one type of man he thoroughly despised was what he called a 'loafer'. By his early thirties he was a multimillionaire but he had little interest in money for its own sake. He generally dressed like a tramp and kept no careful account of his wealth. He wanted money for the power it brought. [**Doc. 19a, p. 122**] In 1880 he plunged into South African politics, becoming MP for a Griqualand constituency, Barkly West.

THE ROLE OF THE BOERS

South African politics were already in a tangled state. The story goes back to the British acquisition of the Cape during the Napoleonic wars. The existing settlers, the Boers, bitterly resented the 'anglicising' policy of the British and, more especially, their 'native policy'. By the famous Fiftieth Ordnance of 1828 the British greatly improved the civil rights of the Hottentots (Khoikhoi), and in 1833 they abolished slavery throughout the empire with what the Boers regarded as totally inadequate compensation. The Boers had always been used to 'trekking' in search of new land and now a mass movement, the Great Trek, began. They went first to Natal but the British disliked the idea of a colony on the South African coast not under their control, which might fall under the influence of another great Power. In 1845 they annexed Natal. The Boers moved on, first to what became the Orange Free State and later to what became the Transvaal. The British, in the middle of the century, were interested only in the Cape as a staging post to India. The fewer responsibilities they had in the interior the better they liked it. By the Sand River Convention of 1852 and the Bloemfontein Convention of 1854 respectively they recognised the independence of the Transvaal and of the Orange Free State. But the tension between the two peoples continued. Many Boers still lived in Cape Colony and some in Natal. The two peoples never saw eye to eye about 'native policy'. The British felt that the Boers by their continual clashes with the 'Bantu' were stirring up trouble for the whole continent of southern Africa, although without fundamentally understanding the very complex population movements of the interior (see Chapter 2). Not only the Boers but some British South Africans felt that the government in London had very little appreciation of the peculiar difficulties they faced, and resentment at what was generally called the 'imperial factor' – that is, intervention in South African affairs from London – grew accordingly.

The situation became more acute in the 1870s. The Transvaal resented the British annexation of Griqualand West after the diamond discoveries. The legal claims of Cape Colony and the Transvaal to the area are not easy to disentangle but confidence was not inspired by the fact that the matter was referred to the arbitration of the British Governor of Natal, Robert Keate. Lord Carnarvon, Colonial Secretary in Disraeli's government of 1874, impressed by the success of Canadian federation in 1867, hoped that all the problems of South Africa might be solved by a federation of the four states, Cape Colony, Natal, the Orange Free State and the Transvaal. Carnarvon's plans broke down, however, on one vital point. The Canadians had actively desired federation; the South Africans did not. Nevertheless, the Transvaalers could no longer go on alone. Their Treasury was almost empty and they were faced with a great new military threat from the resurgent Zulu power under Cetewayo. In these circumstances Sir Theophilus Shepstone, the Secretary for Native Affairs in Natal, was able to rush the Transvaalers into accepting annexation to the British Crown. The new British Governor of Cape Colony, Sir Bartle Frere, who had come to South Africa from India with a high reputation for both efficiency and enlightenment, had now to decide how to deal with the Zulus. London, faced with a probable war in Afghanistan, instructed him to damp down the South African situation. Frere, however, had already issued an ultimatum to the Zulus demanding the demobilisation of their large standing army. The Zulus refused to comply and inflicted a serious defeat on a British force which they caught unprepared at Isandhlwana. A war lasting several months followed which ended with the defeat of the Zulus and the surrender of Cetewayo.

As long as they were threatened by the Zulus, the Boers of the Transvaal remained passive but, after Cetewayo's final defeat, they protested that the annexation of 1877 had been forced upon them and demanded the return of their independence. Gladstone and the Liberal party in England accepted the validity of their arguments but when Gladstone came into office in 1880, Boer independence was not immediately restored. The Liberals, like the Conservatives, hoped that a South African federation might come out of the troubles. The Boers, however, declined to wait. They defeated a British force at Majuba Hill in 1881. Some men in Britain counselled the government to 'avenge Majuba' before making concessions, but Gladstone refused. Instead two Conventions were signed with the Boers, that of Pretoria in 1881 and that of London in 1884. There was unfortunately some ambiguity about these Conventions. They clearly restored internal autonomy to the Transvaal, but the 1881 Convention had a preamble (not repeated in 1884) asserting British suzerainty. The Transvaal was precluded from certain acts which would have been economically damaging to the other South African states. The Transvaal insisted that the Convention had restored them, for all practical purposes, to the status of an independent state. The British government, however, held – and this view was to be very strongly asserted by a later Colonial Secretary, Joseph Chamberlain – that it was a limited and conditional independence that left the British government free, not only to control the Transvaal's external relations with other Powers, but even in some circumstances to intervene in its internal affairs.

The abortive British annexation of the Transvaal was the most spectacular extension of British responsibilities in South Africa in this period but there had been others. In 1868 they annexed Basutoland (the modern Lesotho). This too had been the result of friction between Africans and Boers. The Basuto people were basically the scattered remnants of a number of tribes which had survived the onslaughts of Shaka. They had found a leader of outstanding ability in Moshesh. Their numbers began to increase and in the 1850s they and the advancing Boers began to compete for fertile land. In despair Moshesh appealed for British protection and, reluctantly, the British agreed.

BECHUANALAND

In the 1880s all eyes began to focus on the vast area of Bechuanaland (the modern Botswana). Bechuanaland was, on the whole, an infertile territory but through it passed what was then called the 'Missionaries' Road', although it was an important route long before the Christian missionaries came. Cecil Rhodes himself called it South Africa's 'Suez Canal'. To the west were Damaraland and Namaqualand, which were to become German South West Africa (see above pp. 56–7) To the east were the Boer Republics, themselves in an expansionist mood. If Cape Colony did not act quickly it must resign itself to seeing its route to the north occupied by others. To some this might seem of no great moment but to Cecil Rhodes and his supporters it was vital. Rhodes was already dreaming of an expansion of British South Africa, perhaps as far north as the Great Lakes. Even in the more limited context of the existing South African states it was fundamental to the future balance of power. One day there would almost certainly be some kind of federation. Would it be dominated by the Boers or by the British? It seemed likely that whichever side gained a significant accretion of power now would finally dominate the southern part of the continent. In 1885, startled by German actions in South West Africa, the British government finally moved. Bechuanaland south of the Molopo river became a crown colony, north of the river a British protectorate.

Despite the British acquisition of Bechuanaland, in the following year, 1886, the balance of power in South Africa suddenly began to tilt in favour of the Boers. In that year the great gold discoveries were made on the Witwatersrand. The discoveries were in one sense unwelcome to the traditionalist Boers, led by the old Voortrekker, Paul Kruger. They wanted to live their traditional pastoral life, uninterrupted by a gold rush and the influx of thousands of, in their eyes, undesirable foreigners into their state. On the other hand, if political power followed economic power, the Transvaal was well placed to become the dominant state.

GOLD AND DIAMONDS

Meanwhile Cecil Rhodes was preparing his next move. He was among the first to buy a substantial stake in the Witwatersrand. This gave him a financial edge over some of his old rivals on the diamond fields. In 1888 he persuaded a rather reluctant Nathaniel Rothschild to back him in a financial operation which forced his great rival, Barney Barnato (Rufus Isaacs, the East End Jew who had gone to South Africa in 1873 with forty boxes of dubious cigars belonging to his brother-in-law as his sole asset), to amalgamate his interests with those of Rhodes in the De Beers Consolidated Mines Company, which still virtually controls the world diamond market. The trust deed of the new company was an extraordinary one. It did not confine its activities to diamond mining but deliberately opened the way for Rhodes to 'go north', by allowing its capital to be used to administer and develop any area.

'RHODESIA'

Rhodes had his eyes firmly fixed on the region north of the Transvaal, Mashonaland and Matabeleland. The story of how he secured what was to become Southern Rhodesia (the modern Zimbabwe) is not an edifying one, although the regime that the British replaced was itself a tyranny based on conquest. The area had originally been occupied by the Mashona, a peaceful pastoral people, but some forty years before the British became seriously interested in the area, the Matabele (Ndebele), an offshoot of the Zulus, under Mzilikazi, had turned north and conquered them. Mzilikazi was in time succeeded by his son Lobengula. The nature of Matabele rule was such that contemporaries believed that, in trying to determine the limits of Lobengula's dominions, the only question that could meaningfully be asked was 'Has he raided there?' [**Doc. 21, p. 124**]

Lobengula was, according to all contemporary accounts, an impressive figure; a shrewd man who did all that in him lay to prevent his country being taken by Europeans, whether it was restraining his own young men from a premature challenge or trying to beat the Europeans at their own diplomatic game. That he lost is a reflection of the fact that the odds were too heavily stacked against him. By the 1880s Lobengula was a sorely tried man. It was generally believed that Mashonaland was very rich in gold. Geologically, this seemed to make sense. The gold deposits of the Witwatersrand were now known, the mineral wealth of Katanga suspected. It seemed likely that the crescent of wealth stretched through the future Rhodesia. Moreover, men like the German Karl Peters had argued very persuasively that Mashonaland was probably the site of the legendary gold mines of King Solomon (Peters, 1899). (Rider Haggard incorporated the idea in a famous novel *King Solomon's Mines*.) If the Phoenicians had mined gold there that would explain the ruins of Great Zimbabwe, which the Victorians could not believe that Africans had built. Lobengula was besieged by concession hunters of all nationalities: British, Portuguese, German and Boer. Lobengula rightly discerned that the Boers and the Portuguese were interested in his land as well as in mineral rights. He wrongly concluded that the British were probably only concerned with the minerals. [**Doc. 20, p. 123**]

Rhodes did hope to find gold in Mashonaland. The experience of the British East Africa Company had shown that only reasonable profits quickly would keep investors interested. In Rhodes' own famous phrase, the ideal combination was 'philanthropy plus 5 per cent'. For Rhodes, however, profit was now a secondary consideration – fortunately perhaps for him, since he made no profit out of Rhodesia. He wanted to attract British settlers into the region for a number of reasons; the general principle of expanding the British empire, to keep the balance of South Africa British, to keep alive the dream of an all-red route from the Cape to Cairo which had many attractions for Rhodes. He was influenced too by the general arguments current about the need for empire building. He wrote to W.T. Stead in 1891 that markets were the key question since English home consumption could only support six million workers. Then there is the famous passage, quoted by Lenin, in which Rhodes recounted how he attended a meeting of the unemployed in the East End of London in 1895 and 'listened to the wild speeches, which were just a cry for "bread", "bread", "bread",' and became convinced that the only alternative to civil war was that 'we colonial statesmen must acquire new lands to settle the surplus population, to provide new markets for goods produced in the factories and mines' (Lenin, 1933:96–7). However wild some of his dreams, the empire remained for Rhodes essentially 'a bread and butter question'.

In 1887 two Boers, the Grobler brothers, obtained a treaty from Lobengula which purported to give them very considerable rights of passage through his territory and the right to call on him for military assistance. The treaty was suspect since it was not in a language that Lobengula could understand and there were no independent witnesses to testify that it had been properly translated to him. Lobengula subsequently repudiated it. The incident of the Grobler treaty moved the British authorities to persuade Lobengula to sign a treaty, witnessed by a missionary he trusted, John Moffat, agreeing not to enter into correspondence or treaties with foreign powers, or to sell, alienate or cede any part of his country without the previous agreement of the British High Commissioner in South Africa.

Lobengula now came to the plausible but, as it proved, disastrous conclusion that he could get rid of a lot of quarrelling concession seekers by giving monopoly rights to one group. He signed an agreement, the famous Rudd Concession [**Doc. 20, p. 123**] with C.D. Rudd, the emissary of Cecil Rhodes, by which, in return for money and weapons, he granted exclusive mineral rights to Rudd and his associates with certain vague clauses which conferred ill-defined additional rights to allow them to defend and administer their mining concession.

Rhodes was now ready to take his next step of seeking a Chartered Company to administer the whole region. Many obstacles, however, still remained. Other interested parties, notably the Bechuanaland Exploration Company, had to be bought out or induced to amalgamate their interests with his. Rhodes himself was by no means *persona grata* in England. He was still very active in Cape politics – he became Prime Minister of the Cape in 1890 – and his position was dependent on the close association he maintained with Boer politicians there. Moreover, he had always been an outspoken opponent of the 'imperial factor', if it seemed to encroach in any way upon the autonomy of Cape politics. In the circumstances it is not surprising that he was regarded in London, however mistakenly, as a Boer supporter and therefore suspect from an imperial point of view. He had powerful enemies in London. He had quarrelled with missionary interests over Bechuanaland. The Colonial Secretary, Lord Knutsford, originally supported the claims of the rival Bechuanaland Exploration Company. The London Chamber of Commerce opposed him. So did the Parliamentary South African Committee which included not only Joseph Chamberlain, who deeply distrusted him, but also a number of men later closely associated with Rhodes, such as the Duke of Fife and Albert, later Earl, Grey.

It was the greatest political feat of Rhodes's life that he overcame all this in the summer of 1889 and emerged, in October, with his Charter. The whole story has never transpired but the general reasons why Salisbury's government finally accepted Rhodes' schemes are clear enough. They were convinced that it was necessary to establish a British presence in Mashonaland and Matabeleland to forestall the Germans, Portuguese and Boers. The alternative to a chartered company was direct British administration with all its attendant expenses. The Treasury was not in a generous mood and the government was already experiencing the difficulties of running a colony on a shoestring in Bechuanaland. The change in the government attitude can be traced in Knutsford's communications with Lobengula. In March 1889, in a famous letter, he warned him to be cautious about giving away land or mining rights, reminding him that a prudent king might give a friendly stranger one ox, but not his whole herd of cattle. In November he advised him that, as he could not hope to exclude white men entirely, the safest course would be to agree with 'one approved body'.

The Colonial Office later came to the conclusion that they had been deceived by Rhodes over the whole question of the Charter. They had not understood that the financial assets were retained by another company, the Central Search Association (later the United Concessions Company), which stood behind the Chartered Company. In strict law too, the British government could only grant rights to their subjects as against other British subjects. They could not confer sovereign rights over Africans and African territories, unless these were granted by treaty by the competent authorities. Rhodes had performed a kind of sleight of hand by transforming vague rights connected with mining concessions into a territorial jurisdiction. All in all the Colonial Office concluded in 1892 that they would be legally justified in cancelling the Charter. But it was politically impossible. The Chartered Company was the only body able and willing to keep the area in the British sphere. [**Doc. 21, p. 124**]

If the Colonial Office had reason to complain that they had been deceived by Rhodes, Lobengula had more reason to protest. In his own eyes he repudiated the Rudd Concession by allowing Lotje, the counsellor who advised him to sign it, to be smelt out for witchcraft and by putting to death not only Lotje but his whole household. Lobengula was later to die, probably from smallpox, fleeing from Rhodes' forces, still trying to make clear to Rhodes that he no longer recognised their agreement by returning the money that he had received under it.

All this did nothing to stop Rhodes' advance. He collected his 'Pioneers', a carefully selected body of men who marched into Mashonaland, at this stage avoiding Matabele territory proper, in the summer of 1890. In September 1890 they hoisted the Union Jack at an outpost they named Fort Salisbury, and took possession of Mashonaland in the name of Queen Victoria. The early pioneers suffered acutely from floods and near-starvation conditions. Worse, the hopes of gold proved illusory. For a time Chartered shares boomed. Men and women almost fought for them. But soon they began to drift downwards. Randolph Churchill visited the country and said openly that there was no gold. The radical Henry Labouchere began a great campaign against the Company in *Truth*.

Rhodes' stock was already falling at the time of the Jameson Raid in December 1895. An **uitlander** rising had been confidently expected in Johannesburg, where all new immigrants were denied the franchise and certain other rights by Kruger and the Boers. Joseph Chamberlain, the new British Colonial Secretary, undoubtedly knew of the projected rising – as did every well-informed man in London – and, since he took a very 'high' view of the rights which Britain retained under the 1881 and 1884 Conventions, he saw it as an excellent excuse to intervene on the breakdown of law and order in the Transvaal. Rhodes, however, was the man primarily respons-ible for having a force standing by on the frontier under his old friend Dr Jameson, ready to intervene immediately and present the world with a *fait accompli*. Jameson alone was responsible for the mad act of going ahead with the invasion of the Transvaal when the rising itself had failed to materialise. Jameson was arrested by the Boers and handed over to the British authorities. Rhodes was compelled to resign as Prime Minister of the Cape. The repercussions went deep into British politics. There were many who never trusted Chamberlain again.

Rhodes feared most of all for his Charter and the new 'Rhodesia'. The Pioneers had penetrated, at the cost of war, into Matabeleland proper in 1893 but, with the withdrawal of security forces at the time of the Jameson Raid, first the Matabele and then, to everyone's astonishment, the Mashona, rose. The risings were put down with difficulty and Rhodes who, whatever his other failings, did not lack personal courage, met the African leaders in the Matoppo Hills to arrange a settlement. Mashonaland and Matabeleland were saved for the empire.

There was always an international dimension to the British position in southern Africa. In 1890 and 1891 respectively Salisbury had concluded agreements with Germany and Portugal delimiting their spheres in southern Africa. This enabled Britain in 1891 to include Barotseland, the modern Zambia, in the field of operations of the Chartered Company, to be known a few years later as Northern Rhodesia. The same year, 1891, they proclaimed a protec-torate over Nyasaland (the modern Malawi), where Scottish missions had for some time been active – so active indeed that boys from the Nyasaland mission schools were in demand for clerical positions all over southern Africa.

At the time of the Jameson raid the Kaiser, Wilhelm II, caused a sensation by sending a telegram to President Kruger, congratulating him on defending his independence without calling on the assistance of friendly Powers. The British government tried to pass this off as a royal whim – in fact it had been sanctioned by Wilhelm's political advisers – but it focused attention again on an old threat to Britain's position in South Africa. The British had always been concerned about German sympathy for the Boer Republics. They now concentrated particularly on trying to prevent the Boers getting an outlet to

uitlander: Afrikaans term for a foreigner. It was particularly applied to white residents in the Transvaal, who were not Boers and were refused citizenship.

the sea through the Portuguese port of Lourenço Marques on Delagoa Bay. Despite the British opposition, a railway from the Transvaal to Delagoa Bay was completed in 1894. The Boers were also buying in large stores of Krupps guns from Germany. By the time Alfred Milner went to South Africa as High Commissioner in 1899 both sides were ripe for a showdown. The outcome was the second Boer War which dragged on from October 1899 until the Peace of Vereeniging in May 1902. The war, particularly the early ill-success of the British forces, came as a great shock to British opinion; the Liberal party split open. Some, including David Lloyd George, sympathised with the Boer Republics, which they saw as small independent nations, 'bullied' by the might of the British empire. But the impact was more fundamental than that. Just as the death of Gordon at Khartoum had made men begin to question the whole Egyptian policy, so the Boer war made men begin to question the whole policy of the 'new imperialism' (see Part Three: Assessment). Rhodes himself died a few months before the end of the war, in March 1902, at the age of forty-nine, perhaps, as some of his obituaries said, a conquistador born out of time.

8

Fashoda and the Anglo-French agreements of 1904

By 1898 the greater part of the continent of Africa was divided between the European Powers. Liberia remained independent under the patronage of the United States. The Italians had failed spectacularly at the battle of Adowa in 1896 to make good their bid for Abyssinia. But these were the exceptions. The French had spread steadily over West and North West Africa. Morocco remained independent, but French influence was rapidly increasing there, displacing in some spheres old-established British influence. French colonialists increasingly saw Morocco as the 'missing piece' of their empire, for which they might eventually be prepared to trade even Egypt. [**Doc. 23, p. 127**]

The British had extended their colony of Sierra Leone to include the huge hinterland of the Protectorate in 1896, after a boundary agreement with France the previous year. The Gold Coast was the scene of new wars between the British and the Ashanti in 1895–6 and again in 1900–1901. Ashantiland became a crown colony in 1901. The region north of Ashantiland, the so-called Northern Territories, occupied by a mixture of tribes, had been brought under British protection rather earlier, in 1896–8.

In the Niger region too British territory had considerably expanded. The original British protectorate of 1885 extended only as far as the river Benue. The Royal Niger Company, however, had been active in penetrating into the northern emirates, the well-organised Muslim states such as Nupe and Ilorin, where good trade was expected. They met with many obstacles. The Liverpool men in the delta did not take kindly to the activities of the new Manchester-based group and did their best to discredit them at home until an accommodation was worked out in 1893. The African middlemen too resented a new system of trading that seemed likely to cut out their profits. Some of them, of whom a self-made man, Ja Ja of Opobo, was the most remarkable, put up a strong although ultimately unsuccessful resistance. The northern emirs were suspicious of the Company and examined all trading agreements very carefully. In the end the Company resorted to force of arms to overcome their resistance. But the most dangerous threat to the Company's position was to come from international complications, from the protests of France and Germany. The Company had interpreted the clauses of their Charter and of the Berlin Act, which forbade the setting up of a monopoly and guaranteed free navigation on the Niger, in their own way. [**Docs. 14, 15, pp. 114, 115**] They bore the expenses of administering the area and, they argued, they did not intend to be out of pocket. Free navigation of the river was whittled down until it meant only freedom of transit, and any boat that touched at a wharf was regarded as coming under the Company's jurisdiction in respect of the revenue duties they were entitled to levy. Moreover, the Company evolved very neat book-keeping methods by which customs dues on their own goods were offset against 'administrative costs'. Since trading and government were so closely combined in the Company's activities, almost any expense could be brought under the heading of 'administration'. Naturally there was soon a strong protest from foreign, especially German, traders, who felt themselves discriminated against. One result of the Liverpool and German opposition was the enquiry carried out for the British government by Major Macdonald in 1888. As Professor Flint demonstrated in his *Sir George Goldie and the Making of Nigeria* (1960), Macdonald's enquiry was a landmark in British colonial policy in Africa. Macdonald tried to be fair to all parties including the Company but, in Flint's words, 'For him "Imperial interests" were the interests of the Africans'. (1960: 130) It was the same principle which was to find expression forty years later in the Devonshire White Paper of 1923 which proclaimed without equivocation that 'Kenya is an African country'. Macdonald himself was careful to consult as many Africans as he could. Ideas of 'trusteeship', which had evolved in relation to India during Edmund Burke's great attack on Warren Hastings in the late eighteenth century, were real to many British officials and were translated from India to Africa. In a world where the British government were the 'trustees' of the African masses, the rule of trading companies, primarily interested in their own profits, could have no place. The Royal Niger Company, unlike the British Imperial East African Company, was a financial success but its days were numbered. The Charter was surrendered in 1899 although the Company continued in being as an ordinary trading concern. By 1900 only Cecil Rhodes' South Africa Company remained. It was to last until 1923 and many commentators have traced the different development of Rhodesia in part to the lack of the official element which watched the interests of the weaker party (the Africans) in the new British colonies. A subtle change had come over the whole British position in tropical Africa between the hasty 'grab' of 1884–6 and the end of the century. Initially, the government had had no thought but to establish spheres of influence to prevent the exclusion of British trade by foreign annexations. Now they found themselves ruling a colonial empire in Africa as they did in India. In West Africa the change was symbolised by the winding up of the Chartered Company in 1899 and the establishment in 1900 of the two huge protectorates of North and South Nigeria, joined together and including Lagos by 1914, to form the modern state of Nigeria, then entirely the responsibility of the British government.

The Chartered Company came to an end in 1899 partly because views were changing as to Britain's proper relations with its African possessions, but also partly because the Company had over-extended itself in its conflicts with France. It was inevitable that, as the Company's dominions crept up the Niger, it would eventually clash with the expanding French West African empire. The confrontation came in the 1890s. Although tentative boundaries between the British and French spheres had been drawn up in 1890, many points were left unresolved and, since trade routes and key communication points were now better understood, the French and the Company with Captain Lugard as their champion, manoeuvred for position. In retrospect the contest had its comic side with Lugard and his rival, Captain Decoeur, literally racing to conclude treaties with important chiefs first. But it was also dangerous. The French advance had always been a military one. The British government now allowed the Company to set up the West Africa Frontier Force, under Lugard. It seemed inevitable that, sooner or later, a serious clash would occur. So far the European Powers had avoided any military confrontation among themselves during the whole partition of Africa. The British Prime Minister, Lord Salisbury, was determined that one should not occur now. His Colonial Secretary, Joseph Chamberlain, was by now interested in West Africa for its own sake. It was one of the many 'undeveloped estates' (Hardy, 1968) which Britain had acquired in Africa which must be financed and administered efficiently so that they ceased to be a financial burden and became a great economic asset to the empire as a whole. He was disposed to argue the case in detail and attach importance to retaining a number of crucial positions. Salisbury, however, saw the details of a West African settlement as subordinate to his more general African strategy. To Salisbury at this time the Niger was less important than the Nile. In the event a Niger boundary settlement, reasonably acceptable to all parties, was agreed in June 1898.

FASHODA

A few months later all interest shifted to the Nile with the famous 'Fashoda incident'. The status of the Sudan in international law was unclear after the Egyptian evacuation of 1885. The British held that the area still belonged to the Egyptians although they were temporarily prevented from exercising jurisdiction there. The French on the other hand held that it had become *res nullius*: Latin term, used in international law, to denote a territory which had no apparent owner.

res nullius with no internationally recognised government. This implied that it was open to seizure by the first comer. [**Doc. 22, p. 125**] After 1887 the British had resigned themselves to the fact that they were the government of Egypt for the foreseeable future. They did not want to see any other Power in control of the Upper Nile. Controversy raged then as it has raged since as to whether any occupying Power in the Sudan could have diverted the course of the Nile and so made Britain's position in Egypt untenable. Very possibly the risk was chimerical but it was one the War Office preferred not to have to face. Moreover, the death of Gordon was still unavenged. That tragedy, however, to some extent cut both ways for no one could doubt that the reconquest of the Sudan would be a serious undertaking that might cost a great deal in money and lives.

The British government did not take any steps towards a reconquest until a foreign threat seemed imminent. Just as some Englishmen dreamt of an all-British route from the Cape to Cairo so some Frenchmen began to plan for an all-French route from west to east, from Senegal to the Red Sea. In 1893 this took a more definite form in projects for missions first by Major Monteil and subsequently by Major Liotard from the Ubanghi to the Upper Nile. Liotard consolidated French authority on the Upper Ubanghi but it was another French officer, Major Marchand, who between 1896 and 1898 made an epic overland journey from the Congo to Fashoda, a small outpost on the Upper Nile above Khartoum. [**Doc. 22, p. 125**] Already in 1895 Sir Edward Grey, then Under Secretary at the Foreign Office, had warned the French that any encroachment on the Upper Nile would be regarded as an 'unfriendly act' by the British government. By now Britain had reason to be worried. The Italians had tried to establish a protectorate over Abyssinia. They had been severely defeated at the battle of Adowa in March 1896. The British did not object to an Italian presence in Abyssinia – they had gone some way towards recognising it by an agreement of 1890 – but they were disturbed by the fact that the Abyssinians had had some backing from France. The plight of Italian nationals cut off at Kassala in 1896 gave the British a rather transparent excuse to re-enter the Sudan. In fact there is no doubt that this was part of a carefully conceived strategy by Salisbury to make the Upper Nile safe once and for all. The campaign was entrusted to General Kitchener who was already familiar with the area. Kitchener advanced with great caution, securing his communications at each step by building a railway (see above p. 68) His tactics paid off. When he finally met the Dervishes at the great battle of Omdurman in September 1898, he won a decisive victory. The Sudan was now safe for Britain although legal complications remained. The British government had been careful to instruct Kitchener to act always in the name of the Egyptian government and Kitchener had made this clear to all by flying the British and Egyptian flags side by side. [**Doc. 22a, p. 125**] The French, however, were still reluctant to admit the continuing validity of the Egyptian claim and, after the battle of Omdurman, the British decided to put their claim on the simpler ground, incontrovertible in international law, of right of conquest. A few days after the battle of Omdurman, Kitchener found Marchand and his small beleaguered force at Fashoda. Very properly, the two men exchanged courtesies and referred the diplomatic question to their governments. The excitement in the two capitals was intense. There was talk of war, even some preparation of fleets. But, in the end, realism prevailed in Paris. The French budget was unbalanced, her army in disarray after the **Dreyfus** scandal. Britain had presented her with a *fait accompli* in the Sudan. The French gave in and signed an agreement with Britain in March 1899 which left Britain in complete control of the Sudan.

Dreyfus affair: Political scandal which split French politicians and society in the late nineteenth century. Captain Dreyfus, a Jewish French army officer, was wrongly convicted of spying for the Germans.

THE 1904 AGREEMENTS

Some doubt exists whether the Fashoda crisis hindered or helped a final understanding between Britain and France about colonial matters. The man who became French Foreign Minister in the middle of the crisis, Théophile Delcassé (who, ironically, had been one of the originators of the Monteil mission), argued that it delayed for some years the reconciliation with England he so much desired. This may be true but it can equally well be argued that it finally cleared the air between them. The partition of Africa was now virtually complete. The French were compelled to admit that the British position in Egypt seemed for the time impregnable. This opened the way for the growing lobby in France who wished to cut their losses in Egypt and concentrate on securing Morocco to complete their West African empire. The Colonial Secretary, Eugéne Étienne, was among their number and, in April 1904, after two years of negotiations, a whole series of colonial bargains was signed between England and France. Some did not relate to Africa at all but the crux of the agreements was the bargain struck over Egypt and Morocco. The French would cease to obstruct British administration in Egypt and the British would withdraw any objection to the establishment of French influence in Morocco. [**Doc. 23, p. 127**] West African boundaries were slightly adjusted in return for French concessions in other parts of the world.

The 1904 agreements were very valuable to Britain. It could at last move freely in Egypt. The British Consul General, Lord Cromer, had indeed brought strong pressure to bear on the British Foreign Office to settle with France on almost any terms lest the Egyptian finances break down altogether. But the real importance of the agreements was long term. On paper they were merely a series of colonial bargains. Only on a few very limited questions concerning Egypt and Morocco did they even commit the two Powers to act together.

They certainly did not constitute even an *entente* in European diplomatic terms. What turned them into something much more important were the clumsy German attempts to probe their meaning and the German challenge to the Anglo-French agreement in Morocco, which led first to the Algeciras Conference of 1906 and later to the Agadir incident of 1911. The French were not able to make good their claim to Morocco until 1912 but, in the meantime, their relations with Britain had become closer and closer.

Britain entered the war of 1914 on the side of France and Russia, its two main colonial rivals, against Austria and Germany. With Austria, Britain had no colonial quarrels, with Germany comparatively few. This fact in itself must raise doubts as to whether the 'new imperialism' of the late nineteenth century did, as J.A. Hobson (1902) maintained, distort the diplomatic alignments of Europe. Lenin's contention (1917) that the First World War was an 'imperialist war' was a different point altogether. He believed that the war resulted from the attempted redistribution of territories under 'imperialist' control, defining this to include economic as well as political control, and referring to European and Turkish lands. The swallowing of Africa and large parts of Asia by the European Powers was a mere *aperitif* to this movement. The theories are often confused but the difference was clearly set out in an important article by Professor Stokes (1969). The alignments of the First World War seem to have been determined by traditional European considerations, above all by the balance of power within that continent. Inevitably this raises the question: what was the fundamental significance of the 'new imperialism' for Europe? Was it basically an economic movement or a political one, defining political in the widest possible sense to include diplomatic and strategic considerations? What were its long-term results?

Part 3

ASSESSMENT

9

Conclusion

The Scramble for Africa lasted at most twenty years but, during that period, it went through a number of distinct phases. In the early and mid-1880s no European Power or statesman (with the possible exception of Leopold of the Belgians) had any very clear idea of what territory they wished to acquire in Africa, or indeed whether they wished to acquire any at all. Yet it was during this period that the most critical decisions were taken. Practically all the significant maritime Powers of western Europe (with the important exception of the Dutch who were content with their possessions in the Far East) gathered into their respective 'spheres of influence' those fragments of Africa which history, or other accidental circumstances, placed within their grasp. It was done without enthusiasm. It was also done without effective political opposition at home. It was as if politicians and public alike were so taken by surprise by an unprecedented turn of events that they could not immediately formulate their attitudes.

BRITAIN: CONSERVATIVE AND LIBERAL OPINION

This was particularly true in Britain. The fact that a Liberal government, under William Gladstone, was in power from 1880 to 1885 added to the confusion. Nothing could be more mistaken than to see a simple division between right (imperialist) and left (anti-imperialist) in British politics in the late nineteenth century. Both Conservatives and Liberals had been perfectly happy with the situation in the middle of the century when 'moral suasion' seemed to give Britain strong influence on both the east and the west coast of Africa without the expense and possible danger of direct intervention. Both Conservatives and Liberals had to face the situation after about 1870 when the rise of powerful new industrial states challenged their old-established trading supremacy. The change in British thinking can be discerned as early as Gladstone's first administration of 1868–74. Previously it had been fashionable to express mildly 'separatist' views, to believe that Britain's existing colonies, mainly colonies of settlement, would 'grow to maturity' and separate from the mother country in, it was hoped, an amiable and mutually agreeable manner. The first reaction against this was anything but extravagant and jingoistic. It represented a sober realisation that colonies might have their uses and it concerned itself almost entirely with the colonies of settlement. It found expression in the establishment of the Colonial Society (later the Royal Colonial Institute) in 1868, where eminent men met to read papers and discuss questions of imperial interest. Its members represented a wide political spectrum. Lord Granville, Edward Cardwell and H.C.E. Childers from the Liberal side and Lord Salisbury, Lord Carnarvon and Sir Stafford Northcote from the Conservative side were among its founders. The Society had no thought of advocating an extension of empire but, once it is admitted that existing colonies are of value and should be defended, certain consequences begin to flow. In African terms it was Gladstone's government of 1868–74, not their Conservative successors, who inaugurated a forward policy on the Gold Coast. The Conservatives were responsible for the British forward policy in South Africa but they subsequently maintained, with some plausibility, that they had successfully pursued the old policy of 'influence' in Egypt, with French co-operation, in the 1870s and that it had been Liberal blunders which led to the breakdown of that policy in the 1880s. In West and East Africa and as far south as Bechuanaland it was Gladstone's government which committed the country to the acquisition of spheres of influence and 'protectorates' in the critical period of 1884–6. Their reluctance and even bewilderment at this turn of events is obvious from both their official despatches and their private letters.

CONTINENTAL OPINION TOO WAS DIVIDED

Similar uncertainty is discernible in France and Germany. France, like Britain, had a long colonial history but, after their decisive defeat by Germany in 1871, Frenchmen were deeply divided between those who wished to seek compensation overseas and those who saw overseas adventures as a distraction from the reassertion of their true role in Europe. Some, like Camille Pelletan, lamented 'Alsace-Lorraine is under the Prussian jackboot and our army is leaving for Tonkin'. Some saw all overseas commitments as a Bismarckian trap into which France must not fall. But a colonial lobby can be identified even in the 1860s. Jules Ferry, himself a Lorrainer, defended the French advance in Tunis and in Indo-China. Freycinet was much more interested in grandiose schemes in West Africa than was once realised. Army and navy officers were active in both West Africa and Indo-China. But the French public was by no means convinced in the mid-1880s. When things went wrong in Tunis in 1881 or in Tonkin in 1885, governments fell and politicians' heads rolled – very nearly literally on the latter occasion.

Germany, too, was divided. Many Germans saw their country as essentially a continental one and could generate no enthusiasm for overseas adventures. Others felt that the next step after the German victory of 1871 was the estab-lishment of Germany as a world Power. A few even advocated that Germany should annex the French colonies as part of the peace settlement of 1871. They elicited little response at that time from Bismarck. But a substantial colonial lobby grew up centred on the great trading ports of Hamburg and Bremen. By 1884 Bismarck himself conceded that colonialism was a significant election issue.

This period of indiscriminate grab and bewildered politicians and public did not last long. Bismarck was the first to see that these new African issues could be harnessed to the general purposes of European diplomacy. Domestic pressures undoubtedly played a part in Bismarck's actions in 1884–5 but he also seized the opportunity to try, however unsuccessfully, to reach a new understanding with France. In Britain Salisbury and Rosebery were men of a different stamp from Granville and Gladstone. In the late 1880s and the 1890s the diplomatic game in Africa took on more ordered forms, culminating in the British case with the carefully planned conquest of the Sudan. In France politicians like Hanotaux, Étienne and Delcassé had equally carefully formu-lated objectives that they tried with varying degrees of success to obtain.

THE DEBATE BEGINS IN EARNEST

But if governments and imperial enthusiasts began to marshal their arguments and plan their campaigns, so too did the critics and opponents of imperialism. The British occupation of Egypt in 1882 occurred without effective opposition at home but within two years it had become regarded as the classic case of the radical charge that governments had allowed themselves to become the pawns of the financiers. One of the earliest manifestations of this was a pamphlet by Seymour Keys, *Spoiling the Egyptians: a Tale of Shame*, published in 1882. It was further developed by T. Rothstein in his *Egypt's Ruin* (1910). It was referred to by H.N. Brailsford in his *The War of Steel and Gold* (1914) and by Leonard Woolf in his *Empire and Commerce in Africa* (1920). It appeared almost unchanged as late as 1959 in John Strachey's *The End of Empire* in which he asserted:

> What the British Government really wanted was that somehow or other the interest should be collected without Britain having to involve herself in the complications and responsibilities of conquering Egypt. But when it became clear that that was impossible, Britain occupied and ruled Egypt and the Soudan rather than that the bondholders should lose their money. (1959: 82)

The Boer War was an even greater shock to British opinion and virtually brought to an end the brief popular enthusiasm for empire-building which had found expression in the Jubilee celebrations of 1897. It produced one great anti-imperialist book, J.A. Hobson's *Imperialism: A Study*. It is significant that Hobson was a Liberal (with some socialist leanings) who was primarily interested in the social question at home. His condemnation of imperialism arose from his diagnosis of domestic economic ills. He popularised, although he did not originate, the 'surplus capital' theory of imperialism, which is that when industry produced more capital than could profitably be reinvested at home, financiers were compelled or encouraged to invest abroad. Having invested in unstable countries they demanded, successfully, that their governments should intervene, by force if necessary, to protect their investments. [**Doc. 24, p. 128**]

LENIN TAKES A HAND

Lenin, on his own statement, took Hobson's work as the starting point for his own famous pamphlet, *Imperialism, the Highest Stage of Capitalism* (1917). There were, however, essential differences between the two men, and it is misleading to speak of the Hobson–Lenin theory of imperialism as if their arguments were the same. First, Lenin was primarily interested in the German situation, where the finance capital provided by the banks operated in a somewhat different fashion from the industrial capital, generated by industry itself, which provided the source of most British investment abroad in this period. Second, and more importantly, Hobson saw imperialism as an aberration, a mal-functioning of the capitalist system, which ought to be corrected and which could be corrected if it was properly understood. Lenin saw it as the inevitable result of the capitalist system and an important symptom of its ultimate and inescapable decay. [**Doc. 25, p. 129**] It was in this sense that he interpreted the First World War as the final 'imperialist war'.

Hobson's theories and some of Lenin's theories gained wide acceptance, far beyond the ranks of the orthodox Left. A reaction against the view that imperialism was essentially an economic phenomenon in which financiers played a particularly murky role began after the Second World War. The debate became entangled with the ideological positions of the Cold War between the West and the Soviet Union. Financial explanations in particular came to be regarded as 'Marxist' and anathema to more conservative scholars. Some even shied away from accepting an economic basis for the whole phenomenon.

There are obvious errors and omissions in the earlier theories. Professor Sir Keith Hancock made a telling attack on Lenin's theory in a lecture, 'Wealth of Colonies' (1949), in which he pointed out that the particular stage of capitalist development which Lenin associated with imperialism – that of monopolies and cartels – came after 1900, that is after the Scramble for Africa was complete. In an article in the *Economic History Review* in 1961, D.K. Fieldhouse gathered together and analysed an impressive array of arguments casting doubt on financial explanations of the 'new imperialism'. If such explanations were correct, he argued, one would expect a clear correlation between financial involvement and new annexations. No such correlation exists. On the contrary, 'the places now to be taken over had hitherto attracted little capital, and did not attract it in any quantity subsequently' (1961: 190). There was undoubtedly considerable investment abroad by all the European Powers, and above all by Britain, in this period but most of this went to traditional investment areas like the United States. The whole German investment in Africa before 1914 amounted to only two-thirds of their investment in Austria-Hungary. D.C.M. Platt (1968) questioned whether individual financiers had any more influence on the British Foreign Office at the end of the nineteenth century than they did on Palmerston's Foreign Office or Cobden's Board of Trade. The Foreign Office, he maintained, had narrowly defined the circumstances in which the government would assist overseas investors and it adhered rigidly to these.

Unhappy with economic explanations, a number of western writers began to offer alternative theories which emphasised political, strategic and diplomatic explanations. Detailed studies began to suggest that there was no over-arching theory which explained modern imperialism – or even one particular dramatic case such as the Scramble for Africa. Multi-causal explanations and an emphasis on events on 'the periphery' – that is outside Europe – became popular.

Dealing with the new imperialism as a whole, D.K. Fieldhouse saw it as a natural outcome of the militant nationalism which came to dominate Europe after the victory of Bismarck's blood-and-iron policy in the Franco-Prussian War, This allowed for a considerable psychological element. Empire was a popular cause and this 'ideological fervour [was the] natural outcome of this fevered nationalism, not the artefact of vested economic interests'. Further, it was one

consequence of the tight alliance system that Bismarck imposed upon Europe
– the system which caused Professor Medlicott to conclude that Bismarck
'made a deadlock and called it peace' (1956: 337). Fieldhouse suggested:

> Imperialism may best be seen as the extension into the periphery of the
> political struggles in Europe. At the centre the balance was so nicely adjusted
> that no positive action, no major change in the status or territory of either
> side was possible. Colonies thus became a means out of the impasse.
> (1961: 205)

Professors Robinson and Gallagher in a seminal book in 1961 put forward
a specific explanation of the phenomenon of the Scramble for Africa. They
were certainly not unaware of an economic dimension to the struggle but in
their view 'as an explanation of European rule in tropical Africa, the theory
of economic imperialism puts the trade before the flag, the capital before
the conquest, the cart before the horse' (1961: 409). From one point of view
the Scramble could be seen as a great extension of the Eastern Question.
Defending its traditional interest in the route to India, Britain stumbled into
Egypt in 1882. This caused a breakdown of its long-standing 'gentleman's
agreement' with France on their respective spheres in West Africa. Concern
for its route to India also compelled Britain to defend its established position
in South Africa and to undertake new commitments in East Africa. Only after
Africa had been partitioned for strategic reasons did the British government
try to develop their sphere economically and the British public try to convince themselves that what they had done was a good thing. In a later article
Robinson and Gallagher went further and suggested that the whole partition of Africa was a 'remarkable freak'. It was always an aberration and the
surprising thing was not that it collapsed in three-quarters of a century but
that it survived so long. 'It would be a gullible historiography', they concluded,
'which could see such gimcrack creations as necessary functions of the balance
of power or as the highest stage of capitalism'. [**Doc. 27, p. 130**]

Marxists fought back. There was now the additional embarrassment that
Lenin appeared to have regarded imperialism as an apocalyptic sign of the
approach of the great revolution and the triumph of the proletariat but fifty
years later the European Powers were dismantling their empires and capitalism
still flourished. Most took the line that Lenin had been misunderstood.
A non-Marxist, Eric Stokes, had suggested that escape route in 1969, arguing
that Lenin saw the partition of Africa and Asia as only the preliminary phase
of imperialism, although Lenin's many ambiguities meant that the whole
argument eventually ran into the sand.

Other historians also resisted the jettisoning of the economic dimension.
In the long controversy that was waged in the academic journals, D.C.M. Platt

had reached the conclusion as early as 1968, 'There is much in late-Victorian imperial expansion which cannot be explained by economic factors but there is much which can' (1968: 138). Fieldhouse himself gave them due weight in his *Economics and Empire*. Undeniably, contemporaries had argued for expansion in economic terms. [**Docs. 12, 17, pp. 111, 119**] For the first time in history there were a number of highly industrialised nations in a situation of cut-throat competition. Many were returning to protectionist policies. Politicians were particularly nervous and business confidence was badly undermined by the widespread and little-understood phenomenon of the 'Great Depression'. Every instinct of the businessmen seemed to be to grab their markets and their sources of raw materials while they could. Politicians dared not resist. They were partially convinced too. So was the general public.

It is not easy to quantify, but the evidence seems to suggest that the working classes had (as both Hobson and Lenin allow) been won for the imperial cause. Hobson and Lenin saw this support as the result of a confidence trick on the part of the tiny minority who were likely actually to benefit by imperialism. This is possible. But it is also possible that there was among the working classes a hard-headed appreciation of the dangers threatening the ordinary worker in the new situation of international competition. It was easier for the investor to switch his investments than for the Lancashire cotton operative to find new employment if the British textile industry lost its markets. Hobson began with an examination of the social problems at home and came to the conclusion that imperialism was a false answer. [**Doc. 24, p. 128**] Other men began with a similar preoccupation with domestic problems – Joseph Chamberlain in Britain, Friedrich Fabri in Germany, for example – and concluded that empire-building was the only safe way out. They did not expect immediate returns. They were 'pegging out claims for posterity', safeguarding 'undeveloped estates'. For a generation they were, on the whole, believed. Imperialism became, as Fieldhouse said, 'the ideology of millions'.

In some instances modern research has confirmed the existence of close relations between bankers and politicians. Stern described the German banker Bleichroder as the 'midwife' of Leopold's Congo (1980: 407) although he also concluded that the financiers were the servants rather than the masters of the politicians. Cain and Hopkins in their important *British Imperialism: Innovation and Expansion, 1688–1914* (1993) showed the close connections between government and the City of London.

A new explanation, essentially economic, appeared (or at least received much greater emphasis) to explain British imperialism in the writings of Bernard Porter (1996). Britain was already a declining Power. Its industry, although still growing, was not keeping pace with those of Germany and the United States. Britain's expansion was not, as it appeared at the time, the result of overflowing confidence, but a desperate rearguard action to retain its place in the world. This view is challenged by Cain and Hopkins, who point out that Britain after all secured 'the most valuable parts' of Africa in competition with Germany and France. Britain, in their view, was proactive, rather than simply reactive, and the necessary dynamism came from the City (of London), the home of 'gentlemanly capitalism'. [**Doc. 28, p. 131**]

The end of the Cold War and its attendant ideologies would seem to have re-opened the whole question of the role of capital in the Scramble. But overarching theories are still in retreat before multi-causal explanations. The defence of India or a rearguard defence of a declining economy might offer a plausible reason for British actions but can hardly be extrapolated to other Powers. Cain and Hopkins' emphasis on the City leaves out of account the role of the northern industrialists.

More intangible factors too may be due for reassessment. The mindset of late Victorians is so alien to the world view of Europeans (especially young Europeans) in the twenty-first century that it can be almost incomprehensible. Yet it was the milieu in which the Victorians operated. Imperialism was believed to be right in the sense that it was in the national interest. It was believed to be right in other ways too. It was benefiting the 'backward' native, bringing him up to the standards of western civilisation. [**Doc. 26, p. 129**] This made imperialism attractive to many liberals and humanitarians. A number of Fabians, including George Bernard Shaw and Sidney Webb, saw great possibilities for good in imperialism, as well as many things to be criticised. Imperialism was accepted as right in a third way too. Although some intellectuals raised doubts, most people in the late nineteenth century accepted the idea of progress in human affairs as self-evident. Theories of evolution were generally applied to societies. Western societies were further advanced than African or Asian societies. It was both proper and inevitable that the more advanced would conquer and rule the less advanced. In the end it would be to the advantage of both. But above all it was inescapable. Many imperialists – Cecil Rhodes was perhaps the most striking example – felt that they were in tune with the *Zeitgeist*, the spirit of the age, and this gave them both a comforting reassurance that they were on the winning side and a kind of absolution for any dubious acts they might commit in fulfilling an inevitable and ultimately benevolent destiny. [**Doc. 19b, p. 123**]

THE ROLE OF AFRICANS

But where in all this did the African stand? Peripheral theories at least opened the way for him to play an active role in his own destiny. Marxist theories were of necessity Eurocentric – it was overripe and failing capitalism in the developed countries that had triggered the whole process. Rather ironically, in rejecting this conservatives began for the first time to take seriously the role of the non-European. Ronald Robinson suggested in 1972 that European intervention often destabilised foreign societies and created warring factions among whom European could find allies. In their article in the *Cambridge Modern History*, vol XI (1962) Robinson and Gallagher had suggested an even more radical explanation. They wrote, 'the crucial changes that set all working took place in Africa itself . . . The last quarter of the nineteenth century had often been called the "Age of imperialism". Yet much of this imperialism was no more than an involuntary reaction of Europe to the various proto-nationalisms of Islam'. [**Doc. 27, p. 130**]

Africans were not passive, as was at one time supposed, in the nineteenth century. They were peoples with a long history who had already held the Europeans at bay for centuries. In the short run, however, the imbalance of technological power was so great that the political decisions of the late nineteenth century do seem to have been those of the Europeans. Even the most casual glance at the modern map of Africa reveals those straight state boundaries along lines of latitude and longitude which were clearly drawn up in the chancelleries of Europe and bore little relationship to African conditions. On the other hand it is true that Islam, originally a foreign importation but one which the Africans had long made their own, began a period of revival in the late nineteenth century. Sometimes this reinforced political resistance to the European invader as in Algeria, Egypt, the Egyptian Sudan or the emirates of the Western Soudan which fought hard against the French advance. Essentially, however, when the Africans sufficiently rallied their forces to throw off the foreign yoke – which they did within a century of the conquest – they fought their conquerors with their own ideological weapons. Their rallying cries were nationalism, self-determination, democracy and socialism. No doubt at least the last three of these had existed in their own forms in African societies in the past but it would be false history to suggest that, as they were formulated in the twentieth century, they did not derive directly from the West. The colonial conquests of the nineteenth century ended Africa's isolation, which had been marked in recent centuries. Rapidly, and sometimes brutally, Africa was dragged into the twentieth century. Not everything the Europeans brought was bad. Medicine and new methods of agriculture were generally good. Political ideas could be used for good or ill. But what is now clear is that in Africa, as in Asia, this was but one more layer superimposed upon an already vigorous people with a long history.

Part 4

DOCUMENTS

THE VICTORIAN IMAGE OF AFRICA

Document 1   DAVID LIVINGSTONE: HUMANITARIAN

Livingstone, the greatest of the missionary explorers of the mid-nineteenth century, commanded a wide audience at home. He was much more sympathetic to the Africans than many of his contemporaries but he saw Africa as a country 'whose history is only just beginning' and felt that the white man had a right, indeed an obligation, to change it.

It has been my object in this work to give as clear an account as I was able to of tracts of country previously unexplored, with their river systems, natural productions, and capabilities; and to bring before my countrymen, and all others interested in the cause of humanity, the misery entailed by the slave-trade in its inland phases; a subject on which I and my companions are the first who have had an opportunity of forming a judgement . . . as regards the future, the first white man cannot but feel [a peculiar interest] in a continent whose history is only just beginning. . . . The slave-trade is the greatest obstacle in existence to civilisation and commercial progress; and as the English are the most philanthropic people in the world, and will probably always have the largest commercial stake in the African continent, the policy for its suppression in every possible way shows thorough wisdom and foresight.

Most writers believe the blacks to be savages, nearly all blacks believe the whites to be cannibals. The nursery hobgoblin of the one is black, of the other white. . . . In reference to the status of the Africans among the nations of the earth, we have seen nothing to justify the notion that they are of a different 'breed' or 'species' from the most civilised. The African is a man with every attribute of human kind. Centuries of barbarism have had the same deteriorating effects on Africans, as Pritchard describes them to have had on certain of the Irish who were driven some generations back, to the hills in Ulster and Connaught.

Source: David and Charles Livingstone, *Narrative of an Expedition to the Zambesi . . . 1858–64*, John Murray, 1865, pp. v, 6, 8, 67, 596.

Document 2   COMMERCE

Livingstone believed not only that legitimate commerce would drive out the slave trade but that a rising standard of living would be the quickest way by which the Africans would attain 'civilisation'.

Pity the market is not supplied with English manufactures in exchange for the legitimate products of the country. If English merchants would come up the Zambesi during the months of June, July and August the slave trader would very soon be driven out of the market . . .

Mr O[swell] thinks that agents or commissioners situated in different parts in that region would in the course of ten years extirpate the slave trade. . . . If it is profitable for those who are engaged in the coast trade to pass along in their ships and pick up ivory, bees wax &c., those who may have enterprise enough to push into the interior and recieve [*sic*] the goods at first hand would surely find it more profitable. The returns of the first year might be small, but those who for the love of their species would run some risk would assuredly be no losers in the end. The natives would readily acquire the habit of saving for a market. . . . Give the people the opportunity they will civilise themselves, and that more effectually than can be done by missionary societies.

Source: D. Livingstone, *Private Journals*, 1851–53, ed. I. Schapera, Chatto & Windus, 1960, pp. 43–4, from 'First Journey to Sebitoane's Country'.

AFRICA AS EL DORADO **Document 3**

Men had long thought that the interior of Africa might hold untold riches. These hopes seemed to be confirmed by the reports of sober and well-trained observers like Lieutenant Verney Lovett Cameron who had learned of the resources of Katanga on his east–west crossing of the continent in 1873–75.

Most of the country from the Tanganyika to the West Coast is one of almost unspeakable richness. Of metals, there are iron, copper, silver and gold; coal is also found; the vegetable products are palm-oil, cotton, nutmegs, besides several sorts of pepper and coffee, all growing wild. The people cultivate several other oil-producing plants, such as ground-nuts and seni seni. The Arabs, as far as they have come, have introduced rice, wheat, onions, and a few fruit trees, all of which seem to flourish well. The countries of Bihé and Bailunda are sufficiently high above the sea to be admirably adapted for European occupation, and would produce whatever may be grown in the south of Europe. The oranges which Señor Goncalves [a Portuguese merchant with whom Cameron had stayed] had planted at Bihé . . . were finer than any I had ever seen in Spain or Italy. He also had roses and grapes growing in luxuriance . . . To the eastward of Lovalé ivory is marvellously plentiful. The price among the Arab traders at Nyangwé was $7^{1}/_{2}$ pounds of beads, or 5 pounds of cowries, for 35 pounds of ivory; and the caravans that went out from there for ivory would obtain tusks, irrespective of weight, for an old knife, a copper bracelet, or any other useless thing which might take the fancy of the natives.

Source: Lieutenant Cameron's report to the Royal Geographical Society, April 1876; *Proceedings of the Royal Geographical Society*, 1st ser., xx, 323–4.

Document 4   DARKEST AFRICA: FULLY DEVELOPED RACISM

H.H. Johnston had extensive experience of tropical Africa, East and West, both as an explorer and as an administrator. He had no doubts about the backwardness of the Negro races. In 1920 he drew up a kind of league table of the nations of the world. Britain, the United States and most countries of western Europe were in the first division; the countries of tropical Africa in the fifth, sixth and seventh divisions.

[a] The chief and obvious distinction between the backward and the forward peoples is that the former, with the exception of about 20,000,000 in the Mediterranean basin and the Near East, are of coloured skin; while the latter are white-skinned or, as in the case of the Japanese and the inhabitants of Northern China, nearly white.

Source: H.H. Johnston, *The Backward Peoples and Our Relations with Them*, Oxford University Press, 1920, pp. 7–9.

Johnston held that the Negro had only himself to blame for his condition.

[b] Yet about the African slave trade, as with most other instinctive human procedure, and the movements of one race against another, there is an underlying sense of justice. The White and Yellow peoples have been the unconscious agents of the Power behind Nature in punishing the Negro for his lazy backwardness. . . . The races that will not work persistently and doggedly are trampled on, and in time displaced, by those who do.

Source: H.H. Johnston, *A History of the Colonization of Africa by Alien Races*, Cambridge University Press, 1913.

But even Johnston did not think that the Negro's condition was hopeless.

[c] There are many tribes of Negroes of the present day who are leading lives not much superior in intellectual advancement to those of the brutes; but there is not an existing race of man in Africa that is not emphatically human and capable of improvement.

Source: Quoted in R. Oliver, *Sir Harry Johnston and the Scramble for Africa*, Chatto & Windus, 1957, p. 351.

On the contrary he warned his fellow white man that the situation might change very rapidly.

[d] But the White people must try to realise that the still Backward races, the once decrepit nations, have travelled far in intellectuality since the middle of the nineteenth century, and that the continuance of an insulting policy towards them will join them some day in a vast league against Europe and America, which will set back the millennium and perhaps even ruin humanity in general.

Source: The Backward Peoples and Our Relations with Them, p. 61.

STANLEY'S ANTIPATHY   **Document 5**

Johnston's racism was tempered by a strong sense of responsibility; not so that of H.M. Stanley who, by the end of his career in Africa, scarcely seems to have regarded the inhabitants as human. The following is from his account of the Enim Pasha rescue expedition.

On the 12th December we left camp at dawn. . . . Villages were seen nestling amid abundance, and we left them unmolested in the hope that the wild people might read that when left alone we were an extremely inoffensive band of men. But at nine o'clock . . . we heard the first war-cries. . . . By 11 a.m. there were two separate bands of natives who followed us very persistently. One had come from the eastward, the other was formed out of the population of the villages in the valley that we had left undamaged and intact [after a previous skirmish].

By noon these bands had increased into numerous and frantic mobs, and some of them cried out, 'We will prove to you before night that we are men, and every one of you shall perish today . . .' The mobs followed us, now and then making demonstrations, and annoying us with their harsh cries and menaces. An expert shot left the line of march, and wounded two of them at a range of 400 yards. This silenced them for a while. . . .

Finally at 3.30, we came in view of the Bavira villages situated on an open plain and occupying both banks of a deep and precipitous ravine hollowed out of the clay by a considerable tributary of the East Ituri. [The Africans tried to prevent the party crossing the river.] Loads were at once dropped . . . and a smart scene of battle-play occurred, at the end of which the natives retreated on the full run. To punish them for four hours per-secution of us we turned about and set fire to every hut on either bank. . . . It should be observed that up to the moment of firing the villages, the fury of the natives seemed to be increasing, but the instant the flames were seen devouring their homes the fury ceased, by which we learned that fire had a remarkable sedative influence on their nerves.

Source: H.M. Stanley, *In Darkest Africa*, London, 1890, i, pp. 299–300.

EGYPT

Document 6   SUEZ CANAL

[a] *Sir Charles Dilke's speech in the House of Commons*, 25 July 1882.

Egypt forms our highway to India and to the East generally . . . As regards the Suez Canal, England has a double interest; it has a predominant commercial interest, because 82 per cent of the trade passing through the Canal is British trade, and it has a predominant political interest caused by the fact that the Canal is the principal highway to India, Ceylon, the Straits and British Burmah, where 250,000,000 people live under our rule; and also to China, where we have vast interests and 84 per cent of the external trade of that still more enormous Empire. It is also one of the roads to our Colonial Empire in Australia and New Zealand.

Source: *Hansard*, 3rd ser., vol. 272, 1720.

[b] *J.C. M'Coan (Liberal MP for County Wicklow) in the same debate.*

The Suez Canal was of paramount and national importance to England, indeed, it was a common thing to say that it formed the gate and key to India. So long, therefore, as we held the Empire of India, we must of necessity, dominate the Suez Canal.

Source: *Ibid.* 1758.

[c] *Henry Labouchère (Radical MP for Northampton) in the same debate,* 27 July 1882.

He considered it absolutely necessary to maintain a supreme and paramount influence over the Canal, and that it was impossible to maintain that influence unless we also had paramount influence at Cairo.

Source: *Ibid.* 2050–1.

Dissident Views

[d] *William Gladstone in August 1877.*

Suppose the very worst. The Canal is stopped [*by Russian action*]. And what then? A heavy blow will have been inflicted on the commerce of the world.

We, as the great carriers, and as the first commercial nation of Christendom, shall be the greatest losers. But it is a question of loss and of loss only. . . . What came and went quickly and cheaply must come and go slow and dearer. . . . I turn then to the military question and ask how much Russia will have gained? The answer is, that she will have introduced an average delay of about three weeks into our military communications with Bombay and less with Calcutta. It seems to be forgotten by many, that there is a route to India round the Cape of Good Hope, as completely as if that route lay by the North-west Passage. [Three weeks' delay] will hardly make the difference to us between life and death in the maintenance of our Indian Empire.

Source: *The Nineteenth Century*, ii (1877), 155–6.

[e] *Lord Randolph Churchill's speech at Edinburgh, 18 December 1883.*

Egypt is not the high road to India. The Suez Canal is a commercial route to India, and a good route too, in time of peace: but it never was, and never could be, a military route for Great Britain in time of war.

Source: L.J. Jennings, *Speeches of Rt. Hon. Randolph Churchill*, 1880–88, i, 74: extracts in W.S. Churchill, *Lord Randolph Churchill*, Macmillan, 1906, pp. 219–20.

THE EGYPTIAN FINANCES: STEPHEN CAVE'S REPORT   **Document 7**

The critical state of the finances of Egypt is due to the combination of two opposite causes.

Egypt may be said to be in a transition state, and she suffers from the defects of the system out of which she is passing, as well as from those of the system into which she is attempting to enter. She suffers from the ignorance, dishonesty, waste, and extravagance of the East, such as have brought her Suzerain [the Sultan of Turkey] to the verge of ruin, and at the same time from the vast expense caused by hasty and inconsiderate endeavours to adopt the civilization of the West.

Immense sums are expended on unproductive works after the manner of the East, and on productive works carried out in the wrong way, or too soon. This last is a fault which Egypt shares with other new countries (for she may be considered a new country in this respect) a fault which has seriously embarrassed both the United States and Canada; but probably nothing in Egypt has ever approached the profligate expenditure which characterized the commencement of the Railway system in England.

Fundamentally, Cave found the Egyptian economy sound. The Egyptian revenue had risen from £55,000 in 1804 to £7,377,912 in 1871. If one compared the two periods, 1850–62 and 1863–75, imports had doubled and exports quadrupled – the latter from £36,339,543 to £145,939,736. The population was rising. There had been a great drive for education. In 1862 there had been only 185 European-type schools, in 1875 there were 4,817. Although mistakes had been made in building up the Egyptian cotton and sugar industries – for example siting factories in the wrong place – the potential was great.

The expenditure, though heavy, would not of itself have produced the present crisis, which may be attributed almost entirely to the ruinous conditions of loans raised for pressing requirements. . . .

In 1862 Said Pasha contracted the first loan. The nominal amount was £3,292,800, repayable in thirty years; the interest 7 per cent and the sinking fund 1 per cent. We have no particulars of the amount really received on this loan.

In 1864 the first of the present Viceroy's [Ismail] loans was contracted. The nominal amount was £5,704,200, of which, however, only £4,864,063 was received. The interest and sinking fund on the nominal amount were respectively 7 and 3.87 per cent, but on the amount received they were 8.2 and 4.5, or, together, 12.7 per cent, instead of 10.87 per cent on the nominal value.

Similar real interest rates were exacted on the loans of 1868 and 1873 but the worst example of extortion was the railway loan of 1866:

A loan was raised for the construction of railways in 1866. Its nominal amount was £3,000,000 at 7 per cent. The amount received by the State was £2,640,000, which raised the interest to 8 per cent. The full amount of £3,000,000 was repaid by six annual instalments of £500,000 each, from 1 January 1869, to 1 January 1874, a rate equivalent to a sinking fund of 18.9 per cent, so that during six years this loan entailed on the State an average charge of equal to 26.9 per cent of the amount realised.

After various technical proposals for ameliorating the situation Cave concluded:

It would appear from these calculations that the resources of Egypt are sufficient, if properly managed, to meet her liabilities, but that as all her available assets are pledged for the charges of existing loans, some fresh combination is necessary in order to fund at a moderate rate the present onerous floating debt.

Cave was prepared to see a European official brought in to control the levying of taxation. He was aware that the increasing employment of European officials was a source of criticism but his own views, expressed earlier in his Report were:

They would be checks upon the adventurers who have preyed upon Egypt.
. . . An official of high rank said to us that the great want in Egypt is a body
of high-class Europeans, not those who compete with each other to make
money, and put pressure upon the Khedive, but men like our Indian
officials, who have done so much to raise the tone of the native races.

Source: Report by Mr Cave on the Financial Condition of Egypt, 23 March 1876,
Parliamentary Papers, lxxxiii (1876), *99*.

DIVIDED OPINIONS   **Document 8**

[a] *Joseph Chamberlain's memorandum.*

I think that Liberal opinion in the country will be extremely restive at the
idea of armed intervention either for the maintenance of the [Anglo-French]
Control in the interests of the bondholders or for the enforcement of restric-
tions on the right of the Egyptian people to manage their own affairs. [No
doubt the Control has done good work] but if the people of Egypt prefer
native administration with all its consequences to the inflexible security and
honesty of European control, it is not England's business or right to force on
them an unpopular system which could only be permanently maintained
against their wishes by practically assuming the Government of the country.
On the other hand, if a change is to be made in a system which has the
sanction of International agreement it should be on the demand of some
body entitled to speak for the Egyptian people, and not at the dictation of
a military adventurer supported by an army which he is forced to keep in a
good temper by bribes of pay and promotion, and whose action compromises
the welfare and liberties of the people as well as the interests of foreigners.
The Notables have shown some independence and seem to be the nucleus
of a really national and patriotic party. Should not intervention, whether
by the Sultan or anyone else, have for its chief object the liberation of this
body from the military tyranny to which they have been subjected – with
the understanding that any recommendations it may make for revision of
existing institutions will be favourably considered?

Source: Memorandum for the Cabinet, 21 June 1882, Joseph Chamberlain Papers,
File 7/1/3, Birmingham University Library. Cf. extracts in Garvin, *Life of Joseph
Chamberlain* (1935) Macmillan, 448.

[b] *Evelyn Baring to Lord Northbrook, 27 March 1882.*

It does not seem to me that we ought to interfere *vi et armis* because the
Egyptians want to levy their taxes, vote their Budget etc. etc. in a different

way to that which at present obtained. I daresay the movement may not now be thoroughly national, but I should think it would become so directly we begin to suppress it by force.

Source: Granville Papers, National Archives, P.R.O. 30/29/138.

[c] *Frederic Harrison at a meeting of the Anti-Aggression League, 26 June 1882.*

When two years ago, the great appeal to the nation was made, we thought it was decided for ever that England should renounce the policy of injustice, and cease to undertake the control of half the human race in the name of civilisation in general and Great Britain in particular. We were all, perhaps, a little too confident that the policy we rejected was really abandoned. . . . Tell those who are so eager to govern Arabs, and Africans, and Afghans, and Japanese at modest stipends of £4,000 or £5,000 a year – ask them to see what can be done in the better government of our own island. . . . Tell those noisy philanthropists who call heaven and earth to witness of the 'anarchy' on the Nile . . . tell them to go and do something to prevent anarchy in Ireland. . . . Imagine your own feelings, if you had to send every year some forty million sterling out of the taxes of the country to pay Turkish, or Arab, or Chinese bondholders; and then, having paid that regularly, that you had to keep a Turkish pasha and a Chinese mandarin in London to control your expenditure, so that every penny of the Budget had to get the sanction of their excellencies, and if Mr Gladstone or any other Chancellor of the Exchequer wishes to put on or take off a tax, down would come a fleet of iron-clads from the Bosphorus into the Thames, and train their 80 ton guns right in view of the Tower and Somerset House. That is the state of Egypt now.

Source: F. Harrison, *The Crisis in Egypt* (Anti-Aggression League Pamphlet, no. 2), pp. 3, 7, 11.

[d] *Lord Randolph Churchill, speech at Blackpool, 24 January 1884.*

. . . The Suez Canal was at no time in the smallest danger. The Suez Canal will always take care of itself. The whole world, the East and the West, are equally and mutually interested in the freedom of the Suez Canal. Surely, you will not be misled by such an obvious and transparent fiction. It was bonds and bondholders and no other power which diverted Mr Gladstone, greatly hesitating, from his path, and which drew the British fleet to Alexandria. It was bonds and bondholders only which commanded the British troops. I pray you mark this. England has never before interfered with the internal affairs of other nations on account of bonds or debts which might be owing to her people. We have always looked upon these matters as altogether outside the range of active Government interference. The Southern States of America took a lot of money from us which they never paid. Did we go to war with the United States? . . . I am afraid to say how many people in this country lost their all when Turkey repudiated her debts. The Government of England took no action. It has been left for Mr Gladstone's Government to depart from this wise and time-honoured tradition – for this Government, whose cardinal principle of foreign policy was non-intervention; it has been left for them to intervene, and intervene actively and violently, and on the side of oppression as against the cause of freedom, in the one particular sphere in which till now non-intervention had been acquiesced in by both parties in the State.

Source: L.J. Jennings, ed., *Speeches of the Rt. Hon. Lord Randolph Churchill, M.P., 1880–1888*, Longmans, 1889, i, 100.

EGYPT IN INTERNATIONAL DIPLOMACY   **Document 9**

[a] *Lord Salisbury to Sir Stafford Northcote, 16 September 1881.*

As to our policy – the defence of it lies in a nutshell. When you have got a neighbour and faithful ally who is bent on meddling in a country in which you are deeply interested – you have three courses open to you. You may renounce – or monopolise – or share. Renouncing would have been to place the French across our road to India. Monopolising would have been very near the risk of war. So we resolved to share.

Source: Lady Gwendolen Cecil, *Life of Robert, Marquis of Salisbury*, 4 vols, 1921, Hodder & Stoughton, ii, 331–2.

[b] *William Gladstone to the Queen, 2 February 1882.*

In the matter of Egypt it appeared to the Cabinet advisable that Lord Granville should endeavour to draw off the French Government from the idea of an Anglo-French occupation, on account of the likelihood of its raising European difficulties; and should suggest to them the expediency of seeking the aid of the Powers in meeting any serious crisis which may be impending, without prejudice to the subsisting Control; and even the possibility of being found the least perilous method of using force, if unhappily force should be required that Turkey should be employed as the instrument for giving effect to the general will.

Source: National Archives, CAB 41/16.

[c] *Lord Granville to the British Ambassadors at Berlin, Vienna, Rome and St Petersburg, 11 February 1882.*

Her Majesty's Government are now agreed with the Government of France that, in view of events which might occur in Egypt, it is desirable to ascertain whether the other Powers would be willing to enter upon an exchange of views as to the best mode of dealing with the question on the basis of the maintenance of the rights of the Sovereign and of the Khedive; of international engagements and the arrangements existing under them, whether with England and France alone or with those two nations and the other Powers; the preservation of the liberties secured by the Firman of the Sultan; together with the prudent development of Egyptian institutions.

The Governments of England and France do not consider that a case for discussing the expediency of an intervention has at present arisen, since on the part of the Chamber of Notables and of the new Government the intention is avowed to maintain international engagements; but should the case arise, they would wish that any such eventual intervention should represent the united action and authority of Europe.

In that event it would also, in their opinion, be right that the Sultan should be a party to any proceeding or discussion that might ensue.

Source: National Archives, F.O., *Confidential Print*, 4692, F.O. 407/19.

[d] *Lord Hartington to Lord Granville, 30 May 1882.*

The French seem to be behaving worse than badly. Freycinet's communication to Ld Lyons [the British ambassador in Paris] appears to be nothing less than a breach of faith to us; and practically a deception of the Khedive, who will inevitably be killed before English and French troops can possibly intervene. Of course this strengthens my opinion of yesterday that unless the French keep their word to us and are prepared to go in for Turkish intervention at once, we had much better cut ourselves loose from them. What is the use of such allies? They have brought us into the frightful mess we are in, and I believe it would be easier to act with the Turks and the whole of the remaining European Powers, than with them alone.

Source: Granville Papers, National Archives, P.R.O. 30/29/132.

[e] *Lord Ampthill (British Ambassador in Berlin) to Lord Granville, 15 July 1882.*

Let me congratulate you most sincerely and heartily on having so tactfully steered out of the inevitable complications of 'entangling alliances' into the independent prosecution of a truly British national policy. Everybody I meet seems overjoyed that we are asserting our right to protect our own interests, and have taken the lead of the concert into our own hands. Everybody congratulates me on your policy, with the exception of my French colleague, who is quite broken down with disappointment at Freycinet's weakness, and the absence of national pride in the French Chambers. Münster [the German ambassador in London] is probably right in thinking that Bismarck will now be reticent and reserved. Hatzfeldt [formerly the German Ambassador at Constantinople] tells me that Bismarck becomes simply furious at the mere mention of the Egyptian question, and will scarcely even read what is sent to him on the subject. 'Let the Powers interested settle it as they please [he writes to Hatzfeldt], but don't ask me how; for I neither know nor care' . . . Bismarck, I think, will support any action we take, but will refrain from advice, however much he may wish England to go ahead, and settle the question as you think best for Europe.

Source: Lord Edmond Fitzmaurice, *The Life of Lord Granville, 1815–1891*, 2 vols, Longmans, 1906, ii, 268–9.

DEATH OF GORDON AT KHARTOUM   **Document 10**

[a] *The Times, 3 May 1884.*

A study of the papers contained in the Blue Book . . . must produce a general sense of shame and confusion. . . . The anxiety as to General Gordon's safety is not confined to London, or fomented by Opposition prints, as is sometimes suggested; it is discernible in the organs of all classes, those of the working men not excepted, and is plainly manifested in the North of England and Scotland, the strongholds of Liberalism.

Source: Leading article.

[b] *The Archdeacon of Northampton.*

A nation mourned a son, a true son, fallen by a death of betrayal and desertion in the cause. England wept today and felt remorse, for there was no remorse like remorse for long neglect.

The Archdeacon of Northampton preaching on a day of national mourning for Gordon, 13 March 1885, reported in *The Times*, 14 March 1885.

[c] *The Morning Post.*

We cannot turn our backs upon the Mahdi and his hordes without sacrificing Egypt and shaking to its foundation our Indian Empire. Having entered on this struggle, we must go on with it; and having gone to the Soudan, we can quit it only as victors. There is only one course.

Source: Quoted *Annual Register* (1885), pp. 20, 21.

[d] *Sir George Campbell (MP for Kirkcaldy), House of Commons, 23 February 1885, during the debate on the Vote of Censure on the government for its policy in the Sudan.*

He [Campbell] was one of the small band who had consistently opposed the Government policy in Egypt from the bombardment of Alexandria down to the present time. Holding, therefore, the views he did, he had heard the other day with astonishment and alarm the declaration of the Prime Minister that it was the intention of the Government to overthrow and 'smash the Mahdi', but he was glad to say that the speech of the Prime Minister that evening had to a large extent whittled away the most dangerous portion of his previous utterances. . . . They must all feel that the reconquering of that great Empire in the heart of Africa was an enormous undertaking; and, looking to their position with France, Germany and Russia, he thought they would do well to be wise in time.

Source: Hansard, 3rd ser., vol. 244, 1110.

[e] *J.A. Picton (MP for Leicester), in the same debate.*

They heard a great deal about *prestige* in various articles of the Press, and in some of the speeches delivered in that House. *Prestige* was a French word, and it seemed to him to express a very un-English idea. It might be proper for a people who, under the malignant influence of Imperialism, had been trained up to think far more of glory than of truth and right; but if, by *prestige*, Hon. Members meant reputation, he would ask whether, in this ancient Kingdom, we had much need to be nervous about our reputation?

Source: Ibid. 1122–3.

The government survived the censure motion by only 14 votes: 302 to 288.

WEST AFRICA

Document 11   THE DESIRE TO ABANDON RESPONSIBILITIES

Resolved:
That it is the opinion of this Committee
1. That it is not possible to withdraw the British government, wholly or immediately, from any settlements or engagements on the West African Coast. . . .
3. That all further extension of territory or assumption of Government, or new treaties offering any protection to native tribes, would be inexpedient;

and that the object of our policy should be to encourage in the natives the exercise of those qualities which may render it possible for us more and more to transfer to them the administration of all the Governments, with a view to our ultimate withdrawal from all, except, probably, Sierra Leone.

Source: Report from the Select Committee on Africa (Western Coast), Parliamentary Papers, v (1865), iii.

THE FEARS OF BRITISH TRADERS   **Document 12**

[a] *The National African Company on the Niger.*

Foreign annexations of any degree would, as experience teaches us, practically exclude *pro tanto*, British commerce.

. . . we have no need to dwell at length on the importance to Great Britain of keeping open to her commerce the highway to the countries of the Central Soudan, which are both densely populated and fairly civilised, nor on the facts that this waterway was discovered by an Englishman, Lander, was opened up to trade by another Englishman, McGregor Laird, under the continued auspices of Her Majesty's Government, and has had its resources rapidly developed by (until quite recently) exclusively British capital.

Source: G. Goldie Taubman (as he then was), Vice-Chairman of the National African Co. Ltd, to T.V. Lister, Assistant Secretary at the Foreign Office, 26 September 1883, Granville Papers, National Archives, P.R.O. 30/29/269.

[b] *The Liverpool traders on the Congo.*

John Holt, a leading Liverpool merchant who had lived on the West Coast, wrote under the influence of reports that the French had acquired territory near Stanley Pool and that the Portuguese were extending their claims to the whole coastline from the River Loge to the River Quillo.

The effect of a Portuguese extension would be to exterminate the British trade existing in the absorbed territory, as it could not exist under the grinding exactions of a protective Customs Tariff, which would practically prohibit the importation of every manufacture of British origin. A writer who lived for many years in Angola, and who had abundant opportunities of witnessing the miserable state to which that fine country had been reduced by the wretched and corrupt system of government, represents Portuguese rule there as a 'despotic oppression that crushed the whole country under its heel, depopulating it, and stifling any attempt at industrial development'. . . .

France of late years has been making vigorous efforts to extend her influence in Western Africa. . . . If France sets so high a value on her future in Africa as to deem it wise to extend her power, and to accept gladly the responsibilities of an enlarged empire, and if Portugal does not shrink from the additional cares of an increased territory, it is reasonable to hope that England will not allow the trade at present possessed by her to be confiscated for the benefit of protectionist competitors; but that the influence due to her by virtue of her great colonial and trading interests in Western Africa, which far exceed those of all other nations combined, will be maintained, and, if necessary, her territory extended, in order to prevent the encroachments of foreign powers whose interests are antagonistic to those of Great Britain.

Source: John Holt, Liverpool, to Lord Granville, 11 December 1882, Granville Papers, National Archives, P.R.O. 30/29/269.

[c] *The protest against the Anglo-Portuguese Treaty of February 1884.*

This Treaty has been concluded in direct opposition to the expressed views and to the interests of British merchants and manufacturers. . . . In 1856 . . . the commerce of this country with the native territories north of the Portuguese possessions in Angola was of small importance but . . . during the past five years this trade has nearly quadrupled in value. . . . Manchester furnishes the clothes, Birmingham the iron and brass wares, Yorkshire the woollens, London the boats and means of navigation, and Liverpool and London the provisions. . . . As yet this trade is only in its infancy; if it increases at the present rate, five years hence it will be superior to anything on the West Coast of Africa. The Portuguese see this, but they are not wise enough to see that if they come and obtain possession of the Congo, commerce, so fast growing now, cannot thrive under the disadvantages attending their rule. It is only because it is free that it thrives. . . .

Source: Manchester Chamber of Commerce to Lord Granville, 5 March 1884, *Parliamentary Papers*, lvi (1884), 89.

[d] *The German annexation of the Cameroons.*

I am requested by the Directors of this Chamber to draw your attention to the action of the German Government in the Cameroons River and its adjacent territory on the West Coast of Africa.

The Directors view with alarm and anxiety the annexation by Germany of this district, which has for many years been regarded as under British protection.

Your Lordship is probably aware that there are only two firms of German nationality trading in the Cameroons, whilst of English firms there are six. The former have traded only during the last ten or fifteen years; the English firms – or, at all events, certain of them – have been established there for thirty or forty years.

In respect, therefore, of priority of settlement, Great Britain has the prefer-able claim of supremacy. . . .

It is, doubtless, also within your Lordship's cognizance that the natives of the district have repeatedly applied for annexation to this country; and it is well known that they are exasperated at the action of the German Government.

The Directors of the Chamber are impressed with the belief that, when these facts are brought before the Government of His Imperial Majesty the Emperor of Germany, their pretensions will be withdrawn, not alone as an act of courtesy to a nation with whom the Germans are on friendly terms, but in respect of its just claim of prior and permanent occupation.

Should it be found, however, necessary or expedient to allow Germany to take possession of the southern bank of the Cameroons River, it is all-important that the northern bank should continue under the protection, or be formally annexed by, Great Britain, seeing that the district of Victoria (which has already been annexed by the British), as well as the Cameroons Mountains, are on this side.

Source: John McLaren, President, Chamber of Commerce and Manufacturers, Glasgow, to Lord Granville, 10 November 1884, *Parliamentary Papers*, lv (1884–5), 82.

THE BRITISH GOVERNMENT'S REACTION   **Document 13**

[a] *The government's reluctance to act.*

The responsibilities of Her Majesty's Government on the West African Coast are already very heavy, and Lord Kimberley [Colonial Secretary] is of the opinion that it is very undesirable to add to them. As Lord Granville is well aware the climate of all parts of West Africa is very pestilential, and prejudicial to the life and health of Europeans. Past experience shows that the extension of British occupation would probably lead to wars with the interior tribes and heavy demands upon the British taxpayer. The question of domestic slavery and of fugitive slaves from the inland tribes, which must necessarily arise, would, in Lord Kimberley's opinion, be of themselves sufficient to deter Her Majesty's Government from undertaking such a responsibility as is proposed [the annexation of the Cameroons] if it can possibly be avoided.

Source: R.G.W. Herbert (Permanent Under Secretary at the Colonial Office) to the Foreign Office, 3 May 1883, National Archives, F.O. 84/1654.

[b] *The permanent officials begin to become converted.*

T.V. Lister, the Assistant Under Secretary at the Foreign Office with special responsibility for African affairs, was an early convert. He is here replying to a memorandum by R.H. Meade, his opposite number of the Colonial Office who never became converted.

Everybody seems to be agreed that the occupation of any place or river by the French is almost destructive of British trade, and it is therefore of great importance to keep them out of districts which either are or might be favourable to that trade.

Source: Memorandum by T.V. Lister, 24 October 1883, Granville Papers, National Archives, P.R.O. 30/29/269.

Document 14   THE BERLIN WEST AFRICA CONFERENCE LAYS DOWN THE 'RULES' FOR THE SCRAMBLE

Chapter I. The Congo

Article 1
The trade of all nations shall enjoy complete freedom –

1. In all the regions forming the basin of the Congo and its outlets. [The boundaries of this area are then defined in detail.]
2. In the maritime zone extending along the Atlantic Ocean from the Parallel situated in 2°30′ of south latitude to the mouth of the Logé. . . .
3. In the zone stretching eastwards from the Congo Basin, as above defined to the Indian Ocean from the 5° of north latitude to the mouth of the Zambesi in the south. . . .

Article 6
All the Powers exercising sovereign rights or influence in the aforesaid territories bind themselves to watch over the preservation of the native tribes, and to care for the improvement of the conditions of their moral and material wellbeing, and to help in suppressing slavery, and especially the Slave Trade. They shall, without distinction of creed or nation, protect and favour all religions, scientific or charitable institutions, and undertakings created and organised for the above ends, or which aim at instructing the natives and bringing home to them the blessings of civilization. Christian missionaries, scientists, and explorers, with their followers, property, and collections, shall likewise be the objects of special protection. . . .

Chapter V. The Niger

Article 26

The navigation of the Niger, without excepting any of its branches and outlets, is, and shall remain free for the merchant-ships of all nations equally, whether with cargo or ballast, for the transportation of goods and passengers. . . .

Chapter VI. New Occupations

Article 34

Any Power which henceforth takes possession of a tract of land on the coasts of the African Continent outside of its present possessions, or which, being hitherto without such possessions, shall acquire them, as well as the Power which assumes a protectorate there, shall accompany the respective act with a notification thereof, addressed to the other Signatory Powers of the present Act, in order to enable them, if need be, to make good any claim of their own.

Article 35

The Signatory Powers of the present Act recognize the obligations to insure the establishment of authority in the regions occupied by them on the coasts of the African continent sufficient to protect existing rights, and, as the case may be, freedom of trade and of transit under the existing conditions agreed upon.

Source: General Act of the Berlin Conference on West Africa, signed on 26 February 1885, by the representatives of Germany, Austria, Belgium, Denmark, Spain, the United States of America, France, the United Kingdom, Italy, the Netherlands, Portugal, Russia, Sweden and Norway, and Turkey. *Parliamentary Papers*, lv (1884–5), 438.

THE ROYAL NIGER COMPANY   **Document 15**

The Royal Niger Company, based on the British North Borneo Company (1881), itself formed the precedent for the Imperial British East Africa Company (1888) and Cecil Rhodes's South Africa Company (1889).

[a] *The Charter, granted 10 July 1886.*

The following Charter has been granted to the National African Company (Limited), upon a Petition to Her Majesty in Council:

Whereas . . . the capital of the Company is £1,000,000, divided into 100,000 shares of £10 each [of which 97,675 shares have been subscribed for]. And that the objects of the Company . . . are . . .

To carry on business and to act as merchants, bankers, traders, commission agents, ship-owners, carriers, or in any other capacity, in the United Kingdom, Africa, or elsewhere, and to import, export, buy, sell, barter, exchange, pledge, make advances upon or otherwise deal in goods, produce, articles, and merchandize, according to the custom of merchants, or otherwise.

To form or acquire and carry on trading stations, factories, stores, and depots in Africa or elsewhere, and to purchase, lease, or otherwise acquire, carry on, develop, or improve any business, or any real or personal property in the United Kingdom, Africa, or elsewhere, or any undivided or other interest whatsoever therein respectively. . . .

And whereas the Petition further states, that the Kings, Chiefs, and other peoples of various territories in the basin of the River Niger in Africa . . . have ceded the whole of their respective territories to the Company by various Acts of Cession specified in the Schedule thereto. . . .

And whereas the petitioners further state that the Company . . . have purchased the business of all the European traders in the region aforesaid, and are now the sole European traders there and are now engaged in developing the resources of such regions, and in extending trade further into the interior.

And whereas the Petition further states that the Company . . . have, during many years past, expended large sums of money and made great exertions in and about acquiring the confidence of the said native Kings, Chiefs, and peoples, which have resulted in the said cession of territory, and large expenditure will be incurred in carrying the same into effect and discharging the obligations arising thereunder.

And whereas the Petition further states that the condition of the natives inhabiting the aforesaid territories would be materially improved, and the development of such territories and those contiguous to, and the civilization of their people would be greatly advanced if we could think fit to confer on the Company . . . authority to accept the full benefit of the several cessions aforesaid. . . .

And whereas the Petition further states . . . they would be enabled to render our dominions services of much value, and to promote the commercial prosperity of many of our subjects.

Now, therefore, we . . . do hereby will, ordain, grant, and declare as follows, that is to say:

Authorization to Company

1. The said National African Company (Limited) . . . is hereby authorized and empowered to hold and retain the full benefit of the several cessions aforesaid or any of them, and all rights, interests, authorities, and powers for the purposes of government, preservation of public order, protection of the

said territories, or otherwise of what nature or kind soever . . . ceded to or vested in the Company . . . and to hold, use, enjoy, and exercise the same territories, lands, property, rights, interests, authorities and powers respectively for the purposes of the Company, and on the terms of this our Charter.

Further clauses bound the Company to remain British, to suppress slavery, to guarantee religious freedom and to respect local laws and customs.

Prohibition of Monopoly

14. Nothing in this our Charter shall be deemed to authorize the Company to set up or grant any monopoly of trade . . . and there shall be no differential treatment of the subjects of any Power as to settlement or access to markets, but foreigners alike with British subjects will be subject to administrative dispositions in the interests of commerce and order.

The customs duties and charges hereby authorized shall be levied and applied solely for the purpose of defraying the necessary expenses of Government. . . .

Source: *London Gazette*, 13 July 1886.

[b] *Treaties with African Chiefs.*

There were several variants of these but the one given below, the so-called 'Treaty Form No. 5', eventually became the most widely used. 168 treaties in this particular form were signed between 16 April 1884 and 12 September 1888. In the earlier treaties the Royal Niger Company was of course called the National African Company.

We, the undersigned Chiefs of [blank] with the view to the bettering of the condition of our country and people, do this day cede to the Royal Niger Company (Chartered and Limited), for ever, the whole of our territory extending from [blank].

We also give the said Royal Niger Company . . . full power to settle all native disputes arising from any cause whatever, and we pledge ourselves not to enter into any war with other tribes without the sanction of the said Royal Niger Company. . . .

We understand that the said Royal Niger Company . . . have full power to mine, farm, and build in any portion of our country.

We bind ourselves not to have any intercourse with any strangers or foreigners except through the said Royal Niger Company. . . .

In consideration of the foregoing, the said Royal Niger Company . . . bind themselves not to interfere with any of the native laws or customs of the country, consistently with the maintenance of order and good government.

The said Royal Niger Company . . . agree to pay native owners of land a reasonable amount for any portion they may require.

The said Royal Niger Company . . . bind themselves to protect the said Chiefs from the attacks of any neighbouring aggressive tribes.

The said Royal Niger Company . . . also agree to pay the said Chiefs [blank] measures native value.

There followed the signatures of witnesses to the Chiefs' marks and a declaration by an interpreter that he had 'truly and faithfully explained the above agreement to all the Chiefs present, and they understood its meaning'.

Source: Parliamentary Papers, lxiii (1899), 444.

Document 16   THE GREAT DEPRESSION

The Royal Commission appointed to inquire into the Depression of Trade and Industry, 1885–6.

Questions addressed to Chambers of Commerce, Commercial Associations and (with some changes) 'Trade Societies and other Associations representing the interests of the Working Classes'.

6. . . . can the condition of trade and industry, or that of any special trade or industry, in your district at the present time be fairly described as 'depressed'?

7. . . . If so, when did the depression begin; when did it reach its lowest point; and what are its most prominent symptoms?

13. What measures could, in your opinion, be adopted to improve the existing conditions of trade?

14. To what extent do you consider that the present condition of trade and industry in your district has been affected by the operation of any of the following causes: . . .

(h) Foreign competition.

(k) Foreign tariffs and bounties?

Replies
These were immensely varied but the majority regarded foreign tariffs as a serious problem. A significant number spoke of the need for new markets. A few wanted closer links with British colonies, for example:

Birmingham
6. Every trade, special and ordinary, can only be described as depressed.

7. Distinct depression began in 1876–7. Lowest period during the present year.

13. . . . The formation of a trading union between the mother country and her colonies and dependencies.

14. . . . the principal causes of the present depression [include] – Foreign competition in neutral markets, the rate of wages and hours of labour in Germany, France, Belgium, and all other manufacturing countries being lower and longer than in this country, except in America.

Barnsley

13. . . . Opening up of new markets, more particularly by cultivating closer business relations with our colonies.

Manchester

13. The opening up of new markets, and development of those already partially open to Great Britain, should be assisted by Government in every practical way. Such openings now present themselves in Africa. . . .

Source: Parliamentary Papers, xxi (1886), 73, 75, 77, 97, 114, 227.

EAST AFRICA

THE MIXTURE OF ECONOMIC AND STRATEGIC ARGUMENTS   **Document 17**

The businessmen press their case.

[a] The Zanzibar dominions comprise the whole coast line of that part of East Africa lying between 10°40′ S. Lat. and about 3° N., which included upwards of forty harbours which are mostly safe and commodious. . . .

The principal exports of the mainland are ivory, gum copal, copra, semsem, millet, hides, orchella-weed, tobacco and india-rubber; the latter was unknown to the natives as an article of commerce until about 1876, but it is now one of the most valuable exports. . . .

An analysis of the trade of 1878–9, which was an average year . . . will give an approximate estimate of the proportions of the whole trade absorbed by England. The imports for that year were £709,900 and the exports £870,350 . . . fully one-third of the import and one-half of the export trade of the Zanzibar dominions, for 1878–9, was absorbed by Great Britain. [Cheap Indian cottons are tending to drive out British manufactures in the south.] But in the richer and more populous mountain region to the north the cheaper productions find no market. There we find both clothing and ornament of the most solid character. Manchester grey and blue cottons, heavy iron, copper and brass wire are in constant demand, and beyond these, a few beads are the only articles of European manufacture accepted. The manufactures, in short, which are suited for this new market are just those in which England excels, and in which we are, or ought to be, able to defy competition.

Source: Consul Holmwood to James Hutton, 10 April 1885, National Archives, F.O. 84/1737.

[b] The country around and beyond Mount Kilimanjaro as far as Lake Victoria Nyanza is the most fertile, healthy and beautiful in Africa. It bounds . . . with produce of great importance to our Commerce. Portions of it have lately been visited by [G. A.] Fischer, a German Traveller and by [Joseph] Thomson and [Harry] Johnston, Englishmen. Fischer is known to be pressing upon the German Government the expediency of possessing themselves of the District.

Some years ago Mr Mackinnon proposed to form an association for developing the wealth of the Continental portions of the Kingdom of Zanzibar. The negotiations came to nothing. [He suggests that they be revived in the new competitive situation.] It is believed that there would be no difficulty in obtaining funds for making a Railway to Kilimanjaro; and subsequently to Lake Victoria Nyanza, if such a Concession could be obtained from the Sultan of Zanzibar.

Source: Lord Aberdare to Lord Granville, 24 April 1885, National Archives, F.O. 84/1737.

A new Australia as well as a new India.

[c] Here is a new country as large as Switzerland, enjoying a singularly fertile soil and healthy climate, capable of producing every vegetable production of the tropical and temperate zones, free from the tzetze fly, and inhabited sparsely by peaceful agriculturalists, skilled in native manufactures and capable and desirous of instruction: here is a land eminently suited for European colonization, situated near midway between the Equatorial lakes and the Coast. Within a few years it must be either English, French or German. . . . I have only to invite a certain number of chosen colonists, already desirous of joining my expedition, to come and occupy the beautiful sites which will be given to them gratis, and there to cultivate the vine, the coffee plant, the sugar-cane, rice, wheat, oranges and limes – and the principal points of this healthy district will soon be in the hands of Englishmen. . . . Think what a commanding position this hilly district, with its European climate, occupies in Eastern Equatorial Africa. . . . Situated only 180 miles from the Coast, with an intervening district offering no difficulties whatever in the construction of roads and railways, Kilimanjaro offers an admirable centre for that occupation and colonization of Eastern Africa which must inevitably come from one of the European powers.

Source: Harry Johnston to Lord Edmond Fitzmaurice, Under Secretary for Foreign Affairs, Chagga, 10 July 1884, quoted R. Oliver, *Sir Harry Johnston and the Scramble for Africa*, Chatto and Windus, 1957, pp. 66–8.

The Government weighs up the possibilities.

[d] The geographical position of the East Coast lays it more within the general area of our foreign policy than that of the West Coast. Our alternative route by the Cape to India may at any time make it important that we should have possession of, or at least free access to, good harbours: the importance is not less since the French movement in Madagascar. The Mahommedan element on the East Coast and the large Indian trade which is there carried on, with its connection, which if not close is none the less real, with all that concerns the Mahommedan world in the Soudan, on the shores of the Red Sea, and on the Hadramaut littoral and Persian Gulf, make it essential that we should secure a preponderating influence over its political future.

Commercially it has made great strides in the 10 years which have elapsed since the Slave export was checked and an impulse given to legitimate trade. Apart from the mineral wealth which is believed to exist between the coast and the great lakes, there is an unlimited capacity for the production of cattle, cereals, and all the usual articles of tropical trade. The climate, even as at present understood, is less unhealthy than that of the West Coast, and the great mountain ranges of Kilimanjaro and Kenia, situated between the lakes which give birth to the Nile & the fine harbours of Zanzibar, afford a European climate and sanatorium within easy reach, if once roads are made, of the coast. It is needless to dwell on the advantages of this to our navy, to our officials, and to traders. There is very good reason, too, for supposing that the natives are more naturally industrious than most of the West Coast tribes, and that they would welcome the establishment of any Government strong enough to enforce good order and prevent the raids of the more turbulent tribes.

Source: Memorandum by Clement Hill, a Foreign Office official, 20 October 1884 (written to assess the implications of the Berlin West Africa Conference for East Africa), National Archives, F.O. 84/1813.

THE 'LITTLE ENGLANDERS' STAND ON UGANDA   **Document 18**

I am very much exercised in my mind at the news from East Africa and Mombasa. As you will have observed the East African Company have 'thrown up the sponge' (being as I imagine insolvent), and a determined effort is being made to force the British Government to take to the *damnosa haereditas*. Rosebery has circulated a Memo, (for our consideration but not expressing his own sentiments), by Sir P. Anderson (of the F.O.), in the highest jingo tune advocating the annexation of the whole country up to the Albert Lakes with a view to the 'reconquest' of the Sudan via the Upper Nile. . . . Captain Lugard threatens all sorts of horrors if we do not occupy at once. Bishop Tucker swears he will remain at his post and die – in short every sort of bogey is invoked to involve us in this horrible quagmire, which will be as bad as Khartoum. . . . The railway is *projected* but not *built*, and I hope it never will be. If we embark on this desperate business we shall have no end of trouble with the French and Germans, as indeed we already have. *Cui bono*? Is it *trade*? There is no traffic. Is it *religion*? The Catholics and Protestants (as they call themselves) are occupied in nothing but cutting each other's throats, with their bishops at their head. *Is it slavery*? There is no evidence that there is any slave trade question in this region. . . . I see nothing but endless expense, trouble and disaster in prospect if we allow ourselves to drift into any sort of responsibility for this business, and devoutly hope we shall have nothing to do with it.

Source: Sir William Harcourt, Chancellor of the Exchequer, to W.E. Gladstone, 20 September 1892, quoted Gardiner [*Life of Sir William Harcourt*], ii, 191–3.

SOUTH AFRICA

Document 19   CECIL RHODES

[a] *The 'First of the Money Kings'.*

When Mr Rhodes died, the most conspicuous figure left in the English-speaking race since the death of Queen Victoria disappeared. Whether loved or feared, he towered aloft above all his contemporaries. There are many who hold that he would be entitled to a black statue in the Hall of Eblis. But even those who distrusted and disliked him most, pay reluctant homage to the portentous energy of a character which has affected the world so deeply for weal or woe. . . . It was his distinction to be the first of the new Dynasty of Money Kings which has been evolved in these later days as the real rulers of the modern world. There have been many greater millionaires than he. . . . As a rich man Mr Rhodes was not in the running with Mr Carnegie, Mr Rockefeller, or Mr Astor. But although there have been many wealthier men, none of them, before Mr Rhodes, recognised the opportunities of ruling the world which wealth affords its possessor. The great financiers of Europe have no doubt often used their powers to control questions of peace or war and to influence politics, but they always acted from a strictly financial motive. Their aims were primarily the shifting of the value of stocks. To effect that end they have often taken a leading hand in political deals. But

Mr Rhodes inverted the operation. With him political considerations were always paramount. If he used the market he did it in order to secure the means of achieving political ends.

Source: W.T. Stead in *Cecil Rhodes, the Last Will and Testament of Cecil J. Rhodes*, ed. W.T. Stead, Review of Reviews Office, 1902, pp. 51, 55. (W.T. Stead, a journalist, had been a close associate of Rhodes and Rhodes had intended him to be an executor of his Will until they disagreed about the Boer War.)

[b] *Rhodes's dream.*

I contend that we are the first race in the world, and that the more of the world we inhabit the better it is for the human race. I contend that every acre added to our territory means the birth of more of the English race who otherwise would not be brought into existence. Added to this, the absorption of the greater portion of the world under our rule simply means the end of all wars. . . . The furtherance of the British Empire, for the bringing of the whole uncivilised world under British rule, for the recovery of the United States, for the making the Anglo-Saxon race but one Empire. What a dream! but yet it is probable. It is possible.

Source: Rhodes to W.T. Stead, 19 August 1891, quoted in *Cecil Rhodes, the Last Will and Testament of Cecil J. Rhodes*, ed. W.T. Stead, Review of Reviews Office, 1902, pp. 58–9.

THE RUDD CONCESSION **Document 20**

Know all men by these presents that whereas Charles Dunnell Rudd of Kimberley, Rochfort Maguire of London, and Francis Robert Thompson of Kimberley, herein-after called the grantees, have covenanted and agreed . . . to pay to me my heirs and successors the sum of one hundred pounds sterling British currency on the first day of every lunar month, and further to deliver at my Royal Kraal one thousand Martini-Henry breech-loading rifles, together with one hundred thousand rounds of suitable ball cartridges, five hundred of the said rifles and fifty thousand of the said cartridges to be ordered from England forthwith and delivered with reasonable despatch, and the remainder of the said rifles and cartridges to be delivered so soon as the said grantees shall have commenced to work mining machinery within my territory, and further to deliver on the Zambesi River a steamboat with guns suitable for defensive purposes upon the said river, . . . I, Lo Bengula, King of the Matebele, Mashonaland, and other adjoining territories, in the exercise of my sovereign powers, and in the presence and with the consent of my Council of Indunas, do hereby grant and assign unto the said grantees, their heirs, representatives, and assigns, jointly and severally, the complete and exclusive charge over all metals and minerals situated and contained in my kingdom, . . . together with full powers to do all things that they may deem necessary to win and procure the same, and to hold, collect, and enjoy the profits and revenues . . . and whereas I have been much molested of late by divers persons seeking and desiring to obtain grants and concessions of land and mining rights in my territories, I do hereby authorise the said grantees, . . . to take all necessary and lawful steps to exclude from my kingdoms, . . . all persons seeking land, metals, minerals or mining rights therein, and I do hereby undertake to render them such needful assistance as they may from time to time require for the exclusion of such persons and to grant no concessions of land or mining rights from and after this date without their consent and concurrence. . . .

This given under my hand this thirtieth day of October in the year of our Lord eighteen hundred and eighty eight at my Royal Kraal.

his

Lo Bengula   X

mark

Source: Parliamentary Papers, li (1890), 545.

Document 21   THE COLONIAL OFFICE'S DOUBTS ABOUT THE LEGALITY OF THE BRITISH SOUTH AFRICA COMPANY'S POSITION

'Matabeleland' is the territory of Lo Bengula, King of the Amandebele or Matabele . . . it had been argued by Bishop Knight Bruce of Bloemfontein and others that Lo Bengula was no more than a marauder, and had no legitimate claims [over Mashonaland etc.], but it is too late to go into that now. . . .

It should be premised, as accounting for the recent struggle for the possession of Mashonaland, that the whole country between the Limpopo and the Zambesi had long been reported to be rich in gold . . . after the development of the marvellous gold-fields of Witwatersrand in the Transvaal about 1886–7 . . . it was thought that deposits of ore would be found to recur, equalling or exceeding in riches the deposits of 'the Randt', and the country became the theatre of a lively struggle between speculative groups almost too numerous to mention. . . .

On the 18th of March 1889, the High Commissioner [Sir Hercules Robinson] wrote . . . 'The alternatives before us as regards Matabeleland are to recognise a monopoly which may possibly develop into a Royal Charter, or to follow the Swaziland course of allowing a number of competing concession seekers of different nationalities to establish themselves in the country. Lo Bengula would be unable to govern or control such incomers except by a massacre. . . .'

On 30 October 1888 Rhodes and his associates obtained the Rudd Concession [Doc. 20] and on 29 October 1889 a Royal Charter.

It is understood that the concession from Lo Bengula never actually passed, in full proprietary right, to the Chartered Company, but is leased by the 'United Concessions Company' [another company controlled by Rhodes] to the Chartered Company for a payment of one half the net profits of all their present and prospective undertakings, which, however, have to be conducted entirely at the expense of the Chartered Company. . . .

Sir R. Herbert [Permanent Under Secretary at the Colonial Office] wrote, 'It may be safely stated that no persons connected with her Majesty's Government had any idea that such a scheme was in contemplation when the charter was being considered and settled. If it had been disclosed the charter would certainly have been refused. It may even be a question whether the announcement of it now does not render it necessary to consider whether the charter should be revoked. That would be a very objectionable course, because it would involve the establishment of an administrative protectorate over all the Company's territories. . . . Lord Knutsford [Colonial Secretary] wrote . . . 'Although I think we have been misled by the British South Africa Company's founders I am not prepared to take any steps towards putting an end to the charter. This would impose upon this country the responsibility of taking over and administering this enormous territory subject to the concession.'

Source: Memorandum on the Origin and Operations of the British South Africa Chartered Company, 13 October 1892. National Archives, C.O. 879/37.

FASHODA AND THE ANGLO-FRENCH AGREEMENTS OF 1904

THE FASHODA INCIDENT   **Document 22**

[a] *The British case.*

It is desirable that you should be placed in possession of the view of Her Majesty's Government in respect to the line of action to be followed in the event of Khartoum being occupied at an early date by the forces now operating in the Sudan under the command of Sir Herbert Kitchener.

In view of the substantial military and financial co-operation which has recently been afforded by Her Majesty's Government to the Government of the Khedive, Her Majesty's Government have decided that at Khartoum the British and Egyptian flags should be hoisted side by side. This decision will have no reference to the manner in which the occupied countries are to be administered in the future. It is not necessary at present to define their political status with any great precision. . . . You will, however, explain to the Khedive, and to his Ministers that the procedure I have indicated is intended to emphasise the fact that Her Majesty's Government consider that they have a predominant voice in all matters connected with the Soudan, and that they expect that any advice which they may think fit to tender to the Egyptian Government, in respect to Soudan affairs, will be followed. . . .

It is possible that a French force may be found in occupation of some portion of the Nile Valley. Should this contingency arise . . . Her Majesty's Government entertain full confidence in Sir Herbert Kitchener's judgement and discretion. They feel assured that he will endeavour to convince the Commander of any French force with which he may come in contact that the presence of the latter in the Nile Valley is an infringement of the rights of both Great Britain and of the Khedive.

Source: Lord Salisbury to Lord Cromer, 2 August 1898, Secret, Gooch and Temperley, *British Documents on the Origins of the War, 1898–1914*, Documents-HMSO, 1927, i, 159–60.

[b] *The French case.*

Fashoda. Minister for Foreign Affairs [Delcassé] initiated today a conversation on this burning question by stating that French Minister in London was instructed to speak to your Lordship about it. Much of what passed between us was but a repetition of previous conversations, but his Excellency was just as determined as ever upon the right of France to occupy territory practically abandoned by Egypt and contested the right of Great Britain to warn off other Powers which had not recognised her sphere of influence or to assert that France was committing an unfriendly act in advancing on Upper Nile. He at the same time declared his conviction that honest discussion between the two Governments would soon result in an understanding. He reiterated that it is the desire of the present French Government to make a friend of England, adding that between ourselves he would much prefer an Anglo-French to a Franco-Russian alliance. He again entreated me to take account of existing excitement in France, which is becoming dangerous and might in an instant break out into overt acts, repeating what he had said yesterday: 'Do not ask me for the impossible; do not drive me into a corner.' He admitted that he knew feeling in England is strong, but he argued that Englishmen are not so excitable as the French, and felt sentimental considerations less deeply. I replied that he could not exaggerate strength of feeling in England on this subject, both on the part of the Government and the public, and the knowledge of this caused me great apprehension. He said: You surely would not break with us over Fashoda?' To which I answered that it was exactly that which I feared.

Source: Sir E. Monson (British Ambassador in Paris) to Lord Salisbury, 28 September 1898, Telegram, *ibid.*, p. 171.

THE ANGLO-FRENCH AGREEMENTS OF APRIL 1904   **Document 23**

An agreement about colonial questions serves as the basis for a new Anglo–French entente in European diplomacy.

His Britannic Majesty's Government declare that they have no intention of altering the political status of Egypt.

The Government of the French Republic, for their part, declare that they will not obstruct the action of Great Britain in that country by asking that a limit of time be fixed for the British occupation or in any other manner, and that they give their assent to the draft Khedivial Decree annexed to the present Arrangement [for the conversion of the Egyptian debt].

The Government of the French Republic declare that they have no intention of altering the political status of Morocco.

His Britannic Majesty's Government, for their part, recognise that it appertains to France, more particularly as a Power whose dominions are conterminous for a great distance with those of Morocco, to preserve order in that country, and to provide assistance for the purpose of all administrative, economic, financial, and military reforms which it may require.

They declare that they will not obstruct the action taken by France for this purpose, provided that such action shall leave intact the rights which Great Britain in virtue of Treaties, Conventions, and usage, enjoys in Morocco, including the right of coasting trade between the ports of Morocco, enjoyed by British vessels since 1901.

Source: Articles I and II of the Declaration between the United Kingdom and France respecting Egypt and Morocco, signed at London, 8 April 1904, Gooch and Temperley, *ibid.*, ii, 385–7.

INTERPRETATIONS OF IMPERIALISM

Document 24   J.A. HOBSON

Hobson argued that the acquisition of a vast new colonial empire in the late nine-teenth century had brought little profit to the nation as a whole.

Seeing that the Imperialism of the last six decades is clearly condemned as a bad business policy, in that at enormous expense it had procured a small, bad, unsafe increase of markets, and had jeopardised the entire wealth of the nation in rousing the strong resentment of other nations, we may ask, 'How is the British nation induced to embark upon such unsound business?' The only possible answer is that the business interests of the nation as a whole are subordinated to those of certain sectional interests that usurp control of the national resources and use them for their private gain. . . . Careful analysis of the existing relations between business and politics shows that the aggressive Imperialism which we seek to understand is not in the main the product of blind passions of races or of the mixed folly and ambition of politicians. . . . It is not too much to say that the modern foreign policy of Great Britain has been primarily a struggle for profitable markets of investment. To a larger extent every year Great Britain has been becoming a nation living upon tribute from abroad, and the classes who enjoy this tribute have had an ever-increasing incentive to employ the public policy, the public purse, and the public force to extend the field of their private investment, and to safeguard and improve their existing investments. [None of this would be necessary if mal-distribution of wealth did not lead to chronic under-consumption at home.] It is this economic condition of affairs that forms the taproot of Imperialism. If the consuming public in this country raised its standard of consumption to keep pace with every rise of productive powers, there could be no excess of goods or capital clamorous to use Imperialism in order to find markets. . . . It is not industrial progress that demands the opening up of new markets and areas of investment, but mal-distribution of consuming power which prevents the absorption of commodities and capital within the country.

Source: J.A. Hobson, *Imperialism: a Study* (1902), 3rd edn, with Introduction by J. Townshend, Unwin Hyam, 1988, pp. 46, 47–50, 53–4, 81, 85.

V.I. LENIN   **Document 25**

Capitalism is bound to lead to imperialism and so to its own destruction.

It is characteristic of capitalism in general that the ownership of capital is separated from the application of capital to production, that money capital is separated from industrial or productive capital, and that the rentier who lives entirely on income obtained from money capital, is separated from the entrepreneur and from all who are directly concerned in the management of capital. Imperialism, or the domination of finance capital, is that highest stage of capitalism at which this separation reaches vast proportions. . . .

Typical of the old capitalism, when free competition had undivided sway, was the export of *goods*. Typical of the latest stage of capitalism, when monopolies rule, is the export of *capital*. . . .

It goes without saying that if capitalism . . . could raise the standard of living of the masses, who are everywhere still half-starved and poverty-stricken, in spite of the amazing technical progress, there could be no talk of a surplus, of capital. . . . But if capitalism did these things it would not be capitalism. . . . As long as capitalism remains what it is, surplus capital will be utilized not for the purpose of raising the standard of living of the masses in a given country, for this would mean a decline in profits for the capitalists, but for the purpose of increasing profits by exporting capital abroad to backward countries. . . .

But when nine-tenths of Africa had been seized (by 1900), when the whole world had been divided up, there was inevitably ushered in the era of monopoly ownership of colonies and, consequently, of particularly intense struggle for the division and redivision of the world. . . .

From all that has been said in this book on the economic essence of imperialism, it follows that we must define it as capitalism in transition or, more precisely as moribund capitalism.

Source: V.I. Lenin, *Imperialism, the Highest Stage of Capitalism* (1917), Moscow, Foreign Languages Publishing House, n.d., pp. 97–8, 102–4, 214, 218.

LORD CROMER   **Document 26**

The British belief that their rule benefited the world.

No one can fully realise the extent of the change which has come over Egypt since the British occupation took place unless he is in some degree familiar with the system under which the country was governed in the days of Ismail Pasha. The contrast between now and then is, indeed, remarkable. A new spirit has been instilled into the population of Egypt. Even the peasant has learnt to scan his rights. Even the Pasha has learnt that others besides himself have rights which must be respected. The courbash [whip] may hang on the walls of the Moudirieh, but the Moudir [Provincial Governor] no longer dares to employ it on the backs of the fellaheen. For all practical purposes, it may be said that the hateful corvée system has disappeared. Slavery has virtually ceased to exist. The halcyon days of the adventurer and the usurer are past. Fiscal burthens have been greatly relieved. Everywhere law reigns supreme. Justice is no longer bought and sold. Nature, instead of being spurned and neglected, has been wooed to bestow her gifts on mankind. She has responded to the appeal. The waters of the Nile are now utilised in an intelligent manner. Means of locomotion have been improved and extended. The soldier has acquired some pride in the uniform which he wears. He has fought as he has never fought before. The sick man can be nursed in a well-managed hospital. The lunatic is no longer treated like a wild beast. The punishment awarded to the worst criminal is no longer barbarous. Lastly, the schoolmaster is abroad, with results which are as yet uncertain, but which cannot fail to be important.

Source: Cromer, *Modern Egypt*, Macmillan, 1908, ii, 556–7.

Document 27   A MODERN REJECTION OF TRADITIONAL EXPLANATIONS OF THE PARTITION

In all the long annals of imperialism, the partition of Africa is a remarkable freak. Few events that have thrown an entire continent into revolution have been brought about so casually. . . . It used to be supposed that European society must have put out stronger urges to empire in Africa at this time; and all sorts of causes have been suggested to support the supposition. One and all, however, they suffer from a tiresome defect: of powerful new incentives there is remarkably little sign. Only after the partition was long over and done with did capital seek outlets, did industry seek markets in tropical Africa. As late as the end of the century the European economy went on by-passing these poor prospects in favour of the proven fields of America and Asia. Neither is it realistic to explain the movement by some change in the temper of the European mind. The pride and pomps of African empire did not suit the popular taste until late in the 1890s when the partition was all but completed. . . . Scanning Europe for the causes, the theorists of imperialism have been looking for answers in the wrong places. The crucial changes that set all working took place in Africa itself. It was the fall of an old power [the Khedivate in Egypt] in its north, the rise of a new [the Transvaal] in its south, that dragged Africa into modern history . . . Imbroglios with Egyptian proto-nationalists and thence with Islamic revivals across the whole of the Sudan drew the powers into an expansion of their own in East and West Africa. . . . The last quarter of the century has often been called the 'Age of Imperialism'. Yet much of this imperialism was no more than an involuntary reaction of Europe to the various proto-nationalisms of Islam that were already rising in Africa against the encroaching thraldom of the white men. . . .

[The gaudy empires spatch-cocked together] have fallen to pieces only three-quarters of a century after being thrown together. It would be a gullible historiography which could see such gimcrack creations as necessary functions of the balance of power or as the highest stage of capitalism.

Source: R.E. Robinson and J. Gallagher, 'The partition of Africa' in *New Cambridge Modern History*, xi, 593–4, 639.

WAS THE WHOLE PHENOMENON ECONOMIC AFTER ALL?   **Document 28**

After the Cold War ended in 1989 historians began to re-examine economic explanations of imperialism. Professors Cain and Hopkins, while rejecting Marxist explanations, revived the idea that the financial sector, as embodied in the City of London, played a key role.

Nowhere does the weight of historiography press so insistently upon the study of imperialism as in the case of the partition of Africa . . . Marxist and Marxisant interpretations have performed particularly badly . . . largely because of their failure to relate partition to the realities of capitalist development.

Liberal interpretations have flourished on the diversity revealed by recent research [but] to claim that imperialism was the result of crises on the periphery is to report the symptoms, not to diagnose the cause.

By 1900 . . . Britain had secured the most valuable parts of Africa . . . Just as there are well-known difficulties in finding 'surplus' capital and conspiracies of bond-holders, so there are equally serious problems with the currently influential view that Britain was an ageing, defensive power struggling to fend off new challenges to her dominance.

The interpretation advanced here suggests that Britain had independent reasons for taking action to increase her grip on Africa. The impulses motivating policy can be traced to the metropole . . . the main weight of her interests lay in Egypt and Southern Africa, where City and service interests were most prominently represented, and it was there that Britain showed the greatest vigour in promoting her claims.

Source: P. Cain and A.G. Hopkins, *British Imperialism* Vol. 1, *Innovation and Expansion, 1688–1914*, pp. 351–2, 392–3.

Appendix: European colonial background

European claims in Africa in 1870

Portugal

Portugal had extensive historic claims, dating back to the Age of Exploration in the fifteenth and sixteenth centuries. They included:

Angola
Mozambique
Portuguese Guinea
The islands of Principe and Sao Tome
Cape Verde Islands

Spain

Spanish efforts in the Age of Exploration had been mainly concentrated on Latin America but the Spaniards too had some historic claims in Africa:

Ceuta (Morocco)
Melilla (Morocco)
Rio de Oro
Spanish Guinea

Britain

Britain had established colonies of settlement in southern Africa:

Cape Colony (acquired from the Dutch by the Vienna Settlement at the end of the Napoleonic wars in 1814).

Natal (organised as a dependency of Cape Colony in 1845; separated from the Cape in 1856).

Also the Transvaal and Orange Free State. The Boers (Dutch farmers) had 'trekked' out of Cape Colony in the 1840s because they disliked British legislation, including the abolition of slavery in 1833. They were autonomous in their internal affairs and regarded themselves as independent but had acknowledged British suzerainty by the Sand River Convention (1852) and the Bloemfontein Convention (1854) respectively.

Also Basutoland, taken under British 'Protection' in 1868, at the request of the Basutos, who felt pressurised by the Boers.

Britain also had trading bases with some degree of political organisation scattered along the western coasts of Africa:

The Gambia
Sierra Leone
Gold Coast (Cape Coast Castle and other stations)
Lagos (annexed in 1861)

France
Algeria. In 1830 the government of Charles X had sent an expedition to clear out the Barbary pirates, who were terrorising the Mediterranean. The government of his successor, Louis Philippe, found it impossible to withdraw and were drawn into a war in which they conquered the hinterland, mostly in the 1840s.

France also had a number of stations on the west coast:

Senegal, the oldest, founded in the seventeenth century
Grand Bassam (Ivory Coast)
Cotonou (Dahomey)
Port Novo (Dahomey)
Libreville (Gabon)

Ottoman empire
As well as the European Powers, the Ottoman (Turkish) empire still claimed suzerainty over Egypt and the Sudan, Tripoli, Tunis and (theoretically) Algeria.

British administrations, 1868–1914

December 1868–February 1874 – Liberal
Prime Minister: William Gladstone
Foreign Secretary: Earl of Clarendon, 1868–70; Earl Granville, 1870–4
Colonial Secretary: Earl Granville, 1868–70; Lord Kimberley, 1870–4

February 1874–April 1880 – Conservative
Prime Minister: Benjamin Disraeli
Foreign Secretary: Earl of Derby, 1874–8; Marquis of Salisbury, 1878–80
Colonial Secretary: Earl of Carnarvon, 1874–8; Sir Michael Hicks Beach, 1878–80

April 1880–June 1885 – Liberal
Prime Minister: William Gladstone
Foreign Secretary: Lord Granville
Colonial Secretary: Earl of Kimberley

June 1885–February 1886 – Conservative
Prime Minister: Marquis of Salisbury
Foreign Secretary: Marquis of Salisbury
Colonial Secretary: F.A. (later Lord) Stanley

February–August 1886 – Liberal
Prime Minister: William Gladstone
Foreign Secretary: Earl of Rosebery
Colonial Secretary: Earl Granville

August 1886–August 1892 – Conservative
Prime Minister: Marquis of Salisbury
Foreign Secretary: Earl of Iddesleigh, 1886–January 1887; Marquis of Salisbury, January 1887–1892
Colonial Secretary: Edward Stanhope, 1886–January 1887; Lord Knutsford, January 1887–92

August 1892–June 1895 – Liberal
Prime Minister: William Gladstone, 1892–March 1894; Earl of Rosebery, March 1894–1895
Foreign Secretary: Earl of Rosebery, 1892–March 1894; Earl of Kimberley, March 1894–1895
Colonial Secretary: Marquis of Ripon, 1892–1895

June 1895–December 1905 – Conservative
Prime Minister: Marquis of Salisbury, 1895–July 1902; A.J. Balfour, July 1902–1905
Foreign Secretary: Marquis of Salisbury, 1895–October 1900; Marquis of Lansdowne, October 1900–1905
Colonial Secretary: Joseph Chamberlain, 1895–September 1903; Alfred Lyttelton, September 1903–1905

December 1905 (Liberal) – May 1915 – (when war-time coalition government formed)
Prime Minister: Sir Henry Campbell-Bannerman, 1905–April 1908; H.H. Asquith, April 1908–December 1916
Foreign Secretary: Sir Edward Grey, 1905–December 1916
Colonial Secretary: Earl of Elgin, 1905–April 1908; Earl of Crewe, April 1908–November 1910; Lewis Harcourt, November 1910–1915

[*Note: Throughout the Scramble period, it was the Foreign Secretary, rather than the Colonial Secretary, who played the lead role in decision making in Africa.*]

German Chancellors, 1871–1917

Otto von Bismarck, 1871–90
Leo von Caprivi, 1890–4
Chlodwig zu Hohenlohe-Schillingsfürst, 1894–1900
Bernhard von Bülow, 1900–9
Theobald von Bethman-Hollweg, 1909–17

Significant French administrations and politicians, 1870–1906

(The transient nature of most French governments in this period makes a complete listing impractical.)

Presidents of the Republic
Adolphe Thiers, 1871–3
Comte de MacMahon, 1873–9
Jules Grévy, 1879–87
M.F.S. Carnot, 1887–1894
Charles Alexander Dupuy, 1894–5
François Félix Fauré, 1895–9
Emile Loubet, 1899–1906

Prime Ministers
William Henry Waddington, 1879
Comte de Freycinet, 1879–80, 1882, 1886, 1890–2
Jules Ferry, 1880–81, 1883–5
Léon Gambetta, 1881–2
C.T.E. Duclerc, 1882–3
Emile Combes, 1902–5
Georges Clemenceau, 1906–9

Colonial Ministers
Félix Fauré, 1881–2, 1883–5, 1888
Eugene Étienne, 1887–8, 1889–92
Théophile Delcassé, 1893, 1894–5; Foreign Minister, 1898–1905
Gabriel Hanotaux, 1898

Guide to further reading

The place of publication is London unless otherwise stated. The date of first publication is usually given; subsequent editions are noted only for particular reasons, e.g. significant amounts of new material.

African Background

European thinking about African history and civilisation began to change after the Second World War but the 'break through' decade was the 1960s, when so much thinking about society and race relations began to change. Two very important scholarly books were H.A.C. Cairns, *Prelude to Imperialism: British reactions to Central African Society, 1840–1890* (1965) and P.D. Curtin, *The Image of Africa: British Ideas and Actions, 1780–1850* (1964). New ideas reached the general public largely through the writings of Basil Davidson such as *Old Africa Rediscovered* (1959); *Africa in History: Themes and Outlines* (1st edn, lavishly illustrated, 1966; 2nd edn, text extended but no illustrations, 1968) and *The Africans: an Entry to Cultural History* (1969). Radio played its part. Roland Oliver edited a lively collection of broadcast talks by Mortimer Wheeler and other, *The Dawn of African History* (Oxford, 1961). *The Journal of African History*, which has always carried important articles, was established in 1960. Although ranging much more widely than Africa, it is worth consulting C. Bolt, *Victorian Attitudes to Race* (1971).

The new ideas were incorporated in the new histories of the continent, which now began to appear: R. Oliver and J.D. Fage, *A Short History of Africa* (1962, 1990); J. Fage, *History of Africa* (1995); R. Oliver and A. Atmore, *Africa since 1800* (Cambridge, 1967; 1994); *Cambridge History of Africa*, Vol. 3, *1050–1600* (ed. R. Oliver, 1977), Vol. 4, 1600–1790 (ed. R. Gray, 1975), Vol. 5, 1790–1870 (ed. J. Flint, 1976), Vol. 6, 1870–1905 (ed. R. Oliver and G.N. Sanderson, 1985) and Vol. 7, 1905–70 (ed. A.D. Roberts, 1986). An unfashionable, but sometimes thought-provoking rejection of the modern approach to African history, was L.H. Gann and P. Duignan, *Burden of Empire:*

an *Appraisal of Western Colonialism in Africa South of the Sahara* (1968). A good overview, incorporating modern research is J. Iliffe, *Africans: the History of a Continent* (Cambridge, 1995).

The partition of Africa was preceded by a period of European exploration. Almost all the explorers left accounts, often voluminous, of their experiences. They are probably best approached through anthologies such as M. Perham and J. Simmons, *African Discovery: an Anthology of Exploration* (1942, 1963) and R. Oliver and C. Oliver (eds), *Africa in the Days of Exploration* (1965). There is also Christopher Hibbert's very readable account, *Africa Explored: Europeans in the Dark Continent, 1769–1889* (1982). Heinrich Barth's more substantial studies are accessible in English through A.H.M. Kirk-Greene, *Barth's Travels in Nigeria: Extracts from the journal . . . , 1850–1855* (1962).

African intellectual responses to European pressures can be studied in R.W. July, *The Origins of Modern African Thought: its Development in West Africa during the Nineteenth and Twentieth Centuries* (1968); and P.D. Curtin, *Africa and the West: Intellectual Responses to European Culture* (Madison, WI, 1972).

Particular aspects of African history are covered in John Trimingham, *The Influence of Islam upon Africa* (1968); Andrew Porter (ed.) *The Imperial Horizons of British Protestant Missions, 1880–1914* (2003); and Leon Underwood, *The Bronzes of Benin* (1949).

The Atlantic slave trade has been extensively investigated. James Pope-Hennessy, *Sins of the Fathers: the Atlantic Slave Traders, 1441–1807* (1967, 1970) remains a classic. Eric Williams, *Capitalism and Slavery* (1944, 1967) is also a seminal book, although its argument has been strongly countered by others (see, for example, R.T. Anstey, 'Capitalism and slavery: a critique', *Economic History Review*, 2nd ser., xxi, 1968). P. Richardson, *Empire and Slavery* (1968) is still useful. Basil Davidson, *Black Mother* (1961) pioneered the study of the effects on African society. James Walvin's *Black Ivory* (1992) brings an entirely new perspective to bear on the subject. The bicentenary of the outlawing of the Slave Trade by Britain and the United States in 1807 was widely commemorated in TV programmes and exhibitions in various cities. Until very recently much less had been written about the Arab slave trade in East Africa although the subject was covered in R. Coupland, *The Exploitation of East Africa, 1856–1890: The Slave Trade and the Scramble* (1939, 1968), based on the papers of Sir John Kirk. But there is now Humphrey J. Fisher, *Slavery in the History of Muslim Black Africa* (2001): R. Segal, *Islam's Black Slaves* (2003); and L. Farrant, *Tippu Tib* (a notorious slave trader) (1975).

European Imperialism in General

The Scramble for Africa is part of the general story of European imperialism and more especially of the so-called 'new imperialism' of the late nineteenth century. The literature is vast and some of the aspects most relevant to Africa are discussed in the Conclusion; those arguments need not be repeated here.

It is as well to begin with definitions and the best book for this purpose R. Koebner and D.H. Schmidt, *Imperialism: a Political Word, 1840–1960* (Cambridge, 1964).

Explanations for imperialism have swayed between economic (more particularly financial), political and strategic explanations. Social Darwinist theories, although sometimes used to justify imperialism, have not generally been offered as an explanation for it. J.A. Hobson's *Imperialism: a Study* (1900, rev. edn 1938) is a good starting point; although an untidy book, cobbled together from articles and papers, it was immensely influential. V.I. Lenin in his *Imperialism: the Highest Stage of Capitalism* (Moscow, 1917, innumerable English editions) acknowledged his debt to it. It became common to speak of a Hobson–Lenin theory of imperialism but D.K. Fieldhouse, in a devastating article ' "Imperialism": an historiographical revision' (*Economic History Review*, 2nd ser., iv, 1961), demonstrated that the two men were actually arguing different and incompatible cases.

Until the Second World War economic, largely financial, explanations held sway. (For the particular case of Egypt, see below.) It was assumed in H.N. Brailsford, *The War of Steel and Gold* (1914) and Leonard Woolf, *Empire and Commerce in Africa* (1920). It survived, virtually unchanged, in left-wing analyses after the war in, for example, J. Strachey, *End of Empire* (1959). A rare dissenting voice was J.A. Schumpeter, *Capitalism, Socialism, and Democracy* (1943, 3rd edn 1950). After the war, partly although not entirely as a result of the Cold War, Marxist explanations of all kinds began to be challenged by western scholars. A very important challenge came from W.K. Hancock, *Wealth of Colonies* (Cambridge, 1949) pointing out the fundamental flaws in Lenin's analysis. Some Marxists fought back, arguing that Lenin's theories had been misunderstood, see particularly papers in R. Owen and B. Sutcliffe (eds), *Studies in the Theory of Imperialism* (1972). See also A. Brewer, *Marxist Theories of Imperialism: a Critical Survey* (1980).

Other scholars began to look for other explanations. Of particular importance was R. Robinson and J. Gallagher, *Africa and the Victorians: the Official Mind of Imperialism* (1961, 1981). Their ideas were further developed in 'The Partition of Africa' in *New Cambridge Modern History*, vol. xi, 1962 and 'The imperialism of free trade', *Economic History Review*, 2nd ser., vi, 1953. They argued that Britain always preferred 'moral suasion', that is informal influence, to formal empire and that the British Foreign Office was almost impervious to business pressures. Other historians were not prepared to go so far (indeed, Robinson and Gallagher themselves conceded that there was an economic, as well as a strategic and political, dimension to British policy). A lively debate ensued in which the main protagonists were D.C.M. Platt, *Finance, Trade and Politics: British Foreign Policy, 1815–1914* (Oxford, 1968), 'Economic factors in British policy during the "New Imperialism"', *Past and*

Present, xxxix, 1968 'The imperialism of free trade: some reservations', *Economic History Review*, 2nd ser., xxi, 1968; E. Stokes, 'Late nineteenth-century colonial expansion and the attack on the theory of economic imperialism: a case of mistaken identity?', *Historical Journal*, xii, 1969; G.N. Sanderson 'The European partition of Africa: Coincidence or conjuncture?, *Journal of Imperial and Commonwealth History*, 3, 1974; D.K. Fieldhouse, *Economics and Empire* (1973), and W.G. Hynes, *The Economics of Empire: Britain, Africa and the New Imperialism, 1870–1895* (1979). Bernard Porter, *The Lion's Share: a Short History of British Imperialism, 1850–1970* (3rd edn, 1996) also considers this from a different perspective. But the most important reinstatement of the centrality of economic, even financial, motives is in P.J. Cain and A.G. Hopkins, *British Imperialism*, Vol. 1, *Innovation and Expansion, 1688–1914* (1993).

Other books important for understanding various aspects of the imperialist phenomenon are A.H. Imlah, *Economic Elements in the Pax Britannica: Studies in British Foreign Trade in the Nineteenth Century* (Harvard, 1958); B. Semmel, *Imperialism and Social Reform* (1960); and S.B. Saul, *The Myth of the Great Depression* (1969). The diplomatic background can be studied in A.J.P. Taylor, *The Struggle for the Mastery in Europe* (Oxford, 1954) or P. Kennedy, *The Realities behind Diplomacy* (1981).

The British Empire

The most up-to-date comprehensive history of the empire is the *Oxford History of the British Empire*, 5 vols (Oxford, 1998–9). Vol. 3 (ed. Andrew Porter) covers this period but Vol. 5, *Historiography* (ed. R.W. Winks) is also immensely useful. It is also worth consulting the *Cambridge Illustrated History of the British Empire* (ed. P.J. Marshall, Cambridge, 1996). In recent years there have been a number of attempts to completely reassess the impact of the British empire, of which N. Ferguson, *Empire: How Britain Made the Modern World* (2003) is probably the best known.

Relevant books also include H.L. Hoskins, *British Routes to India* (1928, Cass reprint, 1966); C.J. Lowe, *The Reluctant Imperialists: British Foreign Policy, 1878–1902* (1967); G.W. Monger, *The End of Isolation: British Foreign Policy, 1900–1907* (1963); J.A.S. Grenville, *Lord Salisbury and Foreign Policy: the Close of the Nineteenth Century* (1964); C.C. Eldridge, *England's Mission: the Imperial Idea in the Age of Gladstone and Disraeli* (1973); G.Martel, *Imperial Diplomacy: Rosebery and the Failure of Foreign Policy* (1986); B.H. Brown, *The Tariff Reform Movement in Great Britain, 1881–1895* (New York, 1943); S.B. Saul, *Studies in British Overseas Trade, 1870–1914* (1960); L.E. Davis and R.A. Huttenback, *Mammon and the Pursuit of Empire: The Political Economy of British Imperialism, 1860–1912* (Cambridge, 1986); R. Robson, *The Cotton Industry in Britain*, (1957); and A. Redford, *Manchester Men and Foreign Trade,*

Vol. 2, *1850–1939*, (Manchester, 1956). A useful article is S.M. Hardy, 'Joseph Chamberlain and some problems of the "undeveloped estates"', *University of Birmingham Historical Journal*, xi, 1968. Although not directly concerned with this period, G.R. Mellor, *British Imperial Trusteeship, 1783–1850* (1951) explains an important strand in British thinking even at the height of the imperialist period which, in a sense, is taken up in F.D. (Lord) Lugard, *The Dual Mandate in British Tropical Africa* (1922, Cass reprint, 1965). Dissident voices are represented by B. Porter, *Critics of Empire: British Radical Attitudes to Colonialism in Africa, 1895–1914* (1968).

Many near-contemporary biographies (often official and multi-volume) are useful because they usually contain primary material in the form of letters, etc. They include J. Morley, *Life of Gladstone*, 3 vols (1903); Lord Edmond Fitzmaurice, *Life of Lord Granville, 1815–1891*, 2 vols (1906); J.L. Garvin and J Amery, *Life of Joseph Chamberlain*, 6 vols (1933–69); S. Gwynne and G. M. Tuckwell, *Life of Sir Charles W. Dilke*, 2 vols (1917); A.G. Gardiner, *Life of Sir William Harcourt*, 2 vols (1923); and Lady Gwendoline Cecil, *Life of Robert, Marquis of Salisbury*, 4 vols (1921–32); and an autobiography, Lord Grey (Sir Edward Grey), *Twenty-Five Years, 1892–1916* (1926). Modern biographies are less likely to do so but important ones include H.C.G. Matthew, *Gladstone*, 2 vols (1986–95); R. Shannon, *Gladstone: Heroic Minister, 1865–1898*, (1999); R.T. Marsh, *Joseph Chamberlain: Entrepreneur in Politics*, (1994); and A. Roberts, *Salisbury: Victorian Titan* (1999).

(Britain so dominated imperialism in general in this period that many books and articles relating in particular to economic motives are listed in the 'European Imperialism in General' section above.)

The French Empire

A number of older books still provide a useful introduction for English-speaking readers. They include S.H. Roberts, *The History of French Colonial Policy, 1870–1925*, (1929, Cass reprint, 1963). See also H. Brunschwig (trans. W.G. Brown), *French Colonialism, 1871–1914*, (1966); J. Cooke, *New French Imperialism, 1880–1910: the Third Republic and Colonial Expansion* (1973); A.S. Kanya-Forstner, *The Conquest of the Western Sudan: a Study in French Military Imperialism* (Cambridge, 1969); and J.P.T. Bury, 'Gambetta and overseas problems', *English Historical Review*, lxxxii, 1967.

W.B. Cohen, *The French Encounter with Africans: White Response to Blacks, 1550–1880*, (Bloomington, IN 1980) (also relevant to 'African Background' section above) breaks new ground. J.D. Hargreaves, *France and West Africa* (1969) is a useful collection of documents.

(A number of studies of West Africa and of the Fashoda incident, listed below, are also relevant to this section.)

The German Empire

Although the German empire was dismantled after the First World War, its significance in European diplomacy and, particularly, its relevance for Bismarckian studies means that it continues to be studied. H.-U. Wehler, 'Bismarck's Imperialism, 1862–1890' in *Past and Present*, xlviii, 1970 is a useful summary of his massive *Bismarck und der Imperialismus* (1969). H. Pogge von Strandmann, 'The domestic origins of Germany's colonial expansion under Bismarck', *Past and Present*, xlii, 1969, is also relevant to this debate. Among old but still informative studies see W.O. Aydelotte, *Bismarck and British Colonial Policy* (Oxford, 1937); A.J.P. Taylor, *Germany's First Bid for Colonies, 1884–1885* (1938); M.E. Townsend, *The Rise and Fall of Germany's Colonial Empire*, (1930, 2nd edn, 1966); and H.R. Rudin, *The Germans in the Cameroons, 1884–1918* (1938).

Fritz Stern investigates the complex question of Bismarck's relations with the bankers in *Gold and Iron: Bismarck, Bleichroder and the Building of the German Empire* (1977). E.C.M. Breuning and M.E. Chamberlain (eds) (New York, Lampeter, 1998) provides the only English translation (with commentary) of F. Fabri, *Does Germany need Colonies?*, which Fabri believed, exaggeratedly but not altogether wrongly, triggered the German colonial movement.

The Portuguese Empire

This old and moribund empire partially revived during the Scramble period. James Duffy, *Portugal in Africa* (1962) is a useful short introduction. There is also R.J. Hammond, *Portugal and Africa, 1815–1910: a Study in Uneconomic Imperialism* (1966).

The Belgian Empire (Leopold II)

Until 1908 this was a personal venture of Leopold II, in which the Belgian parliament did not participate. The Congo scandal was famously revealed in E.D. Morel, *Red Rubber* (1906). The king's role was dissected in N. Ascherson, *The King Incorporated* (1963).

Comparative Studies of European Empires

These include D.K. Fieldhouse, *The Colonial Empires: A Comparative Survey from the Eighteenth Century* (1966, 1982); H.L. Wesseling, (trans. D. Webb), *The European Colonial Empires, 1815–1919* (2004), both of which range much more widely than Africa. Specifically on Africa, there is P. Gifford and W.R. Louis (eds), *Britain and Germany in Africa: Imperial Rivalry and Colonial Rule* (Yale,

1967) and *France and Britain in Africa: Imperial Rivalry and Colonial Rule* (Yale, 1971) – both useful collections of essays.

The Scramble for Africa

T. Pakenham, *The Scramble for Africa* (1991) is very readable but lacks the depth of his study of the Boer War. H.L. Wesseling (trans. A.J. Pomerans), *Divide and Rule: the Partition of Africa, 1880–1914* (1996) is the best single book.

Egypt and the Sudan

There is an enormous amount of material on this. It is worth starting, if possible, with contemporary books, which give a quite different perspective to that offered by later studies. They include J.C. McCoan, *Egypt As It Is* (1877) and D. Mackenzie Wallace, *Egypt and the Egyptian Question* (1883) (both journalists); and J. Ninet, *Arabi Pacha* (Paris, 1884), written by a close friend of the Egyptian leader. A little later but in the same category is M. Sabri, *La Genèse de l'esprit national Égyptien, 1863–1882* (Paris, 1924).

What might almost be called the official British case was set out by Lord Cromer himself in *Modern Egypt*, 2 vols (1908). This was reinforced by Alfred Milner, *England in Egypt* (1892) (see also V. Halperin, *Lord Milner and the Empire*, 1952), and Auckland Colvin, *The Making of Modern Egypt* (1906). This was countered by W.S. Blunt, *The Secret History of the English Occupation of Egypt* (1907) – a highly partisan account but with much genuine 'inside information'. The conviction that it had been a 'bondholders' war' had a long history, beginning with Seymour Keay, *Spoiling the Egyptians: A Tale of Shame* (1882) and T. Rothstein, *Egypt's Ruin* (1910).

But the Suez Canal was obviously an important factor. There is the massive D.A. Farnie, *East and West of Suez: the Suez Canal in History, 1854–1956* (Oxford, 1969), as well as the more manageable J. Marlowe, *The Making of the Suez Canal* (1964); and J. Pudney, *Suez: De Lesseps Canal* (1968).

There are a number of popular, but good, accounts of Anglo-Egyptian relations in this period in P. Mansfield, *The British in Egypt* (1971); and J. Marlowe, *Anglo-Egyptian Relations, 1800–1953* (1954) and *Cromer in Egypt* (1970).

Many articles deal with particular aspects of Britain's involvement in Egypt; among them, R.A. Atkins, 'The Conservatives and Egypt, 1875–1880', *Journal of Imperial and Commonwealth History*, 2, 1974; A. Scholch, 'The "Man on the Spot" and the English Occupation of Egypt in 1882', *Historical Journal*, XIX, 1976; M.E. Chamberlain, 'Sir Charles Dilke and the British Intervention in Egypt, 1882: decision-making in a nineteenth-century Cabinet', *British Journal of International Studies*, 2, 1976, and 'The Alexandria Massacre of

11 June 1882 and the British Occupation of Egypt', *Middle Eastern Studies*, 13, 1977; and A.G. Hopkins, 'The Victorians and Africa: a reconsideration of the occupation of Egypt, 1882', *Journal of African History*, 27, 1986.

On the Egyptian Sudan P. Holt, *The Mahdist State in the Sudan, 1881–1898* (Oxford, 1958) is a standard work. Another comprehensive study is G.N. Sanderson, *England, Europe and the Upper Nile, 1882–1899*, (Edinburgh, 1965). A. Nutting, *Gordon: Martyr and Misfit* (1966) is a stimulating biography, although not all scholars would accept his interpretation of Gordon. (For later history see the 'Fashoda' section.)

West and Equatorial Africa

For glimpses of earlier contacts between Europeans and the West Coast see R. Hallett (ed.) *Records of the African Association, 1788–1831* (1964). This is followed up by C.W. Newbury, *The Western Slave Coast and its Rulers* (Oxford, 1961). For a good overview of the Scramble period, see J. Hargreaves, *Prelude to the Partition of West Africa*, (1963) and *West Africa Partitioned*, Vol. 1, *The Loaded Pause, 1885–1890* (1974).

On the Niger region there are K.O. Dike, *Trade and Politics in the Niger Delta, 1830–1885*, (Oxford, 1956), a pioneering work by an eminent African historian; G.I. Jones, *The Trading States of the Oil Rivers* (Oxford, 1963), important because it studies the African politics of the region; and J.E. Flint, *Sir George Goldie and the Making of Nigeria* (Oxford, 1960). M. Perham, *Lugard: the Life of Frederick Dealtry Lugard*, vol. 1 (1956), *The Years of Adventure, 1858–1898*, and vol. 2 (1960), *The Years of Authority, 1898–1945*, deal with his whole life but are particularly important for his period in the Niger region.

The history of Ghana is covered in W.E.F. Ward, *A History of the Gold Coast* (1958) D. Kimble, *A Political History of Ghana: the Rise of Gold Coast Nationalism, 1850–1928* (Oxford, 1963). W.D. McIntyre's *The Imperial Factor in the Tropics, 1856–1875* (1967), although mainly concerned with Asia, has interesting things to say about West Africa. Sierra Leone is comprehensively dealt with in C. Fyfe, *A History of Sierra Leone* (Oxford, 1962). R. Anstey, *Britain and the Congo in the Nineteenth Century* (Oxford, 1962) deals with a dimension often missed.

French policy is dealt with in a number of articles; C.W. Newbury, 'The development of French policy on the Lower and Upper Niger, 1880–1898', *Journal of Modern History*, xxxi, 1959 and 'The Protectionist revival in French colonial trade: the case of Senegal', *Economic History Review*, 2nd ser., xxi, 1968.

Some historians concerned with West Africa strenuously combated the Robinson and Gallagher thesis that the Egyptian crisis triggered the whole scramble for Africa, believing that completely different trigger mechanisms operated in West Africa, C.W. Newbury, 'Victorians, republicans and the partition of Africa', *Journal of African History*, iii, 1962; H. Brunschwig,

'Les origines du partage de l'Afrique occidentale', *Journal of African* History, v, 1964: and C.W. Newbury and A.S. Kanya-Forstner, 'French policy and the origins of the Scramble for West Africa', *Journal of African History*, x, 1969.

Although a very old book, S.E. Crowe, *The Berlin West Africa Conference, 1884–1885* (1942) is still a good, straightforward account, which understands the European diplomatic background, but is superseded in many ways by S. Forster, W.J. Mommsen and R. Robinson, *Bismarck, Europe and Africa: the Berlin West Africa Conference, 1884–1885, and the Onset of Partition* (Oxford, 1988).

East Africa

R. Coupland, *The Exploitation of East Africa, 1856–1890: the Slave Trade and the Scramble*, (1939, 1968) is unlikely ever to be completely superseded because it is based firmly on the papers of Sir John Kirk, the British Consul General at Zanzibar.

K. Ingham gives an overview of the whole question in his *History of East Africa* (1963). Very detailed coverage of many aspects of the story is given in the two-volume *History of East Africa*, vol. 1 (ed. R. Oliver and G. Mathew, Oxford, 1963, 1966), vol. 2 (ed. V. Harlow and E.M. Chilver, Oxford, 1965), a collection of essays by well-known authorities. Uganda is dealt with in K. Ingham, *The Making of Modern Uganda* (1958). Mackinnon's role is assessed in J.S. Galbraith, *Mackinnon and East Africa, 1878–1895* (1972).

To understand the Anglo-German struggle for the region it is worth reading Karl Peters (trans. F. Karuth), *King Solomon's Golden Ophir* (1899), fanciful although it was. The contest itself is best read in R. Oliver, *Sir Harry Johnston and the Scramble for Africa* (1957). By this time the issues were better understood and policies being formulated. W.R. Louis, 'Sir Percy Anderson's grand African strategy, 1883–96', *English Historical Review*, lxxxi, 1966, reveals a rare example of a British civil servant formulating an overarching design. M.E. Chamberlain, 'Clement Hill's memorandum and the British interest in East Africa', *English Historical Review*, lxxxvii, 1972, also deal with the views of Foreign Office. D.R. Gillard's two articles, 'Salisbury's African policy and the Heligoland offer of 1890', *English Historical Review*, lxxv, 1960, and 'Salisbury's Heligoland offer: the case against the Witu thesis', *English Historical Review*, lxxx, 1965, links Salisbury's African policy with mainstream European diplomacy.

Southern Africa

Older studies concentrated on relations between the British and the Boers, culminating in the second Anglo-Boer War of 1899–1902. A. Keppel-Jones,

South Africa: a Short History (1949, 1963, 1975) provides a lively introduction, that does not entirely ignore other races. In the old mode but still useful are E.A. Walker, *A History of Southern Africa* (1928, rev. 1962); C.W. de Kiewiet, *The Imperial Factor in South Africa*, Cambridge (1937); and G.H.L. Le May, *British Supremacy in South Africa, 1899–1907* (Oxford, 1963). A disproportionate amount has been written about the Jameson Raid. J. Van der Poel, *The Jameson Raid* (Oxford, 1951) is a thorough study. The best book on the Boer War, which is not only very readable but uses previously neglected primary sources, including non-European ones, is T. Pakenham, *The Boer War*, 1979.

The *Oxford History of South Africa*, Vols 1 and 2 (Oxford, 1969, 1971) reflects the changing emphasis; as does N. Worden, *The Making of Modern South Africa: Conquest, Segregation and Apartheid* (Oxford, 1994). A new look is provided by D.M. Schreuder, *The Scramble for Southern Africa, 1877–1895: the Politics of Partition Reappraised* (Cambridge, 1980).

Donald Morris, *The Washing of the Spears* (1966, 1968) gives a lively impression of a non-European society. There is also John Guy, *The Destruction of the Zulu Kingdom, 1879–1884* (1979).

Rhodesia (the modern Zimbabwe) is obviously a central issue. A.J. Hanna, *The Story of the Rhodesias and Nyasaland* (1960) is an old-fashioned view. P. Mason, *The Birth of a Dilemma: the Conquest and Settlement of Rhodesia* (Oxford, 1958) is a good introduction. On Zambia there is A. Roberts, *A History of Zambia* (1976). J.G. Lockhart and C.M. Woodhouse, *Rhodes* (1963) is nowadays regarded as the standard biography but it can never completely replace Basil Williams, *Cecil Rhodes* (1928), which had the advantage of personal knowledge.

Cecil Rhodes (ed. W.T. Stead), *The Last Will and Testament of Cecil J. Rhodes* (1902) gives an interesting insight into Rhodes' peculiar thought processes. It is also worth reading S. Jackson, *The Great Barnarto* (Rufus Isaacs) (1970), an exceptionally lively biography.

The Fashoda Incident and the Anglo-French Entente

For background it is worth reading Winston S. Churchill, *The River War: the Reconquest of the Sudan* (1899, 1960) and Philip Magnus, *Kitchener: Portrait of an Imperialist* (1958, 1968), both very readable.

On the Fashoda crisis itself there is D. Bates, *The Fashoda Incident of 1898: Encounter on the Nile* (Oxford, 1984) and C. Andrew, *Théophile Delcassé and the Making of the Entente Cordiale* (1968). Carrying forward the story of the *entente*, with some implications for Africa, there is K.M. Wilson, *The Policy of Entente: the Determination of British Foreign Policy, 1904–1914* (Cambridge, 1985).

References

Cain, P.J. and Hopkins, A.G., *British Imperialism*, Vol. 1, *Innovation and Expansion, 1688–1914*, Longman, 1993.

Cairns, H.A.C., *Prelude to Imperialism: British Reactions to Central African Society, 1840–1890*, Routledge, 1965.

Curtin, P.D., *The Image of Africa: British Ideas and Actions, 1780–1850*, Macmillan, 1965.

Davidson, Basil, *Old Africa Rediscovered*, Longman, 1959, 1970.

Dike, K.O., *Trade and Politics in the Niger Delta, 1830–1885*, Oxford, Clarendon Press, 1956.

Fieldhouse, D.K., ' "Imperialism": an historiographical revision', *Economic History Review*, 2nd ser., iv, 1961.

Fieldhouse, D.K., *Economics and Empire*, Weidenfeld and Nicolson, 1973.

Flint, J.E, *Sir George Goldie and the Making of Nigeria*, Oxford University Press, 1960.

Gardiner, A.G., The Life of Sir William Harcourt, 2 vols, Constable 1923.

Gwynn, S. and Tuckwell, G.M., *The Life of Sir Charles W. Dilke*, Murray, 1917.

Hancock, Keith, *Wealth of Colonies*, Cambridge University Press, 1949.

Hargreaves, J., *Prelude to the Partition of West Africa*, Macmillan, 1963.

Hardy, S.M., 'Joseph Chamberlain and some problems of the "undeveloped estates"', *University of Birmingham Historical Journal*, xi, 1968.

Hobson, J.A., *Imperialism: A Study*, Unwin Hyam, 1902; 3rd rev. edn, 1938.

James, R.R., *Rosebery*, Weidenfeld and Nicolson, 1964.

Keppel-Jones, A. *South Africa: a short history*, 4th edn., Hutchinson, 1963.

Kiewiet, C.W. *The Imperial Factor in South Africa*, Cambridge University Press, 1937.

Lenin, V.I., *Imperialism: the Highest Stage of Capitalism*, 1917; 3rd edn. English trans. Lawrence and Wishart, 1933.

Lugard, F.D. (Lord), *The Dual Mandate in British Tropical Africa*, 1922; Cass reprint, 1965.

Mansfield, Peter, *The British in Egypt*, Weidenfeld and Nicolson, 1971.

Martel, Gordon, *Imperial Diplomacy: Rosebery and the Failure of Foreign Policy*, McGill-Queens University Press, 1986.

McIntyre, W.D., *The Imperial Frontier in the Tropics*, Macmillan, 1967.

Medlicott, W.N., *Bismarck, Gladstone and the Concert of Europe*, Athlone Press, 1956.

Morel, E.D., *Red Rubber,* Unwin, 1906.

Morley, John, *Life of Gladstone*, Macmillan, 1903.

Morris, Donald R., *The Washing of the Spears*, 1966, Jonathon Cape; Sphere Books, 1968.

Newbury, C.W., 'Victorians, republicans and the partition of Africa', *Journal of African History*, iii, 1962.

Oliver, R. and Fage, J.D., *A Short History of Africa*, 1962, Penguin, 1990.

Oliver, R. and Mathew, G., *History of East Africa*, Vol. 1, Oxford, Clarendon Press, 1966.

Peters, Karl, *King Solomon's Golden Ophir* (trans. F. Karuth), Leadenhall Press, 1899.

Platt, D.C.M., 'Economic factors in British policy during the "New Imperialism"', *Past and Present*, xxxix, 1968.

Platt, D.C.M., *Finance, Trade and Politics: British Foreign Policy, 1815–1914*, Oxford University Press, 1968.

Porter, Bernard, *The Lion's Share*, Longman 1st edn 1975: 3rd edn 1996.

Robinson R. and Gallagher, J., *Africa and the Victorians; the Official Mind of Imperialism*, Macmillan, 1961, rev. 1981.

Robinson R. and Gallagher, J., 'The partition of Africa' in *New Cambridge Modern History*, vol. XI, Cambridge University Press, 1962.

Stengers, J., 'L'Imperialisme colonial de la fin du XIX siècle: mythe ou réalité?', *Journal of African History*, iii, 1962.

Stern, Fritz, *Gold and Iron: Bismarck, Bleichröder and the Building of the German Empire*, Allen & Unwin, 1980.

Stokes, Eric, 'Late nineteenth century colonial expansion and the attack on the theory of economic imperialism: a case of mistaken identity?', *Historical Journal*, xii, 1969.

Strachey, John, *End of Empire*, Gollancz, 1959.

Trevor-Roper, Hugh, 'The rise of Christian Europe', *The Listener*, 28 November 1963; quoted in *Oxford History of South Africa*, vol. 1, ed. M. Wilson and L. Thomson, Oxford, Clarendon Press, 1969.

Williams, Eric, *Capitalism and Slavery*, 2nd edn., Deutsch, 1964.

Index

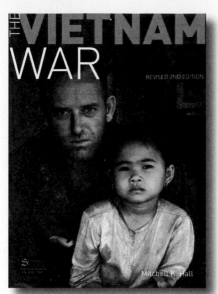

SEMINAR STUDIES
IN HISTORY

9781405874342

9780582771895

9781405874366

9781405874359

9781405840637

9781405874311

9781405874304

9781405846998

9781405840583

9781405874335

9781405824699

9781405812535

SEMINAR
STUDIES

IN HISTORY